D0617040

PRAISE FOR *CULTURAL TRANSFORMATIONS*

"Essential for practicing professionals and academics, *Cultural Transformations* is saturated with insights and findings on organizational leadership that you can apply immediately. Mattone and Vaidya show why some organizational cultures are able to generate long-term sustainability and how you can implement proven turnaround strategies today!"
— Marshall Goldsmith, executive coach and best-selling author
of *Triggers*

"*Cultural Transformations* is a powerful inquiry into the nature of leadership and the increasing role that culture plays in today's business world. Not only is it inspiring to hear from such a distinguished group of CEOs, but authors John Mattone and Nick Vaidya show us how to implement the type of change and evolution they're talking about."
— Deborah DiSanzo, general manager, IBM Watson Health

"Every year new books are published that offer promising solutions to the business challenges that are present in today's complicated global market. What makes this book special is both the high-caliber inquiry that John Mattone (with Nick Vaidya) bring to the table and the talented and diverse group of CEOs he interviews in pursuit of a deeper understanding of the importance and power of a strong corporate culture, as well as the leadership dynamics required to see it thrive.
I recommend this book to anyone looking for inspiration and creative thought stimulation to bring their company to the next level."
— Bill Logue, former president and CEO of FedEx Freight

"By mining the expert opinions of many successful CEOs and entrepreneurs, John Mattone and Nick Vaidya distill the essential practices for successful leadership derived from their journeys through failure and success. This book is a tale of hard work and dedication. It is a call to action, a reminder to bow our heads and give deference to the expertise of the team. It is a plea for resilience and an invitation to stay strong and positive through hardships. By reading these pages you will feel the humility of leaders who dispel the mythical figure of the 'super CEO' in favor of a humble builder of teams, one who is aware of the constant and ever-changing business environment and who relies on the wisdom of co-workers. The practical habits described in this book will give you a foundation to become an effective leader. "

—Fabio Polenti, MD, chief medical operations officer of The Cleveland Clinic Florida

"I wish that all our leaders—in business and in politics—would read *Cultural Transformations*. It contains invaluable insights from 14 diverse leaders who have each built successful companies and thriving cultures within their organizations. If our leaders digested even a fraction of their wisdom and experience, the world would be a better place."

—Joseph Mancuso, founder of CEO Clubs and author of 27 best-selling business books

"*Cultural Transformations* is a must-read for leaders of companies of any size and industry. John Mattone and Nick Vaidya are progressive, bold, and inspiring in their modern and 'think differently' approach to leadership. They provide constructive and immediate executional steps that any company can use as they navigate the ever-changing, competitive global marketplace. Enriched by actual conversations with successful CEOs from various industries who share both their professional and personal journeys, this book on leadership is valid, real and transforming."

—Ruthie Davis, founder, president, and designer of luxury shoe brand Ruthie Davis

"In *Cultural Transformations* John Mattone and Nick Vaidya treat readers to something very rare—a peek inside the minds of 14 CEOs who have successfully led their organizations through major change initiatives. The authors sit you down in a front row seat and give you an unobstructed view of how senior leaders think about and respond to the challenges of the modern workplace. And drawing on their own experience, John and Nick organize the lessons learned from these masters of culture and leadership into a six-step process that will enable you to design and implement your own cultural transformation. This is a timely book that will stand the test of time."

— Jim Kouzes, coauthor of *The Leadership Challenge* and Dean's Executive Fellow of Leadership, Leavey School of Business, Santa Clara University

"*Cultural Transformations* gets at the underlying roots of organizational malaise and lackluster leadership, two of the biggest issues facing companies today. Mattone and Vaidya describe the mindsets required for effective leaders and cultures to thrive in an environment of constant change. Better yet, the CEO interviews provide pragmatic examples and real-world advice, which are much more relatable than theoretical models. This book is a must-read for anyone embarking on a change program."

— Karen Phelan, author of the international bestseller *I'm Sorry I Broke Your Company*

"Today's leader faces an array of complex challenges not even dreamed about by his or her predecessors. *Cultural Transformations* is a book every leader should read before an organizational transition is on the horizon. It will not only help you to anticipate the future, it will help you to create it in a mature, mindful, and savvy manner – and that's what leadership is all about."

— Lois P. Frankel, Ph.D., author of *See Jane Lead* and *Nice Girls Don't Get the Corner Office*

"One of the business world's biggest Holy Grails is learning how to build a corporate culture that supports long term sustainability and growth. In their new book, John Mattone and Nick Vaidya masterfully weave together their own corporate reinvention experience with 14 thought-provoking interviews with top CEOs to create a practical and inspiring roadmap for achieving effective cultural transformation."

— Vegar Wiik, executive director, Florida Atlantic University School of Business

"In *Cultural Transformations*, John Mattone and Nick Vaidya have brought leadership development to a new level. Through their unique interviews, John and Nick get some of the world's top CEOs to open up and talk about how their values, character, and beliefs have had a dramatic impact on the organizational cultures they have created. This book is a powerful learning vehicle and must-read for all leaders, future leaders, and organizations that know they must transform to survive."

— Dan Hoeyer, founder and president of Leaders Excellence, Inc.

"John Mattone's new book (co-authored by Nick Vaidya) builds on his extensive work with corporate executives and offers us great insight on leadership development and cultural transformation built from conversations with 14 top CEOs. It is not a book of abstract ideas but rather a living inquiry into change and leadership through the actual experience of leaders around the world."

— Alper Utko, president of European Leadership University

"*Cultural Transformations* is packed with sage wisdom from those who have experienced the pain and rewards of transformation in themselves and in leading others through change. This masterpiece is filled with clear realizations that can make the difference between success and failure."

— CB Bowman, CEO of the Association of Corporate Executive Coaches

"*Cultural transformation* is one of the most difficult things to accomplish and, more importantly, to sustain for any serious leader dedicated to bettering themselves and the world. What better way to extract wisdom and usable nuggets than from the shared experiences of 14 successful leaders. A must read."

— Sean Magennis, COO of Young Presidents Organization

"*Cultural Transformations* gives you a fascinating look into the hearts and minds of well-regarded business leaders across the globe, an inspiration to any leader who wants to disrupt their business and themselves."

— Whitney Johnson, author *Disrupt Yourself: Putting the Power of Disruptive Innovation to Work*

"*Cultural Transformation* is a gift to organizations that will help bring your management team to the next level. Mattone and Vaidya distill the essence of many thoughtful business leaders' experiences—gained over the years—into clear steps and strategies that organizations can put into practice immediately! *Cultural Transformations* is a paved road toward a healthy, effective, practical, and essential cultural change."

— Soliman Maher Arab, founder and managing principal, Vigor Enterprises

"*Cultural Transformations* provides a practical and inspiring roadmap for corporate reinvention and leadership development. Through 14 in-depth interviews with some of today's best business minds, John Mattone and Nick Vaidya take you into the heart of what it means to lead and transform your company in today's rapidly evolving business landscape."
— Labeed S. Hamid, president of Middle East Management Centre and co-founder of Management Centre Turkey

"John Mattone and Nick Vaidya's new book is essential reading for CEOs, businesspeople, or anyone interested in learning how to become a better leader. Their conversations with some of today's most interesting and successful business minds bring to light a treasure trove of useful and inspiring insights into what it takes to build and lead a thriving corporate culture."
— Kevin Dunn, chief executive officer, CEO Clubs of America

"In *Cultural Transformations*, John Mattone uses his extraordinary ability to bring out the best in people through 14 intimate interviews with some of the world's most successful CEOs. He and co-author Nick Vaidya plumb the depths of each CEO's experience, weaving together a profound and practical study on leadership, culture, and the need for corporate transformation in today's business world."
— Romeo Ruh, executive board, ZfU International Business School

"When it comes to challenging territory of corporate cultural change, John Mattone is a master. In his new book, *Cultural Transformations*, he and co-author Nick Vaidya engage in 14 thought-provoking conversations with some of the world's top business leaders about their leadership style and how they built successful, thriving, and profitable cultures within their organizations. It's a must-read for anyone interested in business culture and how to change it."
— Dr. Eva Benesova, executive director, Principal Coaching Ltd.

"*Cultural Transformations* is an invaluable resource for entrepreneurs, managers, and future business leaders who want to take their leadership and their culture to the next level. Through this book, you will learn from 14 of today's top CEOs about what makes them tick and how they built the thriving cultures that drive their companies' success."
— Kirat Dhillon, Director of HR & Events, Society for Human Resource Management

"Culture is a key driver for any organization success. In their new book, John Mattone and his co-author Nick Vaidya show you why. Weaving together a series of intimate interviews with some of the world's most successful CEOs with their own in-depth experience, they show us why and how to get started in the challenging process of corporate reinvention."

— Achal Khanna, CEO, Society for Human Resource Management

"In our extensive work with companies of all types, we find culture to be the most significant frontier CEOs have yet to explore. In *Cultural Transformations,* John Mattone and Nick Vaidya masterfully guide us in an in-depth exploration of this new frontier. Mining the experience of their clients and many business leaders, they get to the bottom of what it takes to build, lead, and sustain a thriving corporate culture in today's rapidly changing economies."

— Dr. M. Muneer, CEO of CustomerLab

"In *Cultural Transformations*, John Mattone and Nick Vaidya bring you not one, but fourteen intimate conversations with some of today's most successful business leaders. You'll hear about their leadership styles. You'll learn about how they overcame obstacles. And you'll get an inside look into how they built thriving and profitable enterprises by focusing on the health and vitality of their company's culture."

— Dr. Mukul Kumar, president of UWC-USA

Cultural Transformations

Cultural Transformations

Lessons of Leadership and Corporate Reinvention

JOHN MATTONE AND NICK VAIDYA

WILEY

This book is printed on acid-free paper. ∞

Copyright © 2016 by John Mattone and Nick Vaidya. All rights reserved

Published by John Wiley & Sons, Inc., Hoboken, New Jersey
Published simultaneously in Canada.

No part of this publication may be reproduced, stored in a retrieval system, or transmitted in any form or by any means, electronic, mechanical, photocopying, recording, scanning, or otherwise, except as permitted under Section 107 or 108 of the 1976 United States Copyright Act, without either the prior written permission of the Publisher, or authorization through payment of the appropriate per-copy fee to the Copyright Clearance Center, 222 Rosewood Drive, Danvers, MA 01923, (978) 750-8400, fax (978) 646-8600, or on the web at www.copyright.com. Requests to the Publisher for permission should be addressed to the Permissions Department, John Wiley & Sons, Inc., 111 River Street, Hoboken, NJ 07030, (201) 748-6011, fax (201) 748-6008, or online at www.wiley.com/go/permissions.

Limit of Liability/Disclaimer of Warranty: While the publisher and author have used their best efforts in preparing this book, they make no representations or warranties with respect to the accuracy or completeness of the contents of this book and specifically disclaim any implied warranties of merchantability or fitness for a particular purpose. No warranty may be created or extended by sales representatives or written sales materials. The advice and strategies contained herein may not be suitable for your situation. You should consult with a professional where appropriate. Neither the publisher nor the author shall be liable for damages arising herefrom.

For general information about our other products and services, please contact our Customer Care Department within the United States at (800) 762-2974, outside the United States at (317) 572-3993 or fax (317) 572-4002.

Wiley publishes in a variety of print and electronic formats and by print-on-demand. Some material included with standard print versions of this book may not be included in e-books or in print-on-demand. If this book refers to media such as a CD or DVD that is not included in the version you purchased, you may download this material at http://booksupport.wiley.com. For more information about Wiley products, visit www.wiley.com.

Library of Congress Cataloging-in-Publication Data

Names: Mattone, John, author. | Vaidya, Nick, 1965- author.
Title: Cultural transformations : lessons of leadership & corporate
  reinvention from the C-suite elite / John Mattone and Nick Vaidya.
Description: Hoboken, New Jersey : John Wiley & Sons, Inc., [2016] | Includes
  bibliographical references and index.
Identifiers: LCCN 2015036831 | ISBN 9781119055921 (cloth)
Subjects: LCSH: Corporate culture. | Organizational behavior. | Leadership.
Classification: LCC HD58.7 .M377 2016 | DDC 658.4/2 — dc23 LC record available at
http://lccn.loc.gov/2015036831

Cover Design: Michael J. Freeland
Cover Image: Neil Kendall / iStockphoto

Printed in the United States of America

10 9 8 7 6 5 4 3 2 1

CONTENTS

ABOUT THE AUTHORS

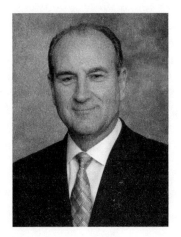

JOHN MATTONE IS WIDELY ACKNOWLEDGED as one of the world's leading authorities on leadership, talent, and culture. He advises Fortune 1000 CEOs and senior leadership teams on how to create and sustain a leadership and talent culture that drives superior operating results.

John is a powerfully engaging, internationally acclaimed keynote speaker and top-ranked CEO executive coach. If you Google the 30 top leadership gurus of 2015, you'll find John Mattone at number nine, after Marshall Goldsmith and ahead of Jim Collins. He was nominated for the prestigious 2013 Thinkers50 Leadership Award, which recognizes the global thinker who has contributed most significantly to our understanding of leadership over the past two years. He was named to the Thinkers50 "Guru Radar" in 2011 and 2013, which recognizes the world's fastest rising stars in the fields of leadership and management thinking. He is also currently recognized by HR.com and Warren Bennis's *Leadership Excellence Magazine* as one of the world's top independent leadership consultants, executive coaches, and speakers. John is one of nine executive coaches in the world who have been awarded the coveted Master Corporate Executive Coach (MCEC) certification from the Association of Corporate Executive Coaches.

John is the author of seven books, including two recent best-sellers. He is the co-author of one of the most respected studies of leadership and talent development in the world, *The Trends in Leadership Development and Talent Management*, which is published biannually by Pearson. John was recently appointed Distinguished Senior Fellow of one of the leading business schools in the world, the Hult International Business School, and he is the host of his own show, *The CEO Magazine's C-Suite Coaching Show*.

John Mattone's work has been featured by the *Wall Street Journal*, *Fast Company*, *BusinessWeek*, *MarketWatch*, *Huffington Post*, *The CEO Magazine*, ChiefExecutive.net, *CLO m*agazine, *CIO* magazine, *The Globe and Mail*, *Harvard Business Review*, and many other respected global news outlets. John Mattone and his work have also been the subject of a 30-minute documentary produced by PBS.

John has over 30 years experience in the fields of executive development, leadership and talent development, and human capital management, as an entrepreneur who has built two successful human capital consulting firms, as the president of a multimillion-dollar leadership consulting firm, and as a leading researcher and author. He is known throughout the Fortune 500 as a cutting-edge thinker regarding trends in executive development and developing high-potential and emerging leaders.

John is the founder and CEO of John Mattone-Global. Prior to this, John was the president of one of the top leadership consulting firms in the world, Executive Development Associates, Inc. (EDA), and prior to EDA he was the vice president of assessments for Linkage, Inc. Prior to Linkage, John was the vice president of sales for Drake Beam Morin (DBM), the global career and outplacement firm. Before joining DBM, John spent 10 years building his first successful consulting firm, Human Resources International.

CAREER HIGHLIGHTS

- Consulted for more than 250 organizations and coached more than 200 executives
- Addressed more than 500,000 people in over 2,000 speeches and seminars in the United States, Canada, and other countries worldwide

- Co-author of *Trends in Executive Development* and *Talent Management* research reports (Pearson 2011, 2013)
- Author of the award-winning "The Role of Assessment in Driving Operating Results," published in Jac Fitz-enz's book, *The New HR Analytics* (AMACOM, 2010)
- Author of "Predictive HR Leadership," published in Jac Fitz-enz's "Workforce Intelligence Report" (2008)
- Author of *Talent Leadership: A Proven Method for Identifying and Developing High-Potential Employees* (AMACOM, 2012), an Amazon best-seller
- Author of *Intelligent Leadership: What You Need to Know to Unlock Your Full Potential* (AMACOM, 2013, foreword by Marshall Goldsmith), a Bloomsberg/Businessweek best-seller
- Author of three e-books: *Powerful Performance Management: The Leader as Coach; Powerful Executive Coaching: A Roadmap to Unleashing Greatness in Your Current and Future Leaders;* and *Powerful Succession Planning* (AMACOM, 2012)
- Author of *Success Yourself* (MasterMedia, 1996) and *Positive Performance Management* (National Press, 1996)
- John has written over 100 professional articles; his work has been featured in the *Wall Street Journal, Globe and Mail, Huffington Post, CEO* magazine, *CIO* magazine, *CLO* magazine, *Leadership Excellence* magazine, *Human Resource Executive* magazine, *Entrepreneurs Digest* (Singapore), *Conocimiento Dirrecion* (South America), and many others
- Written for and performed in numerous audio and video programs, including *Hiring & Performance Management, Focus on Success, The Essentials of Delegation,* and the award-winning *Street Smart Supervision*

PROFESSIONAL QUALIFICATIONS

John Mattone holds a B.S. degree in Management and Organizational Behavior from Babson College and an M.S. in Industrial/Organizational Psychology from the University of Central Florida. John serves as an executive MBA faculty member at Florida Atlantic University, where he teaches his popular course, Global Leadership Assessment and Development. John also serves as a senior talent management consultant and master executive coach for Executive Development Associates (where he formerly served as president), and he was recently named president of the International Center for Business Communication (and is ICBC's first Hall of Fame inductee).

John is a member of numerous professional associations including the Association of Corporate Executive Coaches (ACEC), where he was recently named to the advisory board of the University of Continuing Education Coaching Education and was also appointed as ACEC's Middle East ambassador.

WHAT ELSE ABOUT ME?

I am married to my incredible wife Gayle (we recently celebrated our 37th anniversary). We have four adult children—Jared, Nick, Kristina, and Matthew. Gayle and I enjoy all sports activities, especially skiing and bicycling (we typically ride 80 to 100 miles per week). We travel frequently to visit our children, who live in south Florida and Tennessee, and other family members in Boston, New York, and North Carolina.

NICK VAIDYA

Known as the BlindSpotter, Nick Vaidya is the editor-in-chief of *CEO m*agazine and the managing director of the CEO Leadership Institute. Prior to becoming a serial entrepreneur, he managed a multibillion-dollar product line profitably and was on the Chairman's Strategy Team at a Fortune 50 company. His advice on improving stability and growth is much sought after by C-level executives. Nick's approach is influenced by his doctoral work in empiricism, eclectic life experiences, breadth of business roles, and his in-depth study of the ancient wisdom of the Vedanta.

ACKNOWLEDGMENTS

THIS BOOK WAS TRULY a team effort. I want to thank my incredible wife of 37 years, Gayle, who has stood by me every step of the way. Gayle is the most courageous individual I have ever known. She is a two-time breast cancer survivor who never gave up on life, who persevered and continues to persevere to help others through her work as a registered nurse. Gayle is a remarkable role model for our entire family. Gayle, I love you.

Our four children and their loved ones—Jared, Nick and Brinley, Kristina and Darrin, and Matt and Cassee, and one grandson, Luke Dominic—your love is my strength. I love you. I want to thank my father-in-law, Bill O'Halloran, for his many years of support and love and for giving me the gift of his daughter Gayle. I want to thank my late parents, Dominic and Jane Mattone, and my late mother-in-law, Jean O'Halloran, all of whom I know watch over on our family. We go forward every day with character, conviction, and confidence beneath your wings.

I want to thank all my clients who have attended my speeches and programs and those whom I have had the privilege to coach and consult with throughout the years. I have learned so much from you, and I want to thank you for your contributions to this book. I especially want to thank my co-author Nick Vaidya for his incredible contributions to this book, Joel Pitney, who is one of my closest advisors and who worked tirelessly on our book launch and, of course, I want to thank the 14 CEOs who appear in the book for providing such powerful, rich, and deep perspectives on leadership and culture and truly helping make the book come alive. I want to thank Dr. Kerry Healey, president of Babson College, for writing such a powerful foreword to our book.

I want to thank my close friends and marketing partners—Stefan Speligene, Terri Totty, and the entire *roux* team as well as Jim and

Carla Higgins from the Higgins Marketing Group. I want to thank my close friends and global business partners Bonnie Hagemann, Annette White-Klososky, Dawn Ciarlone, and the team from Executive Development Associates; Dan Hoeyer and team from Leaders Excellence; Vegar Wiik, Sybil Alfred, Natalya Sabga, Debra Delach-Dodd, and the entire team from Florida Atlantic University's Executive Education department; Elaine Eisenman and Joe Weintraub from Babson College's Executive Education team; Romeo Ruh and team from ZfU International Business School in Zurich, Switzerland; Graciela Gonzalez Biondo, Chris Stanley, and team from World of Business Ideas (WOBI); Alper Utko, Didem Gurcuoglu, Labeed Hamid, and team from the Management Centre Turkey in Istanbul; Soliman Arab, Sherihan Hassabo, and team from Vigor Enterprise in Kuwait; Christianna Tsiterou and Marie-Louise Adlercreutz from Innoverto, in Dubai, UAE; Hugo Fernando Gutierrez, Alena Cabova, Lenka Krivkova, and team from Seminarium Mexico; Jorge Venegas and Maria Pia Venegas from Seminarium Costa Rica and Panama; Sven Kroneberg from Seminarium International; Juan Carlos Linares and Paulette Manrique from Lee Hecht Harrison in Bogota, Colombia; Faith Chinogurei and Samantha Mawarire from Manifest HRC in Zimbabwe; Bhaawana Devaraath from Synerggie Events in Oman; Muneer from CustomerLab in India; and CB Bowman and the entire Association of Corporate Executive Coaches family. I want to extend special thanks to Joan Bigham, Des Dearlove, Stuart Crainer, and the team from the Thinkers50 for their belief in me and my work. I want to thank Taha Farhan and the team from Globalgurus for their support and belief in me and my work. And, of course, I want to thank all our global speaker bureau partners for their support as well. Special thanks to all my executive MBA students at Florida Atlantic University. I want to extend a special thank-you to my good friend and personal coach, Linda Mattia Potts, who has given me many gifts along the way, but the ones I most cherish are her honesty, wisdom, and inspiration. I want to thank my colleagues and friends from AlignMark—Cabot Jaffee Sr., Cabot Jaffee, Glen Jaffee, and Mike Struth for what I learned from you and for providing me the wisdom and passion to do what I do today.

Lastly, this project would not have been possible without the outstanding efforts of Senior Editor Matt Davis and his team at Wiley. Thank you very much.

John Mattone

ACKNOWLEDGMENTS

THIS BOOK IS THE CULMINATION of years of effort—and a philosophical and career transformation from a data-centric empiricist to a creative strategist. In many ways it is also a statement of personal growth from the constrained and limiting thought process required of a scientist to the realm of possibilities expected of a philosopher.

I want to specifically thank a few people who were instrumental in helping me make this journey.

My mother, Nirmala Vaidya, has been a pillar of support all my life and has always been there for me and the family in every conceivable way, ensuring difficult times pass in care and love. Her dedication to the family and its well-being has been her sole focus in life and she succeeded splendidly despite incredible odds. She gave up career opportunities because her children needed her at home. A mother like that needs to be saluted and revered. I also want to thank my father, Narendra Vaidya, for his unwavering focus on education and his family's well-being.

My three daughters, Ashima, Ahna, and Anika, bring such incredible joy and learning into my life. Without the lessons their presence in my life brings, I would not be evolving as a human being. They are the source of my strength and happiness in life.

The support of my incredibly loving extended family including my two brothers, sisters-in-law, nephews, and niece is the reason that I have crossed some difficult times without faltering along the way. Nitin, Namit, Sharmila, Soumya, Amol, Priyanka, Apoorv, and Avie Vaidya— I love you all and cannot thank you enough for being there.

I want to thank my late grandparents, Raghubir Saran in particular, for embodying values that I cherish and make efforts to live by—integrity, responsibility, and compassion. They are the reason I am part of an absolutely adorable and loving family of uncles, aunts, and cousins who are always there for me.

Thanks go to Suma Nithya and Faisal Kalim—my closest colleagues, partners, and friends whose unyielding support for the cause of our group is critical to its survival, as well as Abryl Acosta, the au pair for my children and a dear friend, without whom I would not be at work even for a single day. I thank them from the bottom of my heart for being there in my life. I would be remiss if I did not thank my long-time friends Dr. Ranvir Singh, Dr. Sunny Singh, Dr. Sanjay Misra, Dr. Steven Sivo, Punita Srivastava, and Vivek Gujral.

I want to thank my friends Joseph Emmett and Ritu Asatkar, who introduced me to the ancient philosophy of the Vedanta and spent hundreds of hours in discourses that have influenced my thinking about leadership and life in general. Without doubt, this book would not have been possible without my co-author John Mattone, whom I cannot thank enough. He took the project by the horns and made it possible during the most difficult time of my life. I owe thanks to every single person he thanks. I want to thank Dr. Victor Wilson, at Texas A&M University—my doctoral advisor and a huge supporter—and Paul DiModica of Value Forward Marketing Group, my executive coach and advisor who helped me make the transition from a statistician to a strategist.

Thanks also go to my business associates and supporters—David Schmoock, president, Dell, Inc., my former boss and mentor; Tariq Shaukat, chief commercial officer, Caesars Entertainment Corporation; and Alex Vratskides, CEO, Upstream—my colleagues at the start of my career with whom I learned the initial set of tricks; Brett Hurt of Hurt Family Foundation, whom I delight in calling a friend and who means a lot to me.

The role of my guests on *The CEO Show* may not be apparent but is paramount in the development of this book. I could not possibly thank each one of them by name, but they are all in my heart and deserve special thanks. Let me also not forget to thank all the contributors to the *CEO* magazine and all of my readers. Thank you all.

This acknowledgement would not be complete without thanking Missy, my pet Maltese, who sits by me all day long in the office and keeps me company.

Nick Vaidya

FOREWORD

Dr. Kerry Healey
President of Babson College

JOHN MATTONE'S *CULTURAL TRANSFORMATIONS: Lessons of Leadership and Corporate Reinvention from the C-Suite Elite* builds on the wisdom and lessons of his 2013 bestseller, *Intelligent Leadership.* Working with co-author Nick Vaidya, managing editor, *CEO magazine,* they demonstrate how an organization's culture—specifically how it reflects and embodies the values and character of its CEO—is the key to creating an environment that intentionally seeks and embraces change in order to succeed in a global economy that is increasingly globalized, decentralized, and driven by the new, nimble, and bold.

Through revealing and candid interviews with 14 of the top CEOs in the world, John Mattone and Nick Vaidya provide an intimate look at the triumphs and, maybe more importantly, the wisdom gained through failure from some of the world's best CEO mentors. Through their experiences readers will be inspired to achieve more for their organizations—and themselves.

Cultural Transformations is a tremendous resource to teach leaders how to unlock their own potential by being willing to confront hard truths—better known as *the* truth—about themselves and then work relentlessly to improve their personal and professional abilities every day. And, by doing so, these same CEOs set examples and expectations for their leadership teams to emulate, embrace, and disseminate throughout the entire organizational structures. Mattone's leadership development process thoughtfully and thoroughly shows how creating a successful, dynamic, and supportive culture is the cornerstone to building a sustainable, flexible, and competitive business model that can survive and thrive in any market climate.

As president of Babson College—the world's recognized leader in entrepreneurship education, of which John Mattone is a proud alumnus—I, along with my fellow academic leaders, am currently confronting major challenges to the traditional models of higher education. Put simply, we need to transform or be rendered obsolete.

Our customers, students and parents, are increasingly questioning the conventional wisdom of a college education serving as an automatic ticket to career success. As costs continue to rise, student debts mount, and long-term outcomes become less certain there is increasing scrutiny of the return on investment for a college degree.

Adjusting and thriving during this period of rapid evolution requires individuals who can both lead and, more importantly, build leadership teams with the courage to drive a cultural transformation within academia where there is often deep-seated resistance to rapid change. As educators of the next generation of global leaders, the need for academic institutions to lead the charge to create a culture of learning that embraces technology and reflects twenty-first century realities cannot be overstated.

Cultural Transformations is an insightful, understandable, and actionable leadership book for any executive—from young, talented, aspirational Gen Y emerging leaders, to visionary entrepreneurs, to high-potential leaders rising through the ranks making the transition to seasoned executives, all the way to the C-level professional who is looking ahead to what's next and who's next, as they prepare their respective organizations for an uncertain but exciting future.

We have all heard the term "born leader" but the evidence shows that they are, unfortunately, in short supply. This dearth of exceptional leaders and leadership teams will continue to be a drag on economic growth, innovation, and the pursuit of big ideas that will motivate our best leaders and those they mentor to create and take advantage of opportunities others do not see.

What is exciting about *Cultural Transformations* is that it arrives at a time when we desperately need to learn from successful leaders like the CEOs interviewed here. We can learn from their ongoing journeys and see the common thread that runs between their success and John Mattone's unique and powerful approach to leadership development.

Mattone and Vaidya have given CEOs an invaluable tool to address their number one operating and business challenge: the massive leadership and corporate culture gap currently facing global organizations. Competition in the global marketplace is fierce, and companies that want to excel can no longer rely on leaders who are merely good enough. Elite leadership is in short supply across the board from business to government to our civil institutions.

One of the major obstacles to affecting change in any organization is overcoming the embedded resistance that is the predictable result of asking people to purposefully step away from their comfort zones, especially when there is no immediate crisis that requires a response. To overcome this pushback, John Mattone provides a groundbreaking Six-Step Model of Cultural Transformation that can be effectively applied to organizations of any type.

Cultural Transformations will be a cherished resource for executives who understand that while the future is not predictable, it can be expertly navigated if there is a corporate culture that embraces uncertainty and reacts quickly to an ever-changing landscape in order to gain a competitive advantage.

And, as important, the book is a powerful teaching tool and ideal for use in MBA and executive education programs, giving today's students and tomorrow's aspiring leaders an appreciation for how an organization's culture creates measurable results. Imagine the impact on a company that is hiring from a prospect pool and promoting from within candidates who have already embraced the concept of continuous self-improvement and already share this worldview with their mentors.

John Mattone and Nick Vaidya have provided a road map to empower leaders to unlock their potential and then go beyond what they thought was possible. By taking on the responsibility of making an honest self-evaluation of their own strengths and weaknesses, doing the hard work to improve their personal performance each and every day, and having the courage to share what they learn with their leadership teams, CEOs become the catalyst for cultural change throughout every level of their organizations.

INTRODUCTION: THE TRANSFORMATION IMPERATIVE

CHANGE IS THE NEW NORMAL

In today's business world, the rate of change is at an all-time high. Rapid digitization and globalization the likes of which we've never seen before are transforming the face of global business and making the competitive environment far more unpredictable than it was even a decade ago. From smartphones to virtual marketplaces, new technologies are changing consumer behavior, empowering start-ups, and reducing product life cycles. And with the growth in emerging economies like India and Brazil outpacing growth in developed countries, companies are being forced to develop unique strategies for each sector. Within this changing landscape traditional operating models are becoming obsolete and the once-dominant players are increasingly being overtaken by more agile, entrepreneurial companies with business models that are built on change.

In this brave new world, transformation has become an imperative for companies to succeed. In the past, transformation efforts were perceived as emergency solutions to broad and systemic problems. But transformation efforts today have become a basic necessity to keep up with and stay ahead of the ever-changing marketplace. In fact, fewer than 50 percent of the organizations we have worked with directly, including those featured in this book, have been forced to transform due to chronic underperformance. The most forward-thinking companies are launching *preemptive* transformations, retooling themselves to stay *ahead* of their competitors.

CULTURE AND LEADERSHIP: THE KEYS TO TRANSFORMATION

Despite the growing popularity of transformation in the business world, the reality is that most transformation efforts fail. Evidence from global companies undergoing transformations from 2003 through 2015 shows that up to 75 percent fell short of their targets. Only 25 percent were able to capture short-term *and* long-term performance gains compared with their sector average.

Why is transformation so difficult? In our extensive research across a wide variety of industries, we've found that the two key macro levers that make or break transformation efforts are *culture* and *leadership*. When we talk about transforming culture, which we'll explore in Chapter 1, we mean shifting the key values and principles that define corporate cultures into ones that embrace rather than resist change. By leadership, which will be the focus of Chapter 2, we mean finding and developing the right leaders at all levels of the organization who are able to embody and instill these cultural values so they can successfully guide their employees, teams, and organizations through the transformation process. We've found that mastering these two macro levers ultimately determines the success of any transformation effort. The centerpiece of Chapter 2 is our Six-Step Model of Cultural Transformation, which provides a powerful road map for achieving sustained success with any transformation effort by focusing on the micro levers of vision, humility, communication, leadership at all levels, talent, and measurement. These micro levers, if pushed with passion, perseverance, and precision, are the keys to mastering the leadership and culture macro levers which, as we said earlier, are the critical foundation steps to ensuring sustained success with any transformation initiative.

CONVERSATIONS WITH 14 TRANSFORMATIONAL LEADERS

In our conversations with business people from around the world, one of the most common things we hear is that there isn't enough mentorship for aspiring leaders today. In fact, the "leadership gap" is one of the biggest challenges facing companies worldwide. This is a big reason we chose to write this book. We wanted to give you unprecedented access to some of today's most successful business minds and ask them the big questions about success, leadership, corporate culture, and the future of business. Through the following interviews, you'll get to hear from 14

CEOs who have each, in their own way, exemplified transformational leadership within their own companies.

There's the story of Kathy Mazzarella, who started working for Graybar without a college degree and rose through the ranks to become the first female CEO in the company's history. You'll hear from Kris Canekeratne, a Sri Lankan native who instilled a commitment to perpetual improvement into the core business culture of Virtusa from the beginning, allowing the company to survive several evolutions in the tech sector and remain one of the top companies in the world for two decades. There's a conversation with Hap Klopp, who started his company with a group of fellow outdoor enthusiasts and, thanks to an uncompromising commitment to creating products that they love, grew The North Face into the world's most respected outdoor equipment company. And you'll learn how Eddie Machaalani built Bigcommerce on a foundation of hard-working family values that he learned growing up in the Lebanese immigrant community in Sydney, Australia.

Each of these CEOs brings a unique perspective to bear on leadership and cultural transformation. But they all share an uncompromising belief that culture starts from the top and that the success or failure of any company depends on the integrity and vision of its leader. We feel honored to have spoken to such a talented and diverse group of leaders, and hope that by hearing their stories, you'll be better equipped to engage in and lead transformation efforts within your own company.

But before we dive into the interviews, we'd like to talk more in depth about both cultural transformation and leadership, which we'll do in Chapters 1 and 2.

1

Understanding Your Culture and Understanding the Culture You Must Create

YES, CULTURE CAN BE TRANSFORMED.

As we discovered in interviewing some of the top CEOs in the world, successful CEOs and senior leadership teams can and do nurture and reinforce new mind-sets. Individuals, teams, and entire organizations can adapt, mature, and increase preparedness to deal successfully with current and future challenges. They learn to transform successfully what they do and how they do it. As a result, they create and sustain a "think different, think big" culture that is matched only by a "do different, do big" culture. The magic is not in espousing a bold vision or executing an untargeted strategy, but in the match.

Take a client of mine, Claro Colombia, the America Movil subsidiary in Colombia. America Movil has operations in 18 countries throughout South and Central America, the Caribbean, Mexico, and the United States as well as in eight countries in Europe through its Austria Telekom operation. Partly as a result of a corporate-wide initiative to laser focus on enhancing customer experience but also to sustain its leadership position, Claro required a game-changing think-big vision and strategy to ignite its cultural change initiative. Led by Claro Colombia CEO Juan Carlos Archila (see his interview in Chapter 11), Claro started its transformation journey by leveraging its considerable corporate people strengths—an unwavering focus, discipline, and flawless execution in such areas as product development and work processes—into a laser focus on the customer, including building customer relationships based on rapport and trust, creating memorable customer experiences, and building and sustaining a culture based on customer advocacy. Claro's new value proposition emphasizes an almost maniacal focus on enhancing a customer's experience and providing instantaneous turnaround on most services and products, delivered with consistent quality by an entrepreneurial and engaged staff. In conjunction with these transformations, the company launched a new, far simpler business model geared to growth. While still early in its transformation journey, these measures have brought new energy to the organization and inspired a stronger and more vibrant culture of leader and individual contributor *capability*, *commitment*, and *alignment* that is driving impressive operating results. Again, Claro Colombia's shift was big, but the shift required a laser focus on fewer levers—not more—enabling leaders and all employees to focus on what really matters.

Organizations that want to adapt during turbulent times cannot force these transformations purely through programmatic approaches such as restructuring and reengineering. They need a new kind of leadership capability—one that can reframe dilemmas; reinterpret options; and reform, revitalize, and renew operations. They must achieve all of these capabilities at once.

Transforming organizational culture is not for the weak or the quick-change artist. Real, serious, sustained transformation requires real, serious, sustained leadership.

WHAT IS CULTURE? LET'S START HERE

Your organization's culture represents the collective character, values, thoughts, emotions, beliefs, and behaviors of your leaders and individual contributors. Your organization's culture is a product of such factors as its history and how your leaders and individual contributors ascribe meaning and value to it as well as leadership style (legacy and current), which is then reflected in the creation and implementation of your organization's values, vision, mission, purpose, strategy, structure, and roles.

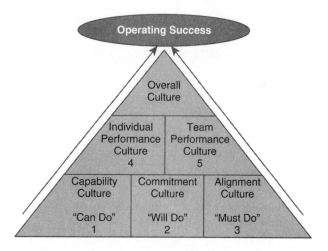

Figure 1.1   The Five Cultures of Culture

Ultimately, your overall culture and the relative health and vibrancy of your culture comprises five cultures as shown in Figure 1.1.

Capability Culture "Can Do"

To what extent does your organization develop the inner core (that is, values, character, thoughts, beliefs, emotional makeup) and outer core competencies and skills of employees and leaders at all levels? Is there a passion and diligence displayed on the part of the senior leadership team to equip leaders and individual contributors with the skills required for individual and organizational effectiveness now and into the future, skills that increase people's learning agility, change/transformation agility, and people agility? To what extent is your organization creating a culture of can do, in which people truly believe they have the skills and capabilities required to be successful and help the organization be successful?

Commitment Culture "Will Do"

To what extent do your organization's vision, mission, and purpose excite and motivate leaders and employees? To what extent is authority and responsibility delegated to those who have the best and most up-to-date information to make the best decisions? To what extent do people truly believe that they can impact the business in a positive way and add value for customers and society? Are people motivated, passionate, and inspired to do great things for the organization? To what extent is there a reasonable risk-taking culture in place in which people believe they can take risks and failure is seen as an opportunity to grow and become better?

Alignment Culture "Must Do"

To what extent is there a clear vision and strategy for the organization? To what extent do different parts of the organization and different levels share the same vision for the organization? To what extent is cooperation and consensus possible when different parts of the organization and different levels work together? To what extent are leaders visionary and possessed of a long-term view? To what extent has the vision, mission, and strategy been translated into a structure with key roles identified so that all employees know their roles and the link between their contributions and the contributions of the whole? To what extent are people so connected and aligned with the vision that they feel they must execute at a high level?

Individual Performance Culture

To what extent is there a culture of individual excellence and execution? To what extent are leaders and employees truly role models? To what extent does everyone "walk the talk"? Does everyone operate with strong character and values? Are they effective leaders in how they go about their work? Are employees effective in how they go about their work? Are leaders and individual contributors open to receiving feedback from others — including customers? Are leaders and individual contributors actually listening to feedback and making needed adjustments?

Team Performance Culture

To what extent is there a team and collaborative approach to getting things done in your organization? To what extent is there real involvement by everyone in helping shape the organization's vision, mission, purpose, strategy, structure, roles, and key responsibilities associated with those roles? To what extent do you have a cooperative, nonsiloed approach to getting work done? To what extent is there a passion and inclination to work hard to achieve win/win solutions when conflicts and disagreements occur?

Why Is Culture Important?

Your organization's current and future operating success is tied to the health and vibrancy and overall maturity of your culture. Regardless of your unique transformation challenge (for example, the need to be more innovative, collaborative, global, more responsive, more efficient, execute better, become more customer-focused, or even integrate or merge with another organization), your culture and how strong and vibrant it is will determine whether you succeed or fail.

Why Transform Culture?

As we discussed in the Introduction, organizations have no choice but to transform. The business world is shifting fast; progressive CEOs and senior leaders see it, know it, and feel it. Attempting to cope, they apply their best thinking to the structures, systems, and processes they need to compete. Conventional wisdom says that the right business structures will provide the right efficiencies and agility (learning, change, and people) that organizations need to succeed and achieve meaningful longevity. Behind closed doors, however, senior leaders and CEOs are speaking a different truth. Conventional wisdom? Throw it out the door.

Increasingly, companies are questioning the incessant reorganizing, reengineering, and restructuring in the name of efficiency. Strategies and plans that should work instead fall apart, yielding yet again less-than-expected results. Operational decisions that once were clear-cut become more complicated and ambiguous.

Worse, many top executives and teams struggle to agree on outcomes—or even common ground—for moving forward. Talented individual leaders with impressive track records fail to collaborate. They don't know how to work together to understand difficult challenges, much less to resolve them. Instead, they continue to be constrained, operating in silos and defaulting to traditional boundaries and turf battles.

Integrating systems, collaborating with partners, and coordinating across the supply chain remains an elusive skill. Innovation is haphazard or thwarted. Customer-focused strategies become uncoordinated with uneven implementation. In short, organizations are stuck; many are failing. Frustrated executives work harder and longer. People at every level are overwhelmed, guarded, and cynical.

What's the Problem?

Inadequate leadership ability is a huge part of the problem. You'll note we say "leadership"—not just a reference to the individual leader. The shift in focus from development of the individual, heroic leader, to the unfolding, emergent realization of leadership as a collective activity is intentional—and very, very important.

Through my research and coaching I have found that the five most important skills and capabilities needed by organizations (and leaders) of the future—leading people and overall people "agility," strategic planning, inspiring commitment, learning agility, and agility with respect to leading and managing change—are among the weakest competencies of today's individual leaders.

These findings suggest that organizations should prioritize creating more balance between developing leaders through individual competencies and fostering the collective capabilities of teams, groups, networks, and organizational leadership. The culture of team performance is just as real and powerful as the culture of individual capability (can do), the culture of commitment (will do), the culture of alignment (must do), and how these three cultural leading indicators manifest themselves in driving the culture of individual performance (are doing). In fact, as we established earlier in this chapter, an organization's overall culture is the net result of the health and vibrancy of these five cultures.

The common thread that ties together my research, coaching, and what we have learned in our CEO interviews is a powerful one: Thoughtful and deliberate attempts to foster and sustain the appropriate, relevant leadership culture given the current and anticipated demands and challenges your organization faces will, in the end, determine your transformation success or failure.

Different leadership cultures serve different purposes. A hierarchy of culture exists—and each advancing culture is increasingly capable of dealing with greater and greater complexity in leading and gaining the commitment of others, effecting strategy, and being successful in organization change.

As companies face change, they need to invest intentionally in a leadership culture that will match the unfolding challenge. The beliefs that drive leadership behaviors need to align with the operational business strategy. Without that alignment, painful gaps appear in the individual leadership skill set as well as the organization's collective leadership capability.

In contrast, when executives change their leadership culture, they are rewarded with significant, sustainable outcomes, including:

- An accelerating ability to implement emerging, successive business strategies
- Greater speed and flexibility, allowing the organization to move faster in response to change and challenge
- New, stronger core organizational capabilities
- Achievement of bottom-line results
- Improved ability to create shared direction, alignment, and commitment throughout the organization
- Growth of not only individual capabilities but waves of individuals all growing capabilities in a leadership collective
- The development of talent and culture while implementing the business strategy
- Genuine organizational innovation for not only products but also the organizational systems required to sustain innovation
- Effective cross-boundary work and the collaboration required for dealing with complexity and change
- Increased engagement within the top leadership team that links through leadership down to employees throughout the organization
- A rehumanized workplace, balancing technical and operational expertise with beliefs and experience
- Leadership and organizational transformation

Change remains difficult, and the history of change management teaches us that a simple recipe does not work. Our experience with clients and with the CEO interviews in this book has helped us identify themes and patterns, tools, and models that will help leaders and organizations positively transform their cultures.

Here are some of the most important themes and patterns that we will touch upon now but will explore in more detail in later chapters with the help of our CEOs.

Thinking different and thinking big are the nonnegotiable prerequisites that will enable any organization to keep pace with rapidly changing reality. This thinking must start with the CEO.

Reality is way ahead of our collective capability to lead transformation initiatives. What's needed to keep pace with the challenges organizations face are new transformation mind-sets, new behaviors, and new habits.

Most organizations lag behind when it comes to their developing the needed capabilities that will propel them toward achieving a more interconnected culture. It takes an even greater stretch to thrive in the face of change. There is no doubt that thinking different and thinking big are the non-negotiable prerequisites to achieving transformation success and this thinking must begin with the CEO.

Real sustainable transformation requires new mind-sets, not just new skills.

Organizations have become savvy developers of individual leader competencies. In doing so, they have over-relied on the human resource function to manage change through individual skill development. Executives have not considered the need to advance both individual and collective leadership mind-sets.

Values and beliefs drive behavior and habits.

Unexamined beliefs control an organization and prevent any meaningful change. Years of valuing hierarchy, status, authority, and control—even if unstated—can lead to assumptions and behaviors that are out of date, unnecessary, unhelpful, and potentially at odds with stated goals and strategic direction.

Real sustainable transformation requires that all leaders possess a strong, vibrant, and mature inner core.

Change yourself—change your culture. That's the new reality. Senior executives who want to move the needle toward organizational transformation must first experience significant personal transformation. That commitment to personal change is a fundamental part of their readiness to take on the leadership and management challenges of change for a sustainable future.

Transforming culture is the real leadership work. No, culture is not "soft." The culture you create and reinforce will determine your operating success.

The hardest work done by the best leaders is developing new beliefs and mind-sets. Developing a new mind-set is much harder than managing spreadsheets and the next restructuring. If this work were easy, everyone would be doing it and doing it well.

Understanding the Culture of Leadership

Fundamentally, culture is about the meaning that people make of the world and the tools they have to deal with it. Leadership culture is the meaning that people make and the tools they have to create shared direction, alignment, and commitment throughout the organization. The goal of culture change work is to build, purposefully and actively, capability for new ways of working. It allows for the new thinking, beliefs, tools, and processes that will result in the organizational success.

As business strategies get more complex, culture growth is required to meet the level of complexity required to implement it.

Let's start by describing the hierarchy of leadership culture: reliant, self-sufficient, and interconnected. Organizations, like people, tend to evolve along a path from reliant to self-sufficient to interconnected.

Each of the three hierarchical levels of leadership culture is characterized by a set of beliefs, behaviors, and practices. Each successive culture is more sophisticated and can respond more successfully to deeper challenges. The core reason? They can think, learn, and respond to challenges faster and better.

Reliant leadership cultures hold only people in positions of authority responsible for leadership. Authority and control are held at the top. Success depends on obedience to authority and loyalty. Mastery and recognition of work operates primarily at the level of technical expertise.

Self-sufficient leadership cultures assume that leadership emerges from a variety of individuals, based on knowledge and expertise. Authority and control are distributed throughout the ranks. Self-sufficient cultures value decentralized decision-making, individual responsibility and expertise, and competition among experts. Other characteristics associated with self-sufficient cultures include:
- Individual performance as an important source of success and status

- An emphasis on taking calculated risks

- Open disagreement

- Independent actions within functions or work groups

Interconnected leadership cultures view leadership as a collective activity requiring mutual inquiry, learning, and a capacity to work with complex challenges. Authority and control are shared based on strategic competence for the whole organization. The mind-set tends toward collaborating in a changing world so that new organizational orders and structures can emerge through collective work. Other characteristics associated with interconnected cultures include:
- The ability to work effectively across organizational boundaries

- Openness and candor

- Multifaceted standards of success
- Synergies being sought across the whole enterprise

Match the Culture to the Need

While there is nothing inherently wrong with any level of culture, organizations must match the leadership culture to the operational need. Asking a command and control (reliant) culture, for example, to implement an innovative, agile strategy is a recipe for disaster. In contrast, an interconnected organization is better poised to handle a high caliber of complexity and challenge. As a more fluid organization, it will be able to draw on individual talent, connect effectively across boundaries, and adapt as needed. Developing leadership culture is about growing leadership talent. To break through the current capability ceiling, organizational leaders must take time to connect two critical factors.

First, you have to know where, in the hierarchy of cultures, yours sits. The way leaders engage with each other and with others in the organization will depend on the leadership logic that dominates. Knowing what your current culture is capable of will save dollars, and more importantly, time. You might leap to implement the next, new thing only to find out your approach was off the mark. Instead, understand where your leadership culture is today to develop feasible change plans.

Second, you must understand the drivers and core capabilities needed for your business strategy to succeed. What future level of leadership culture is needed to support the business strategy? It is the job of leadership to ensure intelligent strategies are wisely implemented. This is possible only when the culture of beliefs and the focus on readiness to develop capability to implement is real. By choosing the right level of leadership culture that your organization requires for its future, your leadership talent as a collective can advance to new levels of organizational capability, securing success. When the level of leadership culture aligns with your business strategy, your performance will be stellar.

Taking Time to Reflect Is Critical

More and more executives tell us they need increasingly collaborative leadership for working effectively across boundaries inside their organizations and across their value chains. In fact, our executive research shows that it is their highest need and yet least effective organizational capability.

If an interconnected culture is needed, but a company is operating at the reliant or self-sufficient level, how does the senior leadership team start to change culture? How does the senior team start to work more effectively across business and functional boundaries? In a counterintuitive move, they need to pause and reflect more—much more.

Pausing and reflection are vital requirements for leading change. By exploring, reflecting, and understanding the sometimes hidden values and beliefs that drive behavior and culture, executives help the organization to be more nimble and agile in the future.

When leaders and teams pause and reflect effectively, real communication begins to happen that then drives better problem solving and decision-making. Instead of reinforcing speed, the focus is on learning. Better solutions and more frequent right answers arise. Everyone involved is able to reflect on assumptions, understand problems more clearly, and integrate the perspectives of others.

Leaders who create a culture that values pausing and reflection at key times for learning, diagnosis, and dialogue almost always create powerful, positive momentum—creating accurate, focused, valuable decisions. Time lost on the front end translates into speed further along in the process. Pausing and reflection help reduce organizational missteps (both large and small) due to poor communication, hasty decision making, and the faulty assumptions and beliefs that drive them.

Pausing and reflection is also a powerful cultural change marker. The behavior in itself signals to everyone that transformation is not only needed but valued.

The Stealth Cultural Transformation Model (see Figure 1.2) offers a compelling, symbolic way to understand the predictive relationships that exist between your organization's critical talent processes—demarcation, diagnosis, deployment, and development, otherwise known as the 4 Ds—critical cultural leading indicators (capability, commitment, and alignment—more on these later), intermediate outcomes, and ultimate outcomes. The 4 Ds essentially act as the four turbocharged engines that propel the stealth toward its target—your organization's Future Desired State and the required leadership competencies required to execute both the current and future business strategy. By way of analogy—if the four engines are well oiled and functioning at a high level (i.e., optimized) and working together (i.e., integrated), they will propel the stealth (yes, your organization) toward its goal.

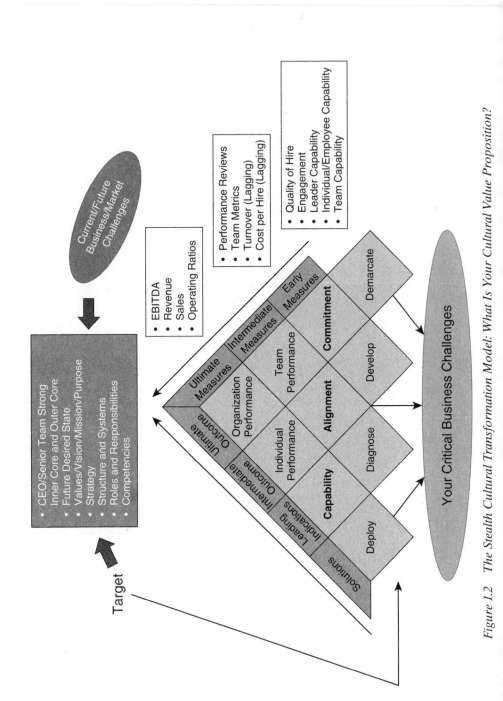

Figure 1.2   The Stealth Cultural Transformation Model: What Is Your Cultural Value Proposition?

In practical terms, your organization's Cultural Value Proposition (CVP) is the holistic sum of the following four talent practices (i.e., tools, processes, etc.) in your organization:

1. *Demarcation*—accurately separating the A, B, and C players (performance management) on those competencies and behaviors that support the new, desired, vibrant culture

2. *Diagnosis*—obsessively and objectively assessing the requisite skills and capabilities of leaders and potential leaders

3. *Deployment*—sourcing, screening, and selecting the best of the best leaders and future leaders but also making sure there are structured "bubble-up" meetings to integrate performance and potential assessments, calibrate capability, determine development options, and identify potential replacement scenarios

4. *Development*—coaching, on-the-job development, and training programs—all in support of the competencies and behaviors required to support the new, desired culture. This is the beginning of your CVP

Beyond this, your organization needs to measure the impact of these four, hopefully turbo-charged, talent engines on multiple levels of outcome—such as capability, commitment, and alignment levels (cultural leading indicators); intermediate outcomes such as individual and team performance, customer satisfaction metrics, bench strength, percentage of women and minorities promotions versus percentage in pool, percentage of women and minority successors, retention rate of successors, percentage of key positions filed internally, promotion rate of successors, success rates of those promoted and cost to fill key roles (lagging indicators); and ultimate outcomes such as organizational revenue, profits, and operating ratios.

Regardless of the exact words used to capture a given organization's CVP, one thing is sure: The elements identified in your stealth need to be continuously well thought out, believed in, communicated, executed, and measured. At its core, a great CVP encompasses everything leaders and future leaders experience and receive as they are employed by your organization—including the degree of engagement they experience, their comfort and fit within the culture, the quality of leadership, and the rewards they experience.

A great CVP always encompasses the ways in which an organization fulfills the needs, expectations, and dreams of leaders and future leaders.

More than anything, an exceptional CVP clearly connects winning talent practices to business and operating metrics. Finally, an exceptional CVP is the very definition of what it means to have a great culture.

As was discussed earlier, there exists no better way to create the belief in the value of talent than by demonstrating the connectedness between winning talent practices and operational success. The research is clear and compelling. The Hackett Group's Talent Management Performance Studies, involving hundreds of Fortune 500 companies and government agencies, gathered both qualitative and quantitative data showing enterprise financial, operational, and process payoffs as a result of having winning talent practices. Others—Boston Consulting Group, the Hay Group, PwC, Executive Development Associates, and others—have replicated these studies. Organizations with the most mature talent capabilities (i.e., the 4Ds) had significantly greater EBITDA, net profit, return on assets, return on equity, and operational results than those organizations that were immature in their talent processes. Additionally, mature talent organizations had leaders who believed in the value of the human capital asset, were passionate about investing in building and growing talent, and were relentless in their assessment of leaders, individuals, and teams.

It is clear that organizations that achieve operating excellence do so because of a sound CVP. They select and promote only those leaders and future leaders who demonstrate (as a result of performance and objective assessments) they have the highest probability of being successful; they benchmark and essentially certify (as a result of assessments) that leaders and future leaders have the capability, commitment, and alignment required to execute strategy; they provide a rich, compelling, engaging, and dynamic learning and performance support environment that motivates leaders and future leaders to become the best they can be; and they recognize and reward those who truly execute what's required in support of the desired culture and current and future operating results.

A strong CVP foundation leads to:

- *Capability*—in which leaders and future leaders possess the *can do* to execute at extraordinary levels
- *Commitment*—in which they possess the *will do*
- *Alignment*—in which they possess the *must do*

Great organizations excel in creating the belief that their leaders and future leaders have the can do (i.e., the skills, the talents, the behaviors) to execute; the will do (i.e., passion, motivation, drive) to execute; and the must do (i.e., an overwhelming sense of connectedness to the culture, mission, strategy, and values of the organization) to execute.

In other words, a strong CVP is the foundation for any organization to build and sustain an overall positive culture in which leaders and future leaders become continuously more capable (the can do culture), committed (the will do culture), and aligned (the must do culture), which then fosters a strong individual and team performance culture (the are doing culture). In fact, organizations that excel in promoting and developing leadership talent—with a focus and unwavering commitment to optimizing all of these cultural leading indicators—achieve impressive operating results.

Identifying and Developing Leaders and Future Leaders: A Critical Element of Your CVP

Current succession planning processes in the global corporate environment are insufficient to do the job. The gap between those in senior executive positions and those prepared to move into them is widening by the day. And just as boards of directors and senior executive teams are beginning to recognize the problem, they are running into new demographic and workforce challenges that make the leadership crisis all the more challenging. This is true especially in the United States, Europe, and the Far East. By some estimates, up to 40 to 70 percent of any organization's management population is currently eligible to retire. While aging thins the ranks of senior executives, other forces have contracted the pool of those available to take over the reins. In the United States, for example, changes in many organizations' pension systems are making it easier for executives to leave senior positions, while downsizing during the 1990s and 2000s have deprived many organizations access to some of the best and the brightest. Therefore, the succession planning debate is not only about the numbers: The quality and state of readiness of those who will take over leadership is also at issue.

A number of big, successful companies have taken action to both upgrade their succession planning practices and address their leadership pipeline issues. General Electric, Procter & Gamble, and IBM have made significant progress. Others, such as FedEx, Office Depot, and Navy Federal Credit Union have launched major projects to improve their succession planning practices. But the record is mixed across. In general, many large companies and most midsize and small companies are struggling with succession challenges. Most U.S. federal agencies and in fact most of other nations' governmental entities are in the same boat. There is little question: Considerable work remains to be done.

Succession planning is about identifying and developing your best talent (present and future) and preparing them to assume higher level roles or other key roles. Succession planning and management can also be interpreted as an organization's intelligent approach to dealing with the inevitable loss of key talent they may be experiencing now or that they project in the future (based on workforce plans). Organizations with succession plans have created intelligent contingencies for successfully combating their present and future losses. Organizations without succession plans have no choice but to react to the inevitable losses they encounter with panic and reactiveness, resulting in ineffective succession decisions. Ultimately, as the Stealth Cultural Model predicts, when organizations are not intelligent about deploying their top talent, individual and team performance suffers and operating results decline—significantly.

Succession planning is needed for several key reasons. The current workforce is aging rapidly. Given the large number of baby boomers nearing retirement, all organizations must prepare for these losses. Compounding this problem are the indisputable generational realities all organizations are facing and the resulting talent gaps, both in sheer number and quality (i.e., readiness) associated with those who belong to Generation X. Not only do organizations need to prepare for a mass exodus of older workers, they must prepare for life with fewer workers in general. Furthermore, many baby boomer executives have the talents and capabilities that many high-potential and emerging leaders do not yet possess. If these talents are not transferred effectively to younger leaders and future leaders, they will become lost forever.

One thing is sure—the attraction and retention of key talent for every organization is no longer a nice-to-have. The Stealth Cultural Transformation Model clearly provides all organizations with a predictive path for achieving breakthrough operating results by successfully executing the four Ds—deployment, diagnosis, development, and demarcation. Clearly, any organization that uses an intelligent approach to optimizing its four Ds—by definition—improves its chances of both attracting and retaining the key talent required to propel the organization to greatness.

No, culture is not soft. Culture predicts operating success. So, what are the critical steps you need to take to transform your culture? Let's answer that question in Chapter 2.

2

The Six Critical Steps to Transforming Your Culture

IT ALL STARTS WITH THE CEO: THINKING DIFFERENT AND THINKING BIG

In a breakthrough executive trends global research study (2011 and 2013) I conducted with my colleague, Bonnie Hagemann, we clearly confirmed that identifying and developing high potential and emerging leaders is and will continue to be one of the top issues facing CEOs. In most organizations in North America, Europe, and the Far East 40 to 70 percent of all executives will become eligible for retirement in the next five years. In other parts of the world like South America, Africa, and the Middle East, the demographics are different, yet the challenge is the same. Most organizations in these regions struggle to accurately identify and develop their future leaders.

In our increasingly knowledge-driven world economy, organizations are right to fear this imminent brain drain, suspecting that when executives leave the firm, business may follow. Conversely, potential and emerging leaders—those most likely to rise to fill those highest positions—account for alarmingly less than 8 to 10 percent of the talent pool. That's just in the United States. In other countries like Canada,

17

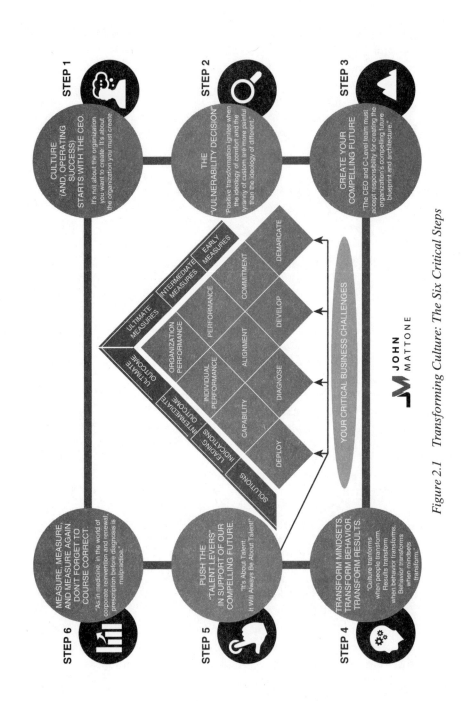

Figure 2.1 Transforming Culture: The Six Critical Steps

18

Australia, the United Kingdom, Japan, and China (and in just about every country except India and various countries in Africa and South America) this issue is as pronounced as it is in the United States, if not more so. And so identifying, developing, and retaining such rare talent truly becomes a mission-critical global challenge for CEOs, senior executives, managers, and HR directors.

Given this indisputable global business challenge, the implication for current and emerging leaders is clear: The demand for outstanding leaders will soon surpass the current supply; therefore, if you are a current or emerging leader, you should be poised and ready to capitalize on substantial opportunities. Regardless of your own desire to ascend the ladder, one thing is certain: All organizations will be asking more of their leaders—expectations, demands, and pressure will only increase. The demand for truly outstanding leaders has never been higher, and, thus, progressive CEOs such as the ones highlighted in this book, are raising the bar—as they must—in order to compete successfully on the global stage.

And, as we learned in our interviews, none of the CEOs we interviewed reserved the demand to raise the bar for everyone else. All 14 were quick to agree that their organization's culture, without question, started with them. Culture and operating success starts in the C-suite. Irv Rothman, the impressive CEO of HP Financial Services, said, "I think culture is absolutely the CEO's job. I spent the first 180 business days in 2002 traveling around the world, talking to the HPA and contact people. All I talked about was our operating philosophy and our business model, not about customers, not about strategy, not about how we're going to do things. Instead, I focused on: This is who we are. This is what you can expect from your leadership. This is why we think this is a good way to go, why we think you're going to be happy working here." Eddie Machalaani, chairman of the fast-growing Bigcommerce, said, "Company culture starts from the top. It starts with the CEO first and foremost. You can't fake a company culture if the CEO doesn't live by that code and doesn't live by the core values of the organization and then also surround himself or herself with the right talent and the right people. I feel really blessed with the talent and the people that we have in our organization. We couldn't do anything we do without them."

Where Are the Outstanding Business Leaders?

As I travel the globe, meeting with senior executive teams, coaching executives, and speaking to various management groups, it is clear to me that the world of business has very few outstanding leaders. There are many very good leaders, as well as a vast supply of good leaders. Outstanding leaders are a rare breed indeed. The distribution of outstanding leadership, like anything else, follows a bell-shaped curve. I always knew this. You know this. Actually, everyone has always known this. But nobody really cared because being a good leader has always been good enough to keep a position and meet its basic requirements. But things are changing quickly. The bell-shaped curve is being completely upended, as all organizations increasingly need to possess a larger percentage of very good and outstanding leaders in order to compete.

I had suspected the need for this critical shift for a couple of years. As we were interviewing executives as part of our "Trends in Executive Development Research Study" (Pearson 2013), it became very clear. Beyond the actual research, an interesting qualitative theme emerged. When I ask executives to identify a great leader in their lives—someone who had a positive impact on them and helped shape their values—roughly 9 times out of 10, they mention a former teacher, coach, parent, grandparent, or friend, as opposed to a business leader. Not only were the leaders mentioned not business associates, many times those executives identify the opposite: the poor managers they've endured, the unkindness, the lack of mentoring, sometimes the nightmares. Why is this?

It's not that those cited as poor leaders were bad people. More often, what became clear is that many managers are promoted far too early—certainly before they are ready to assume leadership roles. They are not adequately trained, coached, or mentored by more seasoned executives, whose experience and insights can dramatically shorten a manager's learning curve. More than anything else, I believe the speed and pace of change in business—technology shifts, demographic shifts, and a more demanding operating environment—present daunting challenges to most leaders. Very few possess both a strong inner core of values, character, beliefs, thoughts, and emotions as well as the outer core leadership competencies that are required to successfully overcome the challenges of today's global environment. In the end, too many executives are beginning to derail or have already derailed because of character flaws or, more likely, sheer immaturity.

Let's look at a couple of real-world examples of outstanding leadership. Transforming culture starts with a CEO who is willing and able to "think different" and "think big." Aside from these qualities, today's CEO must possess a counterbalancing *humility* (which we will learn more about later in this chapter), an unshakable *character* and inner core, and outer core *leadership skills.* Combine all of these elements and you have a great leader, able to walk the talk.

The Role Models of Thinking Different and Thinking Big Leadership

Let's look at two CEOs (one current, one former) who are recognized worldwide as leaders possessing strong character, a strong inner core, superlative leadership skills, and the expertise to positively transform company culture. In the subsequent chapters you will hear from the 14 CEOs we asked to be in this book because of their strong personal and professional leadership reputations and pedigrees. Let's start, though, with Jeff Bezos, the current CEO of the wildly successful U.S. online retailer Amazon, who founded his company in 1994 as an online bookstore. Bezos has built Amazon into the largest retailer on the web, selling everything from groceries to electronics to shoes. Bezos thinks *differently* and he thinks *big.* And, he is mature. Amazon consistently succeeds with risky new ventures, an achievement that Bezos credits to tenacity and obsession with customer needs. Excerpts from an interview in *U.S. News & World Report,* which David LaGesse conducted with Bezos in 2011, contained numerous examples of his strong inner core (i.e., character, values, positive beliefs, positive emotions, self-concept) and outer core (i.e., leadership competencies) that, together, form the foundation of what I refer to as *leadership maturity.*

When Bezos was asked about the need for a long-term view, he replied:

> My own view is that every company needs a long-term view. If you're going to take a long-term orientation, you have to be willing to stay "heads down" and ignore a wide array of critics, even well meaning critics. If you don't have a willingness to be misunderstood for a long period of time, then you can't have a long-term orientation. Because we have done it many times and have come out the other side, we have enough internal stories that we can tell ourselves. While we're crossing the desert, we may be thirsty, but we sincerely believe there's an oasis on the other side.

In this answer, Bezos reveals numerous examples of his leadership maturity:

- Strong statements of conviction
- Character elements of diligence and focus

- The ability to handle uncertainty and ambiguity
- An understanding of the value of experience and "references"
- Compelling beliefs about what is possible
- A powerful sense of optimism

Another great example of thinking different and thinking big leadership is Anne Mulcahy, former CEO of Xerox. When Mulcahy took over Xerox in 2000, she famously delivered a blunt message to shareholders:

Xerox's business model is unsustainable. Expenses are too high and profit margins too low to return to profitability.

Shareholders, wanting easy answers to complex problems, dumped their shares in droves, which caused Xerox's stock price to plummet an alarming 26 percent the very next day. Looking back on that dark time, Mulcahy conceded that she could have delivered her message in a more tactful, careful manner; however, she decided it would be more credible (and thus authoritative) if she acknowledged that the company was broken and that dramatic actions to fix it were required.

Although 25 years with Xerox meant Mulcahy knew the company better than most, when she was named CEO, she honestly acknowledged her lack of financial expertise. Enlisting the treasurer's office to tutor her, she wisely acquired detailed knowledge on the fine points of finance before meeting with the company's bankers. Her advisers urged her to file for bankruptcy, which would clear Xerox's staggering $18 billion of debt. Mulcahy, however, resisted insisting, "Bankruptcy is never a win." In fact, Mulcahy believed using bankruptcy to escape debt would make competing as a high-tech player in the future even more difficult for Xerox. Instead, she chose a much more treacherous, risky goal: She planned on "restoring Xerox to a great company again."

To gain support from Xerox's leadership team, she met personally with the top 100 executives. She shared in no uncertain terms how dire the situation was, laying out the facts on the table. Mulcahy then asked them one essential question: Are you ready to commit? A full 98 out 100 answered yes, renewing their commitment to Xerox. The bulk of those executives are still with Xerox today.

Like Bezos, Mulcahy's actions reflect numerous examples of her leadership maturity:

- Character elements of honesty, modesty, humility, and courage
- A powerful sense of vision
- Unwavering forthrightness in the face of difficult circumstances

- Empowering others with insight and skill
- Passion, drive, grit, and incredible zeal

These are great lessons of leadership from Bezos and Mulcahy; however, you will read about other powerful leadership lessons from the 14 CEOs featured in this book. All of them were selected for inclusion in this book because of their positive reputations and their personal and professional pedigrees. As you read about these impressive executives in our compelling interviews, you will learn—as we did—that just like Bezos and Mulcahy, they are the epitome of CEOs who think different and think big but who also counterbalance their sheer conviction with humility. Harib Al Kitani, CEO of the $6 billion Oman LNG, said it best, "For me, success is not just meeting the target. Success is going beyond what is expected of you. You cannot do it alone. Having people marching behind you with enthusiasm and trust, you will achieve great things. However, you need to demonstrate you care for them by being close to them and extend this to all your shareholders and customers and do so with great authenticity and see the results unfold."

THE OTHER END OF THE CONTINUUM: THE CHARACTER AND BEHAVIOR OF AN INEFFECTIVE LEADER

Lance Armstrong's spectacular fall from grace has been swift, far, and harsh. *Sporting News*' headline on October 23, 2012, read "Lance Armstrong's Sterling Legacy Unraveling Myth by Myth, Lie by Lie." Scott Thompson, once CEO of Yahoo!, Inc., was one day sitting on top of the world with a $1 million salary and $5.5 million in stock options. The next? His board asked him to resign in shame and embarrassment for lying about a degree he said he had earned in the early 1980s from Stonehill College in Massachusetts. And who can forget Dennis Kozlowski, one-time CEO of mammoth Tyco International? He, too, was also asked to resign amid strong speculation he was siphoning company money for his personal use. The courts later determined that Kozlowski indeed saw Tyco's bank account as an extension of his personal checking account—to the shameful (and clearly shameless) tune of more than $80 million. Kozlowski served six and a half years in a New York State correctional facility.

These three former leaders are not just examples of careers gone wrong, they clearly demonstrate extreme *leadership immaturity*. Character flaws drove this lack of leadership skills and illegal behavior. There are so many other examples—executives, CEOs, senior executives, managers, and emerging executives (some of whom I have coached) who were skyrocketing one day and falling from grace the next. You can likely think of a few examples from your own experience. When character is involved—even the question of character—my experience is that the executive may never recover. Honor is nonnegotiable. When executives reach the ultimate pinnacle and then suddenly plummet, there are no limbs to break their fall—their drop from the corporate cliff is as swift as it is unforgiving.

One of the messages I delivered to leaders and future leaders in my last book, *Intelligent Leadership,* is this: *Character doesn't determine your destiny; it determines your ultimate destiny.* Your character, or lack thereof, will impact strongly not just how you are viewed but how you are talked about. The stories told about you are your legacy: not just what you did, but how others speak of what you did (or perhaps did not do) will ultimately determine how you're remembered. The good news? All of us retain total control over how we will be remembered. It is a conscious choice we make. The question I ask all executives is, "Will you make the right choice?"

Identifying Leaders and Future Leaders You Want on Your "Transformation Bus"

CEOs often ask me what they should look for in identifying their leaders (including their fellow C-level executives and leadership teams) and future leaders. My answer is always clear: look for people possessing both a strong inner core set of values, thinking patterns, and emotional makeup, and a strong outer core set of competencies. This inner core and outer core duality provides leaders the capability to be agile—learning agile, change agile, and people agile. These three elements must exist in all your leaders, future leaders, and your entire employee population if you are to succeed in your transformation efforts.

The most critical thing to look for and measure, however, is character. This attribute is critically important for all leaders if they are going to be successful transforming culture. This attribute is the foundation that will support—and reinforce—a think different and think big culture.

The essence of character is undoubtedly multifaceted and complex. When working with executives who possess extraordinary character, I see the qualities exemplified by Jeff Bezos, Ann Mulcahy, and our other 14 CEOs. When it's time for me to help an organization identify the right leaders and emerging leaders who belong on their transformation bus, I look for evidence that they are, at a minimum, *courageous.*

I look for leaders who have the guts to make the tough decisions but the ethical foundation to make the right ones. I look for a willingness and a readiness to sometimes stand alone, in the teeth of pressure (possibly even from their own managers) to follow what may initially seem like a tougher, less forgiving path but in the end proves to be the right path—the only path—because it was the most ethical path to follow. I explain, in my coaching, that saying no to the easy route, the rewarding route, when that decision doesn't align with what you know is the correct one, may seem difficult. However, the minute you begin flirting with such decisions—those that yield better operating results, greater revenue, and greater profits yet clearly compromise you ethically and morally—you enter a world of agony and stress. Making choices such as these will lead you to painful long-term consequences, not the least of which is an increased probability you will say yes to yet more insidious acts in time. That is the danger of the unethical slippery slope—the farther you traverse it, the slipperier it becomes. This is exactly what happened to Dennis Kozlowski. Great leaders—truly great leaders—have the courage to make the right decision not just in the easy times, not just in the obvious times, but every time. Every. Single. Time.

Great leaders (and future leaders) also possess the character traits of diligence, gratitude, honesty, modesty, and loyalty.

Most Poor Leadership Is Just Plain Immaturity

Leaders generally derail not because of an inherent character flaw but rather because they respond with astounding immaturity to mounting stress and change. Immature leaders whose thoughts, beliefs, attitudes, and habits leave much to be desired can, however, recover. Unlike the poor character exhibited by the leaders in the previous section, immature leaders can, and sometimes do, recover. For example, one of the most important traits universally possessed by successful leaders who are able to lead culture transformation efforts is their *helper* trait. They are selfless; they are giving. They possess an altruistic element to their inner core that demonstrates the mature behaviors associated with the helper trait. Beware, however, that when help is executed in a less than authentic way—say, with strings attached—leaders demonstrate the immature behaviors associated with that trait. As you read the subsequent chapters, you will see that while a lot of our 14 CEOs' leadership success comes from their own strong conviction about their own abilities, more of their own success and their organizations' success is directly attributable to the altruistic, giving, selfless cultures they have created and continue to cultivate. Kathy Mazzarella, chairman and CEO of Fortune 500 company Graybar, said it best: "I know there is always a lot expected of me in my role. I am committed to helping others including our employee/owners, our company, our customers, and our community. I am driven to help more than anything."

I believe that organizations that do not compulsively develop their leaders and future leaders to be agile in the face of accelerating change and turbulence — through coaching, mentoring, executive development programs, action learning projects, and the like — unknowingly create and advance leaders with a high probability for derailment and failure. This is the real prescription for leadership disaster, and almost certainly is the prescription for organizational failure. At a minimum, when an organization, leader, or future leader leaves things to chance, the probability of leader derailment or success is nearly the same. However, with targeted coaching and real prescriptions for strengthening inner and outer core leadership capability, leaders and future leaders (and organizations) can seize the massive opportunities that await them, while mitigating the enormous risks inherent in the unrelenting pace and complexity of change in the global business environment.

The Vulnerability Decision

Kris Canekeratne, chairman and CEO of Virtusa, said this about vulnerability: "Clearly we learn a lot from mistakes, whether in life or at work. I think what's important is to make sure that the same mistakes don't happen again, that you learn from them and institutionalize them so the organization can evolve. I have found that when things don't work well, looking in the mirror and reflecting deeply on what I could have done better or differently is a terrific exercise. This is easier said than done, because strong individuals often feel that failure was not theirs but someone else's. But I believe that the best, most able leaders first look at themselves. They introspect and try to learn from their mistakes. They're willing to accept the fact that they erred. Being able to confront and acknowledge one's mistakes transmits one of the most important of all leadership tenets, humility. This further strengthens the trust between leaders and their team members."

Create Your Compelling Future

- What does your organization's future *must* state look like?
- What are the legacy aspects of your business (i.e., operational, structural, cultural "gifts") that you *must* sustain?
- What are the *values* you *must* all live by?

- What *must* be your *vision?*
- What *must* be your *mission?*
- What *must* be your *purpose?*
- What *must* be your *strategy?*
- What *must* be your *structure?*
- What *must* be the *roles* you need?
- What does greatness look like in the roles you need? What are the competencies, skills, and attributes you *must* have in the roles you need?

Here's a great quote from NV "Tiger" Tyagarajan, CEO of Genpact:

There are times when your belief is that something is going to happen and it's about the way the world is going to go in the future, the way something is going to happen, et cetera. Even though it's only in the future, the more you say it and the more it then matches your belief, which means your belief and your sayings all come together, and the more you continue to do that, the more the chances are [that it] actually will happen. I'm a big believer that in the world, in spheres about control, we can will things to happen as long as there is conviction and there is a belief and you keep saying it and then you get everyone to gravitate around it and then it happens.

And, Russ Klein, CEO of the massive American Marketing Association (AMA), had this to say when I asked how he is approaching his transformation challenge:

Well, I've taken many steps but the beginning steps center around communication, starting with a vision in which people could see themselves in a starring role working for AMA. To me, that was an important foundation piece to lay out. So we went through a process of what I call a "stakeholder-built strategic plan." It was the function of lots of listings, lots of input, and ultimately, allowed us to articulate a vision in which people could see their own ideas and their own inputs reflected in it, and they could see how they fit into that vision.

Transform Mind-Sets, Transform Behavior, Transform Culture

The most effective way for your employees to change how they view themselves and what they are capable of achieving is helping them change their references. In doing so, you help them learn to succeed.

The more successes you can help them create, the more chances they will have to interpret these wins as *permanent, pervasive,* and *personal.* The key to successfully internalizing these crucial connections lies in how often, how effectively you lead them to create positively charged references. As they rack up—with your leadership—yet more and more positive references, they're faced with no choice but to interpret both the causes and the consequences of those references in permanent, pervasive, and personal terms.

Likewise, continuing to build on these experiences allows them to build a stronger, more powerful reference system. By definition, they begin to correctly interpret whatever inevitable setbacks and failures they experience as being less permanent, pervasive, and personal. All leaders much have the courage to help their employees become more courageous in the face of transformation, to take reasonable risks in instances of peril, to make positive choices based on the strength of their inner core, and to accept the consequences of their choices. When things go wrong, they must have the resilience to course-correct, course-correct again, and indeed never give up their pursuit of positive, constructive change. This is the course of a leader, a course essential to the company's success and to that leader's personal leadership success.

Achieving this is certainly easier said than done. Where do you start? That's easy. It starts with you. Ask yourself this: Do I possess a positive, self-affirming value system? Is my inner core mature, strong, and vibrant? Notice in the Wheel of Intelligent Leadership™, your self-concept is truly multifaceted and complex, consisting of many elements, including your references and belief systems. Also included is your value system, within which your character plays out. Once you have isolated and identified your character, the two facets are intertwined, never to be separated again.

Visualize an iceberg. Beneath the water's surface is the larger volume of ice, which constitutes your character. Above the water's surface, the smaller volume of ice represents your values. Your character is always evidenced through your values and—as a leader—you must consciously appreciate the interplay between the two. To value something is to place importance on it, to show genuine interest. If you, for example, value money, you are interested in money. You will, therefore, tend to read about money, talk about money, seek to earn money, save money, spend money, and invest to hopefully make money. You honor what you value by your attention. And when you display this focused interest, you, in turn, create a favorable *attitude.* Your attitude, in turn, moves you to *act.* You find pleasures associated with some values more than with others.

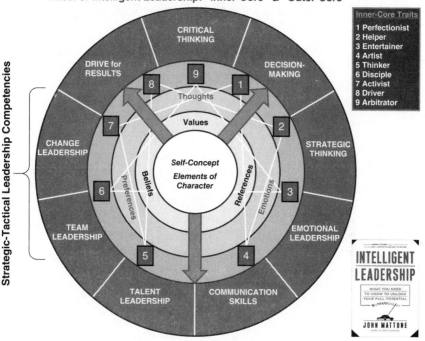

Figure 2.2   Wheel of Intelligent Leadership

There are two types: ultimate values and immediate values. Ask yourself this: What do I value most? You may answer, for example, love, security, or independence. These, then, are ultimate values. That is, they represent what you ultimately desire.

On the other hand, if you answered, "I want money and family," these are more immediate values, and you should probe further. Ask yourself this: What will money do for me? And: What is the importance of family in my life? To achieve greater levels of maturity and success, leaders must:

- Recognize the difference between immediate and ultimate values.
- Understand their own hierarchy of values.
- Understand where their hierarchy of values may deviate from or align with elements of their character.
- Set goals for sustaining their strengths and improving development needs in alignment only with ultimate values that support the elements of character.

This is no easy task; however, the journey you take to strengthen your inner core can be one of the most rewarding ones of your life. It will show you the signs for unlocking and unleashing your massive potential as the foundation for helping others unlock and unleash *their* massive potential. This is how we grow leaders. This is how we solve the leadership crisis we currently face. It's the path to better understanding not just yourself but others, as well. And, it's the direct path to helping others become more *capable* (can do), *committed* (will do), and *aligned*.(must do).

As we discussed earlier, these are the three leading indicators that provide the foundation for how people perform individually and collectively, all of which defines your current culture and how strong or weak it is. What do you have to do? Like the CEOs we have highlighted in this book, you need only do one thing: Commit to becoming the best leader you can be—every day.

I had the honor of speaking at Claro Colombia's management conference in Cartagena, Colombia, at the beginning of the culture transformation work we were doing with CEO Juan Carlos Archila and his executive team. Before I delivered my speech, Archila beautifully demonstrated this to the 1,000 managers in attendance when he said, "This marks the beginning of our coming together as a company and we must commit to becoming better. We must commit to being better today than we were yesterday. This applies to all of us individually and collectively. I take nothing for granted. I have been the CEO of our company since 2012, but I stand here today and say that this feels like the start of my career."

The Secret to Changing Mind-Sets and Changing Behavior

Once you, the leader, isolate your individual values, you can then better understand why you act and behave as you do. And the same principle holds for your employees. Once you understand their values, you then understand why they behave as they do. When you start exploring your own unique value hierarchy and assess the degree to which that hierarchy either supports or deviates from the elements of your character, you then more clearly see why you sometimes make bad decisions, fail to make a decision, or even why your make decisions that create conflict. Consider this: If your number one value is security and your second value is power, you have inherently conflicting values so close in rank that you are extremely likely to experience stress in making *any* decision. When you do make a decision, you likely measure and weigh the relative probabilities that the choice will deliver one of two things—pleasure or pain.

In other words, in addition to your values driving you to act in particular ways, the pleasure to pain ratio that you perceive and associate with those experiences is also at play. That is, whatever pain you associate with making a tough decision or implementing a risky change immediately creates a variety of complex emotional states. So many feelings in contradiction can be counterproductive, leading to avoidance, abdicating responsibility, and making hasty decisions out of fear. On the other hand, if the perceived pleasure you associate with the same action is stronger and more powerful than the pain, you'll likely be motivated to take immediate action. But which decision is correct? Clearly, if you have a strong inner core and a strong outer core working in tandem, you increase the probability that you'll make the right choice. These are the elements that great leaders practice and eventually internalize, coaching their employees to do the same.

As the CEOs in this book reveal, to make true breakthrough change that endures, you and your employees must experience these six critical elements:

1. Visualize in vivid detail new positively charged references that result from the execution of the new, desired behaviors.

2. Associate and connect the new positively charged references, as seen in your mind's eye, with generating a stronger pleasure to pain ratio than the ones associated with past experience, behaviors, and skills.

3. Cultivate only positive thinking and a relentless sense of optimism.

4. Take action, even when it's small steps, to generate momentum. Associate the forward movement with pleasure.

5. Relentlessly and fastidiously remove obstacles that impede your progress.

6. Work with key stakeholders such as managers, peers, and employees, showing humility and an uncompromising desire to improve. Ask for help, ask for support, and genuinely seek ongoing feedback.

As you move through these steps and coach others to move through these steps, remember that real, sustained transformation is based on positive behavioral change; however, the process must begin with you looking within yourself and making the commitment to strengthen your inner core. If you work hard every day—passionately and diligently taking the necessary steps to build a strong self-concept, character, belief system, references, and values—your strengthened inner core will drive positive thoughts (e.g., "I can," "I will," "I must"). In turn, your positive thoughts will drive positive emotions, such as happiness, anticipation, excitement, exhilaration, and empowerment—which are exactly the emotions that activate and incite positive action. Likewise, as we will learn from our 14 CEOs, being a great leader who can transform a business to become more innovative, customer-focused, collaborative, agile, or whatever, requires a collective "we can," "we will," and "we must." There are five cultures that drive the health and vibrancy of your overall culture. Great leaders and great leadership teams foster powerful individual and collective can do, will do, must do cultures that in turn drive both a powerful execution culture composed of individual and team performance. But, if the C-level team is composed of individual leaders who are weak in their inner core and outer core and similarly if there is leadership weakness throughout the ranks of the organization, there is little chance that any organization can succeed in its transformation efforts unless these issues are addressed—directly and swiftly.

You cannot experience any emotion without first experiencing a thought. In your brain, the cognitive element *always* precedes the emotional element. For example, suppose you were at work. Say a call came in that one of your children got sick at school, but, for some reason, nobody could get that message to you. Would you experience the emotion associated with your child getting sick? Of course you wouldn't, because you were unaware that your child was sick! The event never creates stress, conflict, or concern; only the thought about the event does that.

So, if you want to change your emotions, clearly you must first change your thoughts. In turn, positive emotions—because they incite and activate—drive positive behavior, such as constructive problem solving, relationship building, and the like, and, of course, positive behavior drives the execution of the skills and competencies that define the outer core of leadership success. Yes, if you want to change your behavior you must first change your mind-set; if you want your employees to change their behavior, you must get them to change their mind-sets!

The Nuts and Bolts of Getting Your Team on Board

Turbulence and transformation have become a way of life in organizations. Here's how to get people on board.

Part 1: Design the Transformation To understand how to do this first requires an understanding of how to manage the three major activities involved with transformation:

1. *Defining and designing* what the end result of the transformation *must* look like.

2. *Assessing* the current situation in relation to the desired transformation (this always includes a survey or assessment of the health and vibrancy of the current culture).

3. *Planning and managing* the transition from the current situation to the desired future state.

Fifteen or more years ago, most so-called change leaders first assessed the current situation and then they designed the future state. Often this strategy created only small improvements because it was based on what-is and did not take into account the desired what-if of a future state. Today, leaders of transformation efforts should create their compelling future in general terms, defining what they must see, how they want to see it, and when they want the future to arrive. This is the architecture. Planning the future is possible, even when change is constantly a challenge. Next, leaders design the future in more specific terms. A thoughtful, meticulously planned transition is critical; otherwise, there's no road map for moving from the present to the future. In addition, ongoing, everyday business must be managed and led at the same time as the change. This can put a great deal of pressure on leaders to execute the required change and manage business as well.

Part 2: Develop a Transformation Strategy

$$D \times V \times P > R = T$$

D = demand and desire for transformation and the dissatisfaction with the current situation. A high D provides the motivation for the change (a critical requirement here in establishing a high D is to assess the current culture with a cultural assessment tool).

V = the vision for the transformation, stated in a clear, compelling way that is well and widely communicated. Without a strong V, there is neither a shared direction nor a belief that those in charge of the transformation know where it's going.

P = the plan and process for transformation. This is similar to transition, but it also includes concrete information about what the organization will look like after the change occurs. Thus, P has some elements in it from design the future.

R = resistance to the transformation. Almost every transformation effort incurs resistance. With too much R, either the transformation effort will never materialize, or the change will occur but implementation will be very difficult. With no obvious resistance, a leader should begin to wonder why. Where is the resistance? Are we really doing something different enough?

T = the transformation that actually occurs. The transformation strategy formula says this: for successful transformation to occur, there must be sufficient D (demand, desire, dissatisfaction), and sufficient V (a clear and compelling vision for the transformation), sufficient P (plan and process for how to get to the end results), and all three (D, V, and P) must be greater than R (resistance to the transformation). These are the elements of the transformation that leaders must oversee. Notice that there is a multiplication sign between the first three elements (D, V, and P) rather than an addition sign. This is because if any of these elements is zero, no transformation will occur, even if the other two elements are strong.

Part 3: Take Charge of Transformation   To take charge of transformation while still leading and managing the ongoing business, you must take the first two areas—designing the transformation and developing a transformation strategy—and add one more element. Leaders must learn how to be change champions. In Figure 2.3, notice that Design the Future includes anchoring or institutionalizing the transformation and addressing resistance. Resistance also emerges when the current situation is being assessed and people are just learning about the need for transformation. This is the time to increase the desire and demand for the transformation. Resistance will also emerge during the transition period. Leaders need to anticipate and respond effectively to the inevitable resistance that occurs during these three periods.

Push the Talent Levers in Support of Your Compelling Future

We talked about establishing the Cultural Value Proposition in Chapter 1 but here are the nuts and bolts of doing just that:

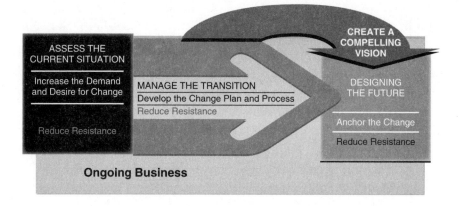

Figure 2.3   Be a Change Champion

- Are we accurate in separating the A, B, and C players and are we differentiating compensation and rewards correctly?

- Are we passionately and diligently measuring the competencies, skills, and talents of our leaders, future leaders, and employees and are we leveraging this critical leading indicator information?

- Are we creating a strong, vibrant learning environment in which our people have the resources, tools, and support to become the best they can be in support of the organization we must create?

- Are we selecting and promoting those leaders, future leaders, and individual contributors who possess what it takes to help us create the organization we must create?

All 14 of our CEOs cited the absolute importance of pushing talent levers in support of building the organization you must create. The impressive and respected Nabil Alawi, CEO from AlMansoori Specialized Engineering, based in Abu Dhabi, UAE (see his interview in Chapter 12), talks so passionately about his people and his care for his people that it is easy to see why he is one of the most respected CEOs in the Middle East.

Measure and Course-Correct

Prescription before diagnosis is malpractice in medicine, but it's also malpractice in the world of leadership development and culture transformation. You must have a passionate and diligent focus on measuring everything and, most importantly, you must measure the strength and vibrancy of your current culture, which has a big impact on your organization's overall readiness to transform (which also must be measured). Here are the elements of measurement that can enable positive transformation; it begins with leaders who make the decision to be vulnerable individually and a leadership team that likewise makes the same decision collectively.

- Are we measuring the strength and vibrancy of our talent levers?
- Are we measuring our leading indicators—the individual capabilities of our leaders, future leaders, and individual contributors? Are we measuring their commitment to our values, vision, and mission? Are we measuring how well they are aligned with the vision of the organization we must all create?
- Are we measuring the strength and vibrancy of our culture? How engaged are our people? How engaged are they with the vision of the new organization we must all create?
- Are we focused externally on getting feedback from customers, suppliers, and competitors?
- Are we measuring the right metrics operationally?
- Are we leveraging this world of feedback and demonstrating the willingness to be vulnerable, so we can create the organization we must create?

3

Kathy Mazzarella
Chairman, President, and CEO, Graybar

Align yourself with people of extraordinary character and
competence.

—John Mattone

WHAT DOES IT MEAN TO align yourself with people of extraordinary character and competence? Who are those people? Are they your mentors? Your bosses? The people who work with you or for you? As a leader, you might read my quote above and immediately think of your team and your peers; however, becoming a leader can happen at any time. It only starts once you commit to it. This builds your foundation, and it happens throughout your life, maybe even early in your life as it did for Kathy Mazzarella.

Born in Pasadena, Kathy Mazzarella was like many other girls growing up in Southern California in the 1960s. Good grades but not great, good looking but yet blending in, shy and soft-spoken. By her own account, Kathy was your average Southern California girl. Following the notorious Watts riots, Kathy's family migrated to the relative peace and calm of Orange County when Orange County was still dotted with actual orange groves, trees swaying in the salty, Pacific Ocean breeze.

Kathy saw the change from fast-paced Los Angeles County to sleepy Orange County as an opportunity for change, a place to start anew.

Her father's strong belief in the power of education to transform one's life inspired him to work extra jobs to earn the money to send Kathy and her siblings to the local parochial school. It was there, at that new private school in Orange County, that Kathy decided to commit herself to transform her life's trajectory. A voice inside her rose up, determined to stand out from the crowd. She committed herself, quite simply, to be extraordinary.

It wasn't easy. It didn't happen overnight. She joined sports teams but won no ribbons. She dedicated herself to her schoolwork but wasn't first in her class. She ran for school office and lost. She auditioned for the school play and did not get the part.

But she didn't give up. Here her character formed.

After trying out for the cheerleading team and making it, she was off and running. This turning point gave her hope and proved that her goal to be not just ordinary, but extraordinary, was not just a dream. She decided to run for student body president. She thought to herself, *I can run, but can I win?*

She'd be running against more popular girls—girls with long-standing social currency, girls who could win without much effort. Was it worth it? Kathy's father gave her some words of wisdom: "Whatever you do, never sell yourself short. Always go for the number one spot."

So, young Kathy ran for student body president and won. She realized then that it is always better to go for it and lose than to settle for second place. She finished third in her class, as a cheerleader and student body president, which was enough to get her a full ride scholarship to the University of Rochester in Rochester, New York. Here her competence developed.

In the fall, Kathy left sunny Orange County, her family, and high school boyfriend behind to study pre-med at Rochester. She was achieving extraordinary goals—everything was going as planned. There was just one problem: Kathy was miserable. She was earning good grades and doing exactly what was expected of her, but she wasn't happy. The science classes felt wrong, the cold felt wrong, it all felt wrong. Kathy did the unthinkable: she dropped out, forfeiting her scholarship. It wasn't the rational choice, but Kathy was following something deeper—her instincts. As she returned to her parents' new home in Northern California, she had that nagging feeling of failure she remembered having as a teenager.

Recognizing she needed to find work, Kathy, the 19-year-old college dropout, got polished up one morning and set out for an appointment at an employment agency. Not knowing the area, she got lost. She stopped in at an office building to ask directions. At the desk, the receptionist asked if she was looking for work. She said, "yes." And so, at 19 years old, with less than a year of college under her belt, Kathy became a customer service rep at Graybar, a North American distributor of electrical and data communications products. During the interview, they asked her what she wanted to do at Graybar. Kathy answered: "I want to run the company." The hiring manager laughed, not knowing Kathy's inner drive. The words of her father echoed in her head: *You always go for number one.*

She committed herself to being extraordinary, and it would become her destiny.

Graybar is an employee-owned Fortune 500 company whose secret to success is a promote-from-within culture that values and recognizes the contributions of its more than 8,200 employees. Kathy Mazzarella was hired at 19 as a customer service rep and, over 35 years of dedicated service, rose through the ranks to become Graybar's chairman, president, and CEO. In addition to being Graybar's first female chairman, president, and CEO, she is one of the 23 female CEOs on the 2015 Fortune 500 list.

Many things have changed at Graybar over the three decades since 19-year-old Kathy arrived. But one thing remains the same: Graybar's values. Core values of integrity, employee ownership, long-term view, and customer focus are the very foundation for Graybar's success. With a leader like Kathy—who learned her values from hardworking parents, who honed her values in high school and even her first, failed attempt at college (she would later return, supported by Graybar)—Graybar is in good hands.

Since 1929, Graybar has remained independent and employee-owned. All of its shareholders are either current employees or retirees, many of whom have built successful careers with the company. I sat down with Kathy to talk about how Graybar grows its own leaders and how character and competence continue to play a role in the company's success.

JM: Kathy, under your watch, Graybar has achieved incredible success. What do you attribute this to?

KM: I believe one thing that makes Graybar so special is how each person in the company can truly make a difference. It doesn't matter whether you're a senior executive or an entry-level employee; we all have the ability to contribute to Graybar's success. As fellow employee owners, we have a special level of commitment to each other to contribute our efforts and skills. This is a unique mind-set that is foundational to our Graybar culture.

Over the past few years, we've brought a lot of new talent into the organization, including many recent college graduates. When I talk to these newer employees, they are enthusiastic and confident in their ability to make a positive impact. I find that attitude inspiring and want to nurture this kind of mind-set throughout the organization to maintain real, sustainable transformation.

Let's face it. Work can be tough, and we all get knocked down by the everyday demands of our jobs. If we can stay focused on a broader purpose, it helps develop a mind-set that puts those everyday challenges into perspective.

JM: Thanks Kathy. As the CEO of Graybar, you've really led the way in developing the culture you just described. What would you say is your leadership style?

KM: One of my top priorities as a leader is to stay connected with employees, to talk about where the company is headed, answer their questions, listen to their concerns, and reinforce how important their work is to our success. One way I do that is by recognizing people and sharing their success stories on my national "town hall" web conferences. I also make time to meet with as many employees as I can, by visiting our branches and talking with groups when they come to headquarters for training or other meetings.

JM: You're really passionate about your employees. Why is that?

KM: First and foremost, because Graybar is employee owned, we all have a stake in the future of our company. The only way we'll succeed is by working together toward a shared purpose. In addition, our employees are the reason why customers do business with us. They are the heart and soul of our organization, working to build relationships and serve our customers every day. I know how hard their jobs are because I've been there, and I want them to know they're valued and appreciated. I also want them to see how they can be part of creating an even brighter future for our company.

JM: You've never forgotten where you're from.

KM: I think that's one of the main advantages of Graybar's tradition of growing our own leaders from within the organization. Think about it. I was just like our employees earlier in my career, doing the same type of work in a very similar environment. In fact, I clearly remember my first visit to Graybar's corporate headquarters. I was 27 years old and won one of the company's biggest awards. I bought a new suit and tried to be on my best behavior. It was intimidating to be at the corporate office with all of the executives, and I felt so nervous and out of place.

When I came in as CEO, I wanted to break down those perceived barriers. I wanted people to understand that we're all on the same team and that they're always welcome to visit and to reach out to anyone within the company—including me.

JM: Let me ask you this. What do you see as your greatest leadership strengths? And what one or two areas would you want to improve?

KM: I believe one of my strengths is that I am extremely values driven. To me, it's important to work for a company where my personal values align with the organization's culture and values. I'm incredibly fortunate to work for a company like Graybar, because I've never had to compromise my values to advance my career.

I'm also highly competitive and am always looking for ways to improve and grow. That helps me achieve more on a personal level, and also from a business perspective, as we seek out new opportunities and big ideas that can transform our company for the future.

Finally, I believe my ability to be real and authentic is an important strength. I realized this not too long ago when I went to visit my dad in the hospital. As I waited for my dad, I sat next to a man who was homeless and wanted to find a nearby shelter. The nurse was talking to him and I pulled out my computer to try and help him find the information he needed.

Later, my mom said to me, "Never lose that, because it's your biggest strength." I didn't know she meant and asked, "What?" She said, "You're real. You're the CEO of a major corporation and you treated that man as your equal."

I never consciously thought about how important it is to see and value the humanity in others until my mother made that statement. It made me realize that, at the end of the day, we are alike in far more ways than we are different.

As leaders, I think it's so important to be human, to treat others with respect and forge connections, even when it appears we have very little in common.

In terms of areas for improvement, I am my own toughest critic and I constantly worry that I might fail or let others down. I feel an immense responsibility for the long-term health of my company and for all of the customers and families that depend on us. Every day, I do my best to make Graybar stronger for the next generation.

JM: You've always been very driven to achieve. What's the next challenge on your list?

KM: While it's true that I've always been driven, I'm also very grateful for everything I have. I've been married to my husband—my best friend—for more than 30 years. We have two remarkable daughters and I have a fantastic job with a great company. I truly have an amazing life.

But I know there's more expected of me as a leader. I am committed to helping others, our company, and our community to reach our next goals … to continue being extraordinary.

From a company perspective, Graybar is in a highly competitive industry that is grappling with dramatic changes in the ways customers want to interact, the services they need, and the measurable results they expect. Advancements in technology are impacting all aspects of our business, and like most companies, we expect talent to be one of the most critical challenges in the years to come. Navigating these changes and leading the company to a whole new level of success is my primary focus right now.

On a personal level, one of the things I'd like to do in the future is to earn my PhD. I have this constant hunger to learn. And the more I learn, the more I realize I don't know. I also have a long list of places to visit, mountains to climb, and goals to accomplish.

JM: Do you have balance in your life?

KM: No, I don't think it's realistic to have balance in this role. In fact, a friend of mine who runs another company was asked the same thing, and she responded that "being a CEO is a lifestyle." I think that's a perfect way to describe it, because as CEO you're always on. You have to be careful what you say because you're representing more than your own opinions. You're representing your whole company and it's your responsibility to make sure you do that well.

JM: Would you describe yourself as happy? Or would you use another word?

KM: I'd probably describe myself as *centered*. There are plenty of times when I feel happy, but the feeling can be fleeting. I do try to keep a sense of humor about the things that happen to me. Life can be really funny if you keep the right perspective.

But I think *centered* is a good word. I am more at peace with myself than I was in the past, and some of that just comes with age. You reach a point in your life when you start recognizing that your time is limited. And you realize that what matters is more than just your own achievements. It's the legacy. And the legacy in itself is the achievement and what you want to be known for.

JM: The idea of leaving a legacy is one of the reasons you're doing this interview, one of the reasons I'm doing this book. It's a chance to really let the world know the essence of who you are how you've become who you are.

KM: When I was younger, my goals were more about me: *I want to do something great. I want to do something that's never been done before. I want to make this big impact. I want to be famous.*

But at the end of the day, I've learned that it's about making life better for those who will follow. It's about showing that you care and want to make a positive impact.

When I think about what I want my legacy to be, I would say this: I want to be known for building an organization that honors its past while inspiring a new era of employee ownership that provides opportunities for the future growth and success of Graybar. On a more personal level, I want to be known as someone who improved the lives of others.

JM: That's fantastic. The hard thing about your legacy, though, is how will you know you've accomplished it?

KM: As someone who's driven and achievement-oriented, I want to solve problems and accomplish goals and finish well. That's one of the hardest things about this. There is no finish line and no way to know for sure if I've succeeded. All I can do is strive to live up to my potential in making a positive difference for my company, my family, and my community.

JM: Talk to me about cultural transformation. When I say cultural transformation, what does that mean to you?

KM: Culture is an interesting concept and one that can be hard to define. As I've learned more about culture, I reached the conclusion that values define culture and behaviors drive culture. So, as we think about transforming our organizations, our focus should be on changing behavior while holding firm to our values and leveraging the strengths of our culture.

At Graybar, we have a very strong culture. Our people are engaged. They do what they need to do, and they're very committed to the company and our customers.

But over time, we can see how certain behaviors begin to form patterns and develop into habits. We sometimes forget *why* we do what we do, because it's just the way we've always done things.

If we're going to compete and grow our business profitably, we need to change the way we work. We can leverage the positive aspects of our culture, such as loyalty, dedication, and engagement, and just shift some behaviors to begin transforming the organization.

JM: Great approach. It's simple too.

KM: Right, I find that a simple approach usually works best. If you want to go in a new direction, it has to be clear how we're going to get there. I have to make the transition. My executive team has to be able to transition and then it cascades throughout the organization.

As leaders, we also have to understand that a true transformation takes time and effort. If we want to raise the level of performance, it's not enough to just tell people to do it. They need to go through the stages of letting go of the old ways of working, dealing with uncertainty and relearning something new. You have to manage their fear and earn their trust before they will follow you to a place where they haven't been. You have to challenge their thinking and their assumptions, while encouraging them to explore new ideas and try new things. And then we'll get the productivity. If you're going to transform an organization or leverage culture, you must first change behavior—individually and then on a broader scale.

JM: Absolutely.

KM: You also can't give up. Sometimes a team will reach a certain level and either stagnate or slide back into an old habit. Sometimes, there's an organizational inertia that creates resistance to change.

It's hard work, but you and your leadership team can't give up. You have to keep constant, steady pressure to move everyone in the same direction.

I wouldn't say we're all in the same place across the organization, but I think overall we're heading in the right direction. The key for us is to keep going and pushing ahead.

JM: How can you tell you're making progress?

KM: I can tell we're making progress when people start to show support and enthusiasm for where the company is headed, and we are definitely seeing that at Graybar. One good indicator is the reaction from some of our long-term employees, some of whom have been with Graybar for 30 to 40 years. Let's face it: after that many years with one company, it can be hard for people to get excited about change.

But over the last few months, I've heard several of these long-term employees share their enthusiasm about the new direction we're going. For example, I met with one of our long-term employees, who said, "I love this new talent we're bringing in. I'm so excited. It's really going to change everything." And I thought, *Wow, that's pretty cool.*

It's great to get that kind of support. What's even better is that many of these long-term employees are highly respected within their spheres of influence. When their direct reports, peers, customers, or suppliers hear them make these comments, it validates the transformation journey and helps us accelerate our progress.

JM: That's great. One of the things I've learned is that people will change when they perceive that staying the same is more painful.

KM: That's very true. I think of it like exercise. It hurts, it's difficult, and it's really easy to give up, but eventually you break through. You reach the point where you realize that resisting change is worse than moving forward and trying something new.

JM: Any other thoughts on transforming culture?

KM: To me, the key to cultural transformation is having the right team in place. It's great for leaders to cast a bold vision for the future, but that doesn't really change anything. At the end of the day, you need people at all levels of your organization with the values, the ability, and the commitment to do what needs to be done.

In a small start-up, leaders can take a very hands-on approach in building their teams from the ground up. But as organizations grow and mature, you have to trust others to build your team.

That's why I think it's vitally important to choose leaders who recognize that leadership is not about promoting their own self-interests, but rather, about making their teams stronger and more successful. You need leaders who believe in your vision and strategy and can translate it into action for their people. And, you need leaders with character and integrity, who set the right example and model the right behaviors.

Leadership isn't limited to a select few at the top of the organization. We need strong leaders at all levels to achieve lasting change.

JM: Leaders have an inner core, which includes things like your belief in yourself, your character, and your value system. And the outer core is what the world sees when you execute as a CEO. What I've discovered is that executives who are willing to exploit their inner core and come to grips with their strengths and weaknesses have a much higher probability of executing the outer core. What are your thoughts on this?

KM: To lead people to extraordinary achievements, leaders must be congruent between their inner and outer core; this is authenticity. Instinctually, people respond to authenticity in their leaders. They will listen to you based on your title; they will only follow you based on your actions. People do not respond to "Do as I say, not as I do" leadership. The stronger the linkage between our inner and outer cores, the more extraordinary the achievement of our teams. The key is we must be humble enough to show our human side and let people know our inner core. People don't expect leaders to be perfect, but they will only follow a leader they trust. That comes from a strong inner core. I am reminded of the words of Vince Poscente: Be honest with yourself, and you will find the motivation to do what you advise others to do.

4

Kris Canekeratne
Chairman and CEO of Virtusa

It is the disciplined pursuit of less that will give you more.

—*John Mattone*

KRISHAN A. CANEKERATNE, ALSO KNOWN as Kris, was a driven young man, excelling in not one but two sports in his native Sri Lanka. In the capital city of Colombo, Kris learned early exactly what it takes to succeed in sports at an elite level. And elite he was, becoming Sri Lanka's number one rated player under 16 years in not just table tennis but golf as well. He achieved this when he was just 15 years old.

What Kris realized very early on was that it wasn't just a high level of commitment, hard work, grit, and determination that was necessary to succeed, but also one elusive element: luck.

Fortunately, luck was—and continues to be—on Kris Canekeratne's side.

Indeed, shortly after ranking number one in Sri Lanka for table tennis, a letter arrived at Kris' ancestral home. It was from China. The Chinese government invited Kris to study and play competitive table tennis on a full scholarship in China. What an honor! But Kris did not immediately accept, and instead, sought guidance from his mother. Though he loved the sport and all that came with it, deep down he had reservations. Yes, he

47

loved the camaraderie of being part of a team. Yes, he loved the dedication required to become the best. Yes, he loved the thrill of victory. More than any of that, he loved the leadership skills learned by being captain of both the table tennis and golf teams. But instinct told him that his future did not lie in table tennis and so, not wanting to deprive another of the opportunity of a lifetime, he gracefully turned the invitation down.

What would he do instead? Recently, he'd had his first experience with a computer. His high school had purchased an early model Apple, and Kris was fascinated by what it could do. He used it simply, tackling word processing and the like, but not programming. A seed of a dream was planted, however. He'd always dreamed of leaving the tiny island of Sri Lanka and coming to the United States. Could he somehow combine the two?

Soon after the idea formed, Kris arrived for the spring semester at Syracuse University in upstate New York to study computer science and mathematics. Syracuse, at the time, was one of the top 30 computer science programs in the nation, and most of Kris' fellow students were four, sometimes five, years ahead of him in experience and knowledge.

Using his well-honed skills of dedication and drive, Kris endeavored to catch up to his classmates and master computer programming. Just like playing a sport, writing a program was completely up to him. If it succeeded, it was because he made it succeed. Likewise, if it failed, Kris knew he could find it in himself to figure out why and self-correct. The immediate gratification of the process was a thrill and a source of inspiration. Before he knew it, it was 1988 and Kris was graduating from Syracuse. He worked near Wall Street and continued to hone not just his skills but also his dreams. He married and, in 1996, not just his first child, but his first business—Virtusa—was born.

Again, Kris went to his mother for a talk. Another life-changing decision was about to be made. He asked if his mother would agree to rent out a room in his parents' home, where software engineers would work to create his company. When she agreed, a global experiment set sail.

Kris co-founded Virtusa Corp., beginning with six engineers working from the basement of his house in the suburbs of Boston, and another 10 working from his parents' home in Colombo. The engineers worked in what used to be the visiting chamber where Kris' grandfather, a judge, met his clients.

When Kris cofounded Virtusa, the software development industry was struggling with coding inefficiencies, cost overruns, and delays in releases. Kris had already proven his mettle by helping launch and grow a successful business venture in New York, INSCI Corporation.

He believed that it was possible for software development practices to embrace the efficiencies that had been achieved by mature industries like manufacturing and automobiles.

His goal was to apply the concept of platforms to software development and when he set sail with Virtusa, he did just that. It has become one of the fastest growing business consulting and IT outsourcing companies in the United States.

As an example, his company helped one of the largest U.S. banks design and develop a check presentment and fulfilment platform for online banking and launched one of the first online and mobile banking experiences including digital check-deposit through a mobile device. This app went on to become very successful, so much so that other banks followed up by developing similar apps of their own.

More recently, Virtusa has been helping this bank reimagine an omni-channel customer experience for its retail consumers through a banking experience that is mobile first and works seamlessly across on-premise, online, and digital channels.

Virtusa Corporation is a leading business consulting and global information technology services company. In 2007, it went public by listing on the NASDAQ. Virtusa's headquarters are located in Westborough, Massachusetts. The company provides business consulting, technology consulting, systems integration, and application outsourcing services to large enterprises and software vendors in banking and financial services, insurance, health care, telecommunications, technology, media, information, and education industries. It has delivery centers in the United States, the United Kingdom, the Netherlands, Germany, Sweden, Hungary, India, Sri Lanka, Malaysia, and Singapore.

With Kris at the helm, Virtusa has become one of the fastest growing software services companies in the United States with a 10-year compounded annual growth rate of over 23 percent, Sri Lanka's largest tech employer, and one of India's top 10 tech employers. Virtusa netted $28 million on a revenue of $333 million for the fiscal year ending March 31, 2013. This was a 40 percent jump in profits over 2012 and got the company listed on Forbes 100 Best Small Companies list in 2013. As of March 31, 2015, Virtusa has just about 10,000 employees, 114 clients worldwide, and grew 22 percent to end the year at $478 million in revenue. I sat down with Kris Canekeratne to find out just how he made it happen.

JM: Let me congratulate you on your incredible success, individually, but also the company. Kris, you obviously have a million things coming at you. You're leading one of the fastest growing companies in the world, plus you've got your personal life. How do you navigate all of this and continue to face the many challenges that are in front of you?

KC: Thank you John, but I might have a contrarian point of view here. I have actually worked diligently to avoid getting into a situation where I feel like too many things are coming at me. In many ways, I've accomplished this by surrounding myself with the right people and making sure that they are empowered. In essence, I'm reliant on others on my team to do the things that they do better. This is not to say I haven't had to step in and play a number of different roles from time to time, but for the most part, I am fortunate to work with some exceptional people who are really outstanding in their specific areas. Because of this, I've never felt like there were so many things coming at me that I was overwhelmed or cut up into a million little pieces.

JM: It's very interesting that you've already brought up a concept I keep hearing repeatedly from all the business leaders that I'm interviewing: that success is all about talent.

KC: It would be very hard for us to grow at the rate that we've grown if it weren't for our ability to attract and retain exceptional talent. We have established a terrific platform where our team members get to innovate and apply themselves. I believe that our employee engagement model is intellectually stimulating, empowering, and attractive to top-tier software engineers who join Virtusa because they have an opportunity to reimagine what our clients can do and transform their businesses.

JM: Kris, tell me about the creation of Virtusa. What was the igniter?

KC: My background is in software engineering, and I've had the good fortune of writing some fairly sophisticated enterprise systems and working with some amazingly talented people. I worked in this sector for eight years after graduating before cofounding Virtusa in 1996 and eDocs in 1997. eDocs was a leading provider of electronic account management and customer care [which Oracle acquired]. During those years, I had the opportunity to work with and then lead a small team of high-performance software engineers dedicated to building a software product platform that supported document management, archival and retrieval of consumer statements. We learned through our initial work that software platforms are inherently more enduring, help accelerate time-to-market, reduce overall costs, and provide a better end-user experience. So we started to experiment with helping our clients to build their own unique software programs.

JM: Excellent.

KC: During this time, my wife and I would make trips over to Sri Lanka to see our parents, and on these trips we would invariably meet software engineers who were quite talented but lacked the opportunity to work on innovation. We felt that there was an opportunity to harness this tremendous global software development talent and direct it towards building software platforms to help our clients accelerate business innovation.

Sri Lanka, because of its education system, was largely similar to India in that it had a significant availability of software engineering talent. So we felt that we would be well served by starting our experiment out of our basement in the suburbs of Boston and my parents' home in Colombo, Sri Lanka. One of the key reasons for seeking out talent in Asia in the mid 1990s was because most of these highly capable and creative software engineers were doing relatively rudimentary tasks such as maintenance and remediation for which they were overqualified. Back then, Y2K was a significant initiative that helped establish the Indian IT offshoring industry. And I found it hard to comprehend how a smart software engineer would be gratified by working on things that were not very interesting—like taking a two-digit year and making it a four-digit year! So the combination of access to good, creative talent in Colombo, and our focus on building software platforms for our clients resulted in the experiment that led to Virtusa.

JM: Amazing story. When did you know the experiment was a success?

KC: Like any start-up we had some growing pains, but we were 100 percent committed to our goal of accelerating innovation for our clients. We soon started to realize the power of our platforming approach as we doubled or tripled our company every year, we had good solid clients, and our team members were enthusiastic and gratified by the work they were doing. We built on our early successes, learnt from our mistakes, and realized in relatively short order that we could compete against very established players and win!

JM: Can you share with me some of your thoughts on the word "success"? What does it mean to you as a leader of Virtusa? What has made you successful?

KC: It goes without saying that Virtusa's accomplishments are directly attributable to our global team members and our leadership team. Each of them is very strong, capable in their own right, talented, and consistently give their best. We have some terrific, talented, high achievers who are outstanding at what they do. But to be honest John, I have personally always believed that success is still ahead of us. It's something that's aspirational, out in the future and seldom attained.

JM: I love it.

KC: So we're always striving towards this somewhat elusive next step—it's out there! Our most successful leaders are not those who believe that they have already attained their full potential but those who are constantly striving to attain their full potential. Our goal is to cherish the unknown and work hard towards finding the next best way to do something. We value being transparent, creating a performance-oriented culture, learning from others, becoming keen students, reinventing ourselves, and being catalysts for change. So for me, success is something we are always seeking.

JM: Absolutely. As a leader, as a person, you can never rest on your laurels. It's like an athlete who has a game today. He has to show up and it doesn't matter what happened in yesterday's game.

KC: That's right. And while we can't control the future, what's in our control is our preparation. We expect our leaders and our teams to give it their absolute best in terms of preparing: leave nothing undone, nothing to chance.

JM: Right.

KC: My view on this is rather pointed. When any of our leaders become too satisfied with their individual success, it transmits the wrong message to the team and creates a rather negative impression. They shift the thinking towards the past as opposed to yearning for what's next. Their motive changes and then you just don't get the same level of intensity. I believe that this is one of the reasons why some established companies become dinosaurs and new companies out-innovate and make obsolete the established ones.

JM: Very true.

KC: Fundamentally, I am a strong believer that success is always ahead of and not behind you. Leaders at Virtusa who have internalized and practiced this principle have done well, while those that have not have struggled.

JM: You have to be able to respect your past and your successes, but ultimately you have to recognize that you're still in pursuit of the next success story. You have to create your future every single day. I'd love to get your perspective on failure or setbacks.

KC: Clearly we learn a lot from mistakes, whether in life or at work. I think what's important is to make sure that the same mistakes don't happen again, that you learn from them and institutionalize them so the organization can evolve. I have found that when things don't work well, looking in the mirror and reflecting deeply on what I could have done better or differently is a terrific exercise. This is easier said than done, because strong individuals often feel that failure was not theirs but someone else's. But I believe that the best, most able leaders first look at themselves. They introspect and try to learn from their mistakes. They're willing to accept the fact that they erred. Being able to confront and acknowledge one's mistakes transmits one of the most important of all leadership tenets, humility. This further strengthens the trust between leaders and their team members.

We made some big mistakes in the early days of our company, which we learned a lot from. After starting in '96, we were making a lot of progress by '99. We had bootstrapped the firm with very limited funding and grown it to be over $10 million without any outside funding. We never turned to a venture firm to get funding until 2000 when we were somewhat seduced by the dot-com frenzy.

JM: Talk to me about that.

KC: By 2000 we had built a very strong global software engineering competency, which we had proven across multiple industries. Our thought at that time was to take what we had built and work with a number of industry strategists so that we could help established enterprises and upstarts to embrace the web in order to transform themselves and disrupt their industries. Specifically, we felt that if we combined our global software engineering capabilities with senior industry strategists, we could really help companies to reinvent themselves and accelerate their time-to-market.

JM: Logical progression, right.

KC: We felt good about the direction we were taking and decided to raise venture capital for the first time in Virtusa's history. We raised venture capital and started hiring business consultants from particular industries to compete against the established dot-com providers. Our differentiation was that we could help our clients think about what they needed to do and execute this effectively through a rapid global delivery model. About nine months into this process, however, we realized that things were not that good. We had a very high burn rate, which made us unprofitable for the first time in our history. Our sales pipelines were taking longer to build and close, and we started to see early signs that the dot-com market was about to collapse.

We were quickly running out of capital because of our expensive burn rate and the fact that the market was quickly drying up for dot-com services. I remember sitting down with our then-CFO Tom Holler, who now is our chief strategy officer, and going over a set of plans that he had developed to take our burn rate down and reorient the company. Tom and I had to make some tough calls, reduce costs, and reestablish our business. We quickly stripped away all of the high-cost strategy consultants, and started the process of rebuilding our company. Luckily for us, we moved quickly, and made the changes we had to make. We were able to live on as one of the very few consulting and services companies of our generation to survive the dot-com melee. I learnt a great deal from this experience. Had it not been for Tom identifying the situation that we were in, and our willingness to make a course correction, I doubt if we'd be here having this conversation today!

JM: That is a great example of the transformation you made. You lost some money, and did you lose people too, Kris?

KC: Yes to both. We lost people and we lost money. At this point we had too many high-cost strategy consultants who were not deployable because the dot-com bubble collapsed. Our goal at this point was to eliminate costs, reorient the business, and return to profitability.

JM: And at that time, the more expensive the consultant, the more respect they actually garnered.

KC: It was a very strange time and we certainly paid a lot of money to a lot of strategy consultants. When the bottom fell out, Tom and I decided to eliminate the entire strategy consulting group, which must have been 40 or 50 strong. We essentially cut the high-cost resources and focused on helping our clients to build software platforms that became the foundation of our products and enterprise processes as we continued to build the company.

JM: Unbelievable lesson. I have a saying that I'd like to share with you: "The greatest leadership truth is that failure almost always precedes success." However, the greatest leadership irony is that success often leads to failure. People and organizations that achieve success end up getting more opportunities. Then what ends up happening is they get distracted into investing their effort and resources into too many new areas, which dilutes the focus of your core business.

KC: I agree with you, John. In our case, we thought we had built a successful business and believed that we had a terrific new opportunity. But the bigger lesson for us ended up being that we had to move very quickly to avoid failure. Fortunately, we did.

JM: Powerful story. What would you say are two leadership strengths that you're most proud of?

KC: I would say the two are focusing on results and building high-performance teams. When I put my mind to something, I take that very seriously. I've learned over the years how much effort is required to be able to at least give yourself a fighting chance to succeed. This is an area that I'm personally very fortunate to have understood early in life as a result of playing sports at a very competitive level.

The other strength is our ambition to build high-performance teams. I've learned a lot of really good lessons about how hard it is to find and hire the right people. In the early years, several senior hires I made didn't work out. In the early years, we would often find a terrific contributor through the interview process only to later be let down either because we hired the wrong person or because the ethos of the firm repelled the individual. Over the years we have become much smarter about hiring, and we look for very specific traits that mirror Virtusa's culture.

JM: Yes, and can you share a little bit more about your ability to hire great leaders?

KC: In the early days, I think my hit/miss ratio was around 50:50. Over the last 10 years, my ratio has improved tremendously and the team members that we have, especially at the executive level, have been truly phenomenal. I also learned what to look for in people through some of the mistakes that I had made earlier.

JM: What do you look for?

KC: At Virtusa, we have a strong culture defined by our core values, which are pursuit of excellence, integrity, respect, and leadership. These values are very explicit and our team members are expected to internalize and practice them. We look for these values in new recruits at the executive level, the mid-manager level, and even at the campus recruit level. We take our values very seriously and have become tougher and tougher on ourselves about strengthening our processes during recruitment. In fact, adhering to our core values is a component of determining each employee's variable compensation. So compensation is based in part on how an individual practices our core values. This is also true during promotion cycles.

JM: Excellent. I love your focus on values because, in my mind, values are the essence of what creates culture in a family, and Virtusa is a family.

KC: In our business it's actually more pronounced than that. Product companies like Apple design, build, and sell products, and their intellectual property is for the most part embedded in the product.

JM: Right.

KC: At Virtusa we don't have a product per se. We provide a service, so our people are our only assets. Our values are what unify us. They're how our team members know to interact with each other. They create the glue that galvanizes us. They promote a common purpose and quickly repel those that don't belong.

JM: I totally agree with that! A lot of people don't understand that the actions and the behaviors of your leaders and your people all originate from your core values. It starts there. So I want to ask you, as a chairman and CEO are there leadership areas that you're trying to improve?

KC: Plenty. Being able to learn from one's mistakes is not easy but it's so important. Having the awareness, strength, and humility to reach within and learn and grow as a leader is critically important. For example, when we were a smaller company I had much more interaction with our people. I knew almost everyone by name until we grew to 300-plus team members. It felt like my extended family. As we scaled, I still wanted to preserve that familial sense of belonging, that open and trustworthy culture. So I decided that we would use video conferencing to celebrate our quarterly successes. We even shared sensitive financial information, which was very unusual for companies that were privately held. I think this has worked well with our people. We also have town hall gatherings where a large cross section of our team members have an opportunity to interact and ask questions.

Now as we look towards the future, we feel that there is a terrific opportunity to continue to leverage new mechanisms including social media, video, and omni-channel communication to reach a broader cross section of our team members. The key is to make our team members feel connected.

JM: Yes.

KC: Making time to be available to our team members is a critical success factor in our business. I enjoy interacting and spending time with people, and I respond to my e-mail messages, Yammer messages, and text messages fairly quickly. This has set a tone of responsiveness in the organization. But while we have succeeded in creating an environment of belonging, we also need to learn about some of the unique needs and expectations of the millennial generation as we develop our internal platforms for the future.

JM: Kris, I am impressed with your willingness to be vulnerable, which I think is very powerful lesson and I appreciate you talking about that. I think that's just a great message for young people to hear.

KC: Thank you!

JM: I believe that positive transformation in any organization starts with the CEO and the chairman. That requires thinking differently and thinking big, but it also requires humility, which you've talked a lot about here today. As leaders, we've got to be vulnerable, willing to look inside and recognize our strengths and our gifts and the things that we need to work on. We also need the ability to change mind-sets, to lead the charge, and create our compelling future. Kris can you talk to me about the compelling future that you are envisioning for Virtusa?

KC: Enterprise IT has come a long way since the dawn of the mainframe era, but we are now at the start of the largest application modernization in history. Two powerful forces drive much of this: the rapid evolution of mobile, social, big data, and cloud and a large and growing consumer base of digital natives who demand 24x7 access to services. In this new era, the enterprise storefront is digital, and enterprises must invest in creating an unparalleled digital presence in order to attract and retain digital natives and digital immigrants (their superset). Unless established enterprises are able to adapt quickly, they will become dinosaurs and be unseated by those that innovate faster. We have just entered an era where the consumer experience through the digital storefront will eclipse other channels as the primary means of attracting and retaining end consumers.

JM: Incredible, wow!

KC: At Virtusa, we are extremely well positioned to capitalize on this paradigm shift, because so much of our heritage is in simplifying, rationalizing, and consolidating our clients' IT application infrastructure to accelerate innovation. We are judicious about leaving no stone unturned to help our clients to reduce application redundancies and to unlock business velocity. We are resolute in our belief that less will get you more. The majority of our experience is based on working in large business-to-consumer industries and helping our clients move from on-premise to online, and from online to digital. Having spent the past two decades working at the intersection of our clients and their end consumers has provided us with a rich heritage of experience in an area that is evolving and transforming rapidly. All enterprises with large consumer-based services—financial services, insurance, health care, media, communication, technology, and retail—are making significant investments into creating a unique digital storefront for their consumers. We are uniquely positioned to help our clients reimagine their digital presence while rationalizing and unlocking the value of their existing IT application infrastructure.

JM: Wonderful.

KC: To effectively take advantage of this opportunity, we are mindful of our own requirement of attracting and retaining talent. In this regard, we have developed an award-winning millennial friendly employee engagement model, V+. Virtusa's V+ employee engagement platform provides our team members a work environment that replicates their weekend social computing experience, including social collaboration, video learning, advanced search techniques, peer review and feedback, gamification, and leaderboards. V+ is a high-performance team member engagement model that provides a rich learning environment that inspires millennials, who make up over 70 percent of our workforce. As a result of our heritage, focus on innovation, and our V+ team member engagement model, we are an attractive employer across all our geographies of operation.

JM: Yes.

KC: Much of V+ is targeted at creating a high-performance environment for our engineers to innovate for our clients, know what best-in-class looks like, and have an opportunity to raise the bar. So our focus is to identify top talent, those who have a natural desire to innovate. This has enabled us to continue to strengthen our DNA and build for the future.

JM: Absolutely yes. What words you would like to share with future leaders about how they can be better leaders and better people and add value to the world?

KC: During my early career as a software designer and engineer, I had the unique opportunity of interacting directly with our clients to determine what was required and then set out to design and write the code. If I got it right I had an immense sense of gratification. But if my solution didn't work, I had no one else to blame but myself. As I moved from software engineering to leadership, I tried to create the same environment for others: intense gratification upon success and introspection when things didn't work well.

JM: Right.

KC: The subtle but significant lesson that I learned was the importance of engaging an engineer directly in developing a solution with the client as opposed to having the team leader simply tell the engineer what is required and how to do it. We saw better results when the requirements were phrased in the form of questions. This approach allowed the engineer to think more deeply about ways of solving the problem, it gave them ownership over the project, and it gave leadership the opportunity to iterate the solution crafted by the engineer.

Simply stated, we stopped telling smart engineers what to do and how to do it. Instead, we explained what the problem was and asked them to come back to us with their solution. This moved the development of solutions and their execution to the engineering team where they belonged. The leadership then took on the role of reviewing and providing feedback, which enabled us to better understand if they were going in the right direction early in the cycle, so we could provide feedback before it was too late.

These early lessons and experiences formed the nucleus of my personal leadership approach. The power of breaking down a problem and then allowing others to take ownership of the solution and the execution of their idea is incredibly empowering. This approach helped me attract and empower smart leaders who could all build on an idea. Failure was not an option for these empowered teams and their commitment to seeing their solution through was terrific governance. We essentially created a force multiplier!

JM: Absolutely.

KC: We implemented this approach early on at Virtusa, and while implementation was easier said than done, we now have a great foundation. It has become an important part of our ethos.

JM: As we close, I want to ask you three final questions. First, what aspects of your culture are you most proud of? Why?

KC: Being in the IT services industry, people are our most important asset. We have made significant investments in building a strong culture within the organization, which not only helps us reinforce the values that define Virtusa but also helps define who we hire. We have built a strong and pervasive culture of collaboration, which allows globally distributed, culturally diverse teams and individuals to seamlessly work with each other to deliver high impact outcomes. This is something we are extremely proud of.

Another aspect of our culture that stands out is the mentality to always put the team ahead of the individual in instances of success while encouraging individuals to stand up and take personal responsibility for failures. A third defining aspect of our culture is the way we encourage innovation.

JM: What aspects of your culture need to transform and why?

KC: While we can always do a better job of reinforcing the above cultural aspects, we continue to invest in programs that help us identify and groom more leaders from within the organization. We are looking for leaders who are already steeped in our culture, are able to inspire their teams to achieve more, and are evangelists for our brand when they engage with our clients.

JM: Finally, what is your strategy for transforming your organizational culture and what kind of progress are you making?

KC: We have put together a foundational program to groom future leaders at Virtusa. This program is based on industry benchmarks and supported by best-in-class frameworks and processes and is already beginning to show significant results with over 65 percent of leadership positions being filled by internal candidates. We expect to continue developing this program to groom world-class leadership within the organization as we continue to grow and scale our operation.

5

Eddie Machaalani

Co-Founder and Executive Chairman of the Board, Bigcommerce, Inc.

Have the guts to look inside and admit that while you may be good, you are not the best you can be.

—*John Mattone*

IN 1975, WHEN FIGHTING BROKE out between the Maronite and Palestinian forces in Lebanon, it launched a civil war that would last 15 long, deadly years. All told, an estimated 120,000 people lost their lives, a devastating blow to the small country. Many who did not perish fled, with a staggering one million people making a mass exodus out of the country.

Eddie Machaalani's family was among those who fled. Immigrants in bustling Sydney, Australia, Eddie, his parents, and both his younger and older brother set out to do what many immigrants do—build a new life. Thrive. As a young boy, Eddie watched his parents work unimaginably hard to create a good life for the family. They worked hard, day after day.

Immigrants don't arrive on foreign shores with a corporate mind-set. Even if they worked for a larger business in their country of origin, many start small, family-run businesses from scratch. It was through this experience, watching family and extended family and even community work together to make a good living, that Eddie Machaalani gained a kind of organic knowledge of the values and grit it takes to build a business from scratch. He saw exactly what it takes to not just survive but to thrive. He learned the values of honesty, fairness, and respect from the elders who came before him, and internalized a universal truth: Do the right thing and good things will come.

As the family thrived, Eddie's father invested (one of the first in their community to do so) in a personal computer for his boys, who spent long hours learning every aspect of how it worked and what magic it held. Gadgets had always fascinated Eddie, who was endlessly tinkering the way certain kids do. When it came time to head off to college, Eddie decided the University of Technology was the place to further explore his passion. It was there he became fascinated with programming.

The instant gratification of programming thrilled him. The creation of making something from nothing, the launch of a website, the immediate reaction—it was a rush. In programming, Eddie found a kind of perfect balance between creativity and science, between the practical and the artistic that was thrilling. He was hooked. When it came time to graduate, students in the program were required to obtain eight months of corporate experience. Not Eddie's passion, but he knew it would bring him insight and knowledge. He just didn't realize how.

Diving in feet first, Eddie was immediately a success. He singlehandedly built and rolled out a technology project and witnessed as it immediately caught fire. He'd won a company contest, even, with his ingenuity and drive. So when a company meeting was called to discuss new projects, Eddie sat in shock as his manager presented their victory.

"I want to share what I have been working on lately."

Eddie sat at the conference table in disbelief. His manager said "what *I* have been working on." He referred to himself alone, as if he'd created it, as if it was his victory. It was a brutal blow to Eddie, his first taste of what he'd later refer to as "toxic culture." Instead of being honored, complimented, rewarded, and appreciated, Eddie was ignored while his manager took full credit for his work. It was a devastating blow, but one he would carry with him when his eight-month term was up.

In 2003, Eddie became a web designer, eventually connecting with his business partner Harper Mitchell, whom he met—where else?—in a chat room. Harper shared Eddie's values and ideals, and together they launched their first company, Insterspire. In 2009, they raised $20,000 on their personal credit cards and launched another company, Bigcommerce.

Working from a rented space above a friend's office in Sydney, Australia, Eddie and Harper have grown Bigcommerce more than

100 percent year-over-year, raising more than $125 million in venture capital along the way. Bigcommerce powers more than 95,000 online stores globally, and has processed more than five billion dollars in sales.

These days, Eddie is an active angel investor and speaker. While running Bigcommerce, investing, blogging, and contributing to well-regarded business outlets, he was named as a finalist for the Ernst & Young Entrepreneur of the Year Central Texas award, as well as for *BRW*'s Entrepreneur of the Year award. Through Bigcommerce, Eddie Machaalani aims to level the commercial playing field such that merchants from all over the world can build scalable businesses and strong brands that are capable of competing with the biggest players in their industries.

I wanted to find out more about this dynamic CEO and discover what drives him to continuously improve and grow.

JM: The first thing I want to say is congratulations on all your success. Your company is growing quickly and you appear to be having a lot of fun.

EM: Yes, thank you. We have been very blessed; we have a great team, we are in the right market, and we are rocking and rolling.

JM: You are indeed. Let's start by talking about the pivotal points in your early life that caused you to move in the direction of being an entrepreneur. Tell me about that experience when your manager took credit for your work.

EM: It was real blow to me, to be completely devalued in an environment like that. It was a toxic culture. There was a lot of infighting, with people taking credit for each other's work and not being held accountable. This was completely foreign to me. It wasn't the way I had been brought up. So I said to myself, *If I start a company I am going to make sure we never have a culture like that.* That was a real pivotal moment for me. I became a web designer. I ran a small web design business, and I recognize we needed to have a special content management system designed just for my clients. So I went to work and ended up building one of the first content management systems on the web. While I was on this journey I met my co-founder, who had similar values. We got together and launched another product, which eventually became Bigcommerce.

JM: That's fantastic. What is the predominant theme you live by? Is there a particular saying or message that repeats itself in your head?

EM: Yes, a really pivotal phrase for me has been: Think like a man of action and act like a man of thought.

JM: I love that—you obviously live that daily. So, let me ask, how are things progressing? And, as the leader of Bigcommerce, what are your leadership challenges? You obviously have a lot going on, many things coming from many directions. Talk to me a little bit about how you approach all of this?

EM: It's a great question. My goal is to constantly look for bottlenecks to growth. I try to focus on the top three bottlenecks in the business and, sure enough, I find that these bottlenecks almost always involve people.

JM: Yes.

EM: There comes a time—especially in the early days of a start-up—when you realize suddenly that you're doing too much yourself. In our case, we wrote our own code, we ran the marketing campaign, we did sales calls. But as we went on our journey, we started to see that we were our own bottlenecks to growth. We started to hire executives who could lead those functions. It's a real mind-set shift to move from doing everything yourself to empowering people. But once you start along that journey, you recognize quickly that the biggest opportunity for growing your company and ensuring that you have the right culture to foster that growth lies in surrounding yourself with great talent. Today, it's less about "how do I solve the problem?" and more about identifying the person or people who possess the skill set that can best solve the problem.

JM: I think you put your finger on something very critical. There are very few start-up entrepreneurs who are able to recognize that once they reach that point of growth in which they can't do everything, they have to find talent and then empower those people to do the things that they once did themselves. They have to feel comfortable enough to have others take over those responsibilities. It's one thing to want to do it, and it's another thing to execute. It sounds like not only did you cognitively recognize this need as the company was growing, but you are executing it. It sounds like you have assembled a great team and you feel comfortable with them.

EM: Yes, I think Richard Branson said that really well in an interview that stuck in my mind. They asked him, "What's the secret of your success?" And he said "Three things: people, people, people." I subscribe to that philosophy, and translating it into your company culture starts from the top. It starts with the CEO first and foremost. You can't fake a company culture if the CEO doesn't live by that code and doesn't live by the core values of the organization and then also surround himself or herself with the right talent and the right people. I feel really blessed with the talent and the people that we have in our organization. We couldn't do anything we do without them. We have a proven philosophy, we call it Bucket One and Bucket Two.

JM: Bucket One, Bucket Two—tell me more about that.

EM: Bucket One is a way of describing somebody who is very skilled and experienced at what they do, a complete A player. They know the industry and they are really, really strong. So if I am hiring a head of engineering, for example, I want someone who has been in high-performance environments before. They can build and recruit a phenomenal team, they have an engineering mind-set, they have all the skills and experience. That's Bucket One.

Bucket Two is evaluating if they are good human beings. Do they live by our core values, are they honest, are they genuine, do they promote their team, do they put the team first, are they passionate about the work, do they have family values that they want to bring into the organization, are they going to hire people who also have the same values? That's Bucket Two.

Understanding the value of Bucket Two has been a big learning process. I have had extremely talented people in the organization who were phenomenal in terms of Bucket One—the skill set, the knowledge, the main expertise. These people were technical geniuses, but they lacked the Bucket Two qualities and hence, couldn't take other people along with them on their journey. As a result, we lost good talent. These kind of people really hurt your culture; they hurt your entire company. And they reflect poorly on you as a leader if they are not supporting the culture you are trying to build with the values you want the company to live by.

We believe we need to hire strong executives who have both Bucket One and Bucket Two. For this reason, we spend a lot of time with reference checks and situational questions. We want to understand how they live, what their values are, will they cut corners, will there be dishonesty? Do they have a team that's worked with them in the past who wants to come on the journey with them? My best executives always bring people that have worked with them in the past. They are phenomenal people and they are phenomenal leaders. I feel confident with the team that we have today. I am constantly on the lookout for great talent. I really focus on people that have the skill set but also are culturally aligned. That is the foundation of creating a phenomenal organizational culture.

JM: Very well said, Eddie. When we look at the word "success" how would you define it?

EM: Defining success is twofold. First and foremost, my family is my number one priority. The way I live my life and the relationships that I have with my children, my friends, my extended family, and God is how I define success. From a business perspective I am a growth-mind-set person. Success means that an organization is growing: customers are increasing, we are building a phenomenal product, we are generating a revenue and profits, and we're doing it all the right way. As long as I am running the company, there will really be no end to growth. That's my definition of success: to continually grow and build and solve problems and help customers.

JM: I want to ask you about failure. Some executives have difficulty discussing even the notion of failure. Can you tell me about the notion of failure as you see it?

EM: I don't believe in failure. I don't think people fail, rather, they make mistakes and in doing so, learn. You may have made a mistake in one area, but I would never say that you failed. In actuality, you made a decision that wasn't the right one at the right time, or perhaps you brought on the right person in the wrong environment. That is the process of growth, not failure: It is only through the process of transformation—which includes invariable missteps—that success arrives.

JM: Very good, you are an optimist. Your mind-set is exactly what I see in successful CEOs all over the world. What are some of the challenges at the top of your mind? Maybe they don't keep you up at night, but they are lingering in your consciousness.

EM: Currently, the leadership change in a lot of our departments is my primary concern. The biggest opportunity with our new leadership team is getting them completely aligned. It's my imperative to make sure they understand and believe that I have complete confidence in them. Having made a lot of changes across the executive team, it is essential that the people who are still here don't feel like they might be next to go. We are constantly communicating with the team, reassuring them that they are performing well and that we have a tremendous amount of confidence in their ability. The key is getting everyone aligned and sharing the same goal. I ensure that every executive in the organization knows where we are going, what we stand for, and what are my expectations. I expect them all to hire world class colleagues—anything less is unacceptable. I expect them to embody our company culture; I expect them to know the company metrics and the growth trajectory of the organization.

Another big challenge that I face is prioritizing. We are striving constantly to meet all our goals while also streamlining our core objectives. That requires us to recognize the three or four things we need to do exceptionally well in order to achieve our goal.

JM: Very well said. I appreciate your openness about that.

EM: I am a big believer in allowing your team to make mistakes and giving them the freedom to test things out. I want to support them by helping them to focus on their strengths rather than their weaknesses. We all have weaknesses, but if we focus on telling our team where their weaknesses lie, that is the wrong approach. To bring true transformation amongst our leaders, it is far better to focus on their strengths.

JM: Absolutely. If you are gifted in a certain area, you have to polish that gift. That's not to say that we can't focus on one or two development needs. But let's take those strong qualities that unleash us and focus on that. On that note, what are your leadership strengths? What would they say are the two exceptional qualities that Eddie Machaalani brings to Bigcommerce?

EM: First, I have a tremendous desire to do great things. Secondly, I have an undeniable ability to hire incredible talent.

JM: This business is in your blood, right? I imagine you get up very early in the morning and put in long days, but have fun in the process, is that correct?

EM: Yes, absolutely. Being a founder and a CEO is a roller coaster: You have stunning highs and you have crushing lows, but you appreciate the journey. As you mature in the organization it becomes less about the *what* and *why* and more about the *who*. This is why I say that a great culture is incredibly important—not just at the C-suite, or the executive level, but the entire organization. My co-founder Mitch and I interviewed every single one of the first hundred employees that joined Bigcommerce. We felt that if you set the proper expectation from the outset, those people would help us maintain the culture. From day one, we had people here who knew and valued the organizational culture. As we've continued to grow, those original leaders have been the first to remind us that this is the way culture should be going.

JM: That's very powerful and consistent with what I am seeing among leaders today. Let me ask you this: What would you describe as your greatest professional achievement?

EM: My greatest professional achievement is getting Bigcommerce to where it is today and believing in where it can be tomorrow.

JM: Would you say that at Bigcommerce you have an imperative to transform?

EM: Yes, without a doubt. Absolutely.

JM: When I say cultural transformation what does that mean to you?

EM: When I think about cultural transformation I ask, *do we have a culture that is serving the needs of the company?* The most important thing is understanding the tradition of our current culture and what kind of culture we are striving to create. Do we want a start-up culture? Do we want a high-performance culture? Do we want a cutthroat culture? In every company, the culture you want is one that serves the ambition of the company.

We are constantly going through cultural transformations, because our ambitions and needs are always changing. When we were a start-up, we had unique needs and ambitions. Now we are high performance, and it's incredibly competitive. We must, therefore, shift away from that start-up mind-set and evolve to a high-performance culture. It's similar to playing sports: When you are in high school, you're at one level. When you are in college, you increase your game. With each level, you must increase your training, expertise, and set higher goals. That's exactly the process we use to transform the culture in our organization. Every year you have step back and say, *is the culture we have serving our ambition as a company?*

This year my big focus is combining high-performance culture with one in which each employee really cares about the company. In the past, our culture has been more about what can the company do for the individuals, fulfilling individual needs, getting this fancy new toy or widget or lunch and so on. What I really want to do now is shift our attention away from ourselves and onto what each of us can do for the company. JFK said, "Ask not what your country can do for you, ask what you can do for your country." I want our company focus to shift away from what the company can do for me in the short term to what I can do to make this a phenomenal company to work for. You do that by shifting the focus to the customer and serving them in the best possible way.

JM: That's very powerful—it's very other-oriented. I want to end with two final questions. First, what aspects of your culture are you most proud of and why?

EM: The energy, passion, and camaraderie of our team is second to none. I've had executives and people from outside the organization say our culture is unlike anything they've ever seen. The desire to win across the entire organization is incredibly high. There is an overwhelming respect between our entire executive leadership team that flows on to the organization at large.

JM: I have one last question. Can you share any words of wisdom for the many hopeful leaders and future leaders all over the world? How can they become better leaders?

EM: Humility, curiosity, and desire are an incredible blend of traits. Those three elements are an unstoppable combination. If you have the desire, you continue to grow. If you have the humility, you realize you are never going to be the smartest person in the room. If you have the curiosity, you will realize that you can always learn from every single person that you meet. I learn from others every day, and I think that's something that came natural to my co-founder and me. When we met with an entrepreneur we admired, we spent 5 percent of the time asking questions and 95 percent of the time just soaking it up. We had an intense desire to learn and a tremendous amount of respect for the person.

When you meet with certain people, you know instantly that they are going to be successful. They are asking all the right questions and listening to your answers. They are humble and they have and enormous desire to learn. They are reading, watching videos, attending events and seminars, and constantly on the lookout for better advisers. On the other hand, if you meet with people who want to tell you about how great they are and they talk 90 to 95 percent of the time, you get the sense that they don't have the humility, the curiosity, or the desire to learn. I think that's what makes the best entrepreneurs special. Take Steve Jobs for example. Without a doubt he had vision, conviction, and confidence, but he was also always willing to surround himself with talented people. Successful leaders are constantly willing to learn, be advised, and get coached. Steve Jobs had a coach, the Google guys had a coach, Jeff Bezos had a coach. They were all willing to learn and be hungry. They all had a combination of those three traits—humility, curiosity, and desire—which I think are the magic steps for success.

6

Harib Al Kitani
CEO, Oman LNG

The key to unlocking your massive potential is making the decision to be vulnerable.

—*John Mattone*

HARIB AL KITANI WAS BORN in 1962 on the fabled, uncommonly beautiful islands of Zanzibar. An archipelago off the coast of East Africa, Zanzibar is a dichotomy of winding lanes and ornate architecture and wide, white beaches set off from clear blue sea, the shoreline a near-perfect reflection of the azure sky dotted with pure white cumulus clouds. At the time the Al Kitanis were starting their family, Zanzibar was a colony of Oman, so there were many Omanis who made a life there—some remain today. This rich history has forged strong cultural and economic relationships, relationships that have been forged over centuries.

In January 1964, when a bloody revolution to remove the Omani rule from Zanzibar commenced, Omanis fled in droves to locations far and wide. But the Al Kitanis, a family of intense pride and ethical fortitude, held firm. Harib's parents had a steadfast commitment to education, and for mostly this reason they were determined to stay put. As a result, young Harib had what can only be characterized as a tough upbringing amidst the post-colonial period. Stripped of everything they owned, the family struggled in a myriad of ways.

In these post-revolutionary wilds, young Harib learned quickly that you have to be extremely tough and work incredibly hard to survive. Looking back today, Harib gives thanks to God that his parents upheld their commitment, worked extremely hard for their family, and did so with both an unwavering pride and inarguably elevated ethical ground. It wasn't easy.

There were 10 boys and two girls in the Al Kitani family, all well looked after by their parents in spite of such difficulties. This was a blessing: growing up in such a challenging environment, witnessing the steadfast example of strong parents being good role models was invaluable to his later success in the world of business.

But it was these tough times that Harib and his family had to endure before they would, at last, move to Oman. Harib learned early that working hard to survive was essential, and it's a lesson he took with him through all the phases of his life.

Holding fast to his parents' dedication to and veneration for education, Mr. Kitani earned his MBA from University of Warwick and his engineering degree in biochemical engineering from the University of Birmingham.

Today, Harib Al Kitani is the CEO and director of Oman Liquefied Natural Gas LLC. Starting out at Oman LNG in 1995 as the deputy manager of marketing, Harib quickly advanced to marketing and shipping manager. He was instrumental in strengthening Oman LNG's position in the key markets of Korea and Japan. He also began the company's cargo swapping and diversion with different parties in the global liquefied natural gas trade, creating better value for the company's shareholders in the process.

Later transferred to Shell International in London (where he worked for three years in various positions including LNG Global Business Adviser and Manager of Suape project in Brazil), Harib then served as the president and CEO of Qalhat LNG. Finally, he moved back to Oman LNG, to a plant in Qalhat near Sur, Oman. Established by the Royal Decree of Sultan Qaboos of Oman in 1994, the company is fast becoming a key regional player in the energy industry. With partly state-owned status and notable global backers like Shell, Total, Korea LNG, and Mitsubishi, success is imminent. The government of Oman is its main shareholder, with a 51 percent stake, followed by Royal Dutch Shell (30 percent), Total S.A. (5.54 percent), Korea LNG (5 percent), Mitsubishi Corporation (2.77 percent), Mitsui & Co. (2.77 percent), Partex Oil & Gas (2 percent), and Itochu Corporation (0.92 percent).

The LNG plant receives its exclusive supply from the gas-gathering plant at Saih Rowl in the central Oman gas field complex through a 224-mile-long 1,200 mm pipeline with a capacity of 12 billion cubic meters per annum of gas. It consists of two 3.3 million tons per annum (MTPA) liquefaction trains, which were constructed by Chiyoda-Foster Wheeler.

In October 2013, Oman LNG and Qalhat LNG were merged, making Oman LNG the only face of LNG supply from Oman to the world. As the country's only exporter of liquefied natural gas with 10.4 MTPA capacity, Oman LNG plays a significant role in the sector.

Just as the Zanzibar beaches mirror the Zanzibar skies, Harib Al Kitani's meteoric rise in the world of business mirrors the long struggle and ultimate triumph of his family's story. Holding fast to ideals, conducting one's life with the highest ethical standards, and always striving with an eye to the future served not only the Al Kitani family, but Harib Al Kitani as well. He applied these principles, learned at an early age, to a storied career. I sat down to talk to him about the journey to get where he is today.

JM: Your family history is incredibly fascinating. What were the lessons you internalized from living such a life?

HAK: I learned that respecting people and being persistent in whatever you do is at the utmost importance. Again, from our parents who have never lost respect to anybody, who worked hard and brought us up to be honest, to respect people, and to appreciate life, we had an excellent starting point to shape the character needed to succeed in life.

JM: Without those it would be tough.

HAK: Indeed—hard work, respect, and honesty are three important core values for the family living through these very, very difficult times.

JM: At what age were you when the family moved to Oman?

HAK: I moved to Oman with some of my siblings in 1979, at the age of 17 years. Having finished high school in Zanzibar, it was time to go home, to Oman. Oman was rebuilding after the Renaissance, which started in 1970. Indeed, some of my brothers had already moved and working in Oman.

JM: It sounds like the time was right.

HAK: Absolutely. Schools were opened to help the rebuilding of Oman, and work was abundant. So we returned upon the call of His

Majesty Sultan Qaboos bin Said, as a march toward building Oman. The call implored all Omanis living abroad to come back and rebuild our great country. So when we came back, the natural development was to start seeking out a new job. My plan was to find a job to contribute to the building of the new nation, to help the family, and then move on. I started my first job toward end of 1979 at Petroleum Development Oman [PDO], an oil and gas company. I joined in a refinery operation training program—as the government at that time was looking at building the first oil refinery in the country.

JM: Absolutely. And then what happened?

HAK: What happened was that from that moment on, my career began taking shape.

JM: When you were in high school, did you have an idea about your future? As one of 12 in your family, did your brothers and sisters have an impact on you in terms of direction?

HAK: Yes, absolutely. Truly, we were all working hard to survive when back in Zanzibar—by survival, John, I mean true struggle. Finding food, finding a uniform to wear to school, finding books to read—that was our struggle. A struggle for the basics. There was absolutely no luxury, just the necessities needed to grow and thrive.

JM: Yes. It sounds difficult, but you were determined. How did your siblings play a role in that?

HAK: My senior brothers were all like parents to us—protecting us, guiding us, and providing whatever they could to ensure we received a good education to lay the foundation for a strong career. However, neither they nor I had any idea what career I was going to pursue. When I came to Oman, my thinking was to pursue my dream of becoming a doctor. Like many young men, I had that dream to grow up and be a doctor and serve people; however, when I came to Oman the quickest opportunity and priority was for work instead of study. At that time, again, we have to start a new life and thus earning some money was important for the family to build a new life.

JM: Absolutely.

HAK: Then again, in terms of career, the clearest and quickest path for me to work was to join this oil and gas sector—plenty of opportunities and directly contributing to the economic backbone of our new nation. So I joined PDO as a trainee in the refinery operations.

JM: Amazing, yes.

HAK: That was a new start. The whole family was encouraging all of us to find work. My brothers and I, we all spread out across the country, finding work in banks, in the military, in oil and gas, and in other sectors. Meanwhile, the younger siblings went straight back to school to complete their education. It was an interesting start of new life and a shift of priorities from surviving to thriving.

JM: Fascinating. No easy road, but the lessons of life are learned through the difficulties correct?

HAK: Yes, indeed. Struggles provide an opportunity that only few people get. Out of struggle, opportunity arises.

JM: So with this great foundation from your parents and family, with exceptional values, you come to Oman to work at PDO. Let's fast forward: Where do you go from there? A return to education?

HAK: Yes, it's a winding road. I started working at PDO, where I learned about refining operations. I was trained there, and later in Bahrain, in theory. When the refinery company was formed, the government decided to create a new company called Oman Refinery Company, which would be 100 percent owned by the government. We built the refinery, started it up, and I assumed my function as a process operator. I started as an outside operator, then became a panel man. Quickly I realized it was not enough for me. I knew I wanted to do something better: I wanted to earn a degree. The bad news was there was no scheme to pursue further education.

JM: So what did you do? I know you found a way to make it happen.

HAK: Yes, I did. I worked my way up and paid part of the cost to go to the U.K. to take A levels courses (diploma) so I could get into university to have a degree course in chemical engineering.

JM: Excellent. Always focused toward the future, it seems.

HAK: Exactly. So I went to the U.K. and I did the high school to qualify for the university, and then progressed on to University of Birmingham, where I earned a combined degree of chemical and biochemical engineering. Coming back to Oman in 1988, I moved from operations to become a process engineer. I thought I was a good engineer, but engineering didn't take me long and so I again thought that there is something else there I can do. The fact was, I did not want to end up being "just" an engineer. So, I started to do an MBA course

by distance learning from University of Warwick in the U.K. It was important that I continue to work so I can earn some money, so I completed the MBA in my spare time
at home.

That is when I introduced myself into the leadership world of business. While doing my MBA, with a keen interest in the nonengineering world, I managed to move from being an engineer to become a planning and economics engineer.

JM: Wow, that's great.

HAK: I thrived in the new assignment and achieved some innovative—at that time—changes like third-party crude processing, operational optimization, and the like. I had a chance to train at Ashland Oil in Kentucky and Caltex Oil in Texas. Then LNG business came to Oman, very, very early on in 1995—just as an idea. The competition was either to build an LNG plant in Oman or transport gas by pipeline to India, all dependent on if LNG will find a market for its products and what economic benefit will the country achieve.

The opportunity was to join the LNG group led by Shell, find market for LNG, and build a company *or* fail to find a market and look for another job! I joined Oman LNG as VP marketing in April 1995. In 1997, when we closed deals and signed contracts with Japanese and Korean companies, the government decided there would be an LNG company in Oman. I was also asked to market the new company. I did that successfully and then left Oman LNG in 2004 when Qalhat LNG was formed to be CEO of Qalhat LNG and build the company. In between the two, Shell gave me an opportunity to work with them and, thus, I moved to London to work with them in their gas and power business. I started as business adviser for Southeast Asia where I was advising Shell on developing and monetizing gas in Pakistan, Bangladesh, and India. Then I was promoted to be the LNG manager for Suape project in Brazil. Shell was thinking of building an LNG receiving terminal together with Petrobras of Brazil in Suape in the Recife area in northeastern Brazil. So I had the opportunity to be LNG manager for that project.

I returned home to Oman in 2000 to lead the marketing for Oman LNG, until Qalhat LNG was formed in 2004.

JM: How long were you CEO there?

HAK: I was CEO from 2004 to 2012.

JM: And then CEO at Oman LNG—

HAK: From July 2012.

JM: Unbelievable success. You're not only successful in the business world but obviously family and adding value to the world is important, no? What are the three most important things that have led to your success?

HAK: When people inquire about whom do I follow [as leadership guru] or what leadership theory I follow, I have no answer.

JM: No?

HAK: I am a humble person and don't have a particular guide in my work. But my humbleness goes beyond people's expectation of a CEO. I'm humbled by what I have achieved and what others have achieved. I think of a team following this down-to-earth person who is genuine in whatever he does. I respect everybody. This is very powerful in our achievement of the same goal. My respect for people will never diminish, because I can swear on the results.

Sometimes I have these gut feelings that guide me through what I do. You follow your instinct. You get some sense of this by being close to people, listening to them, and following your instincts.

JM: I agree.

HAK: My belief is that when we treat people well and with respect they will all fall behind you, support, and go with you anywhere to reach the set goal.

JM: Yes, they will.

HAK: For me this is all what we need in life. We have a lot of challenges in Oman, inside or outside the Arab world—we cannot outsmart people, be arrogant or dictatorial in our approach. We need to respect people and hold them and sell to them our dreams, give them our vision to move on!

JM: Amazing insight and humility.

HAK: For me, success is not just meeting your target: Success is going beyond what is expected of you. You cannot do that alone. Having people marching behind you with enthusiasm and trust, you will achieve what you want. However, you need to show you care for them, provide them with good care, and extend it to your shareholders and customers to see the results unfold.

JM: There's no question—I saw that in the limited time that I spent with you. It was evident you cared for your team and they in turn trust you. Talk to me about failure and setbacks. We all have them. Many CEOs I interview talk about the life-changing setbacks and failures that, while difficult, set them on a path to the inevitable future. Did you experience a crucial setback?

HAK: You experience failures and then immediately stand up and move forward. They build your character. For me, it's more than the failure but instead what opportunities you would have left behind. I feel as if I could contribute more toward business, toward human kind, toward our country, but I'm not able to do it all.

I have a job to run, but I always want to do more. I told you about my childhood challenges—I couldn't do anything about them. I wish I went to university earlier than I did. I was a mature student but could I do anything about it? I will not consider it as a failure but as an opportunity missed.

JM: Absolutely. Let me ask you this: What are your strongest leadership strengths?

HAK: Care and respect for people is primary.

It's the people who contribute to all this march of success so we must care about them and respect their contribution.

JM: And second?

HAK: Second is leading by instinct. Even when your gut feeling is out of the norm, it will often lead to success.

Spontaneously doing something that people may never think but it ultimately addresses the issues at hand. I'm lucky to have such good instincts.

JM: And third in your leadership skills?

HAK: Following through. A true leader should have a follow-through, all the way to the end. Without follow-through, nothing can be achieved. Sometimes there will be initiatives in the company or with the government, and they end up in studies or half-done and people lose interest—the follow-through is essential. Following through also leads to new horizons and more opportunity.

JM: Without question those are strong leadership strengths and gifts. A strong mind and heart, combined with well-honed instincts is an undeniable formula for leadership success.

HAK: It's not something you read from a book—you have to practice it and apply it and so forth. Over time, it becomes natural. Without that gut feeling, you will not feel the heartbeat of the organization.

JM: Are there things you're working on about yourself to improve your leadership skills?

HAK: Absolutely there is. At the moment I am working toward increasing my ability to touch people's hearts.

I strive, for example, to, instead of a swift "no" to an employee's request, to sacrifice a bit and please the person.

JM: It's an interesting example of a strength that can also become a weakness.

HAK: Yes, we never stop learning—especially from people like you.

JM: That's ultimately the point. We have a massive gap in leadership and culture all over the world. What was your greatest professional accomplishment, Harib?

HAK: Because I never planned or dreamed of it, becoming a CEO at relatively young age for our culture is a great achievement. Perhaps not in the United States, but to reach the level of CEO in an oil and gas company at a youngish age is an enormous accomplishment. I was the CEO of Qalhat LNG at 42 years of age.

JM: Very impressive. What other accomplishment pleases you?

HAK: I've accomplished a lot in the LNG industry and by marketing our LNG volume. Both companies (Oman LNG and Qalhat LNG) contribute toward our national economy, supplying 10 percent of the GDP of the whole nation. Once you realize the contribution on this, you feel a great sense of achievement!

The final achievement about which I'm very proud is the integration of Oman LNG and Qalhat LNG.

JM: Yes, that an enormous accomplishment, because integration is neither simple nor often successful.

Most integration efforts, as you know, fail. I want to ask you about the culture you've created. Talk to me a little bit about the road map you used to integrate two so different company cultures.

HAK: They companies had not only different cultures, they're of different sizes. Oman LNG was somewhat rigid and double the size of Qalhat LNG. I led Qalhat LNG in a very practical, flexible, and friendly culture. I moved to Oman LNG a few months before the integration to prepare the platform. I planned what we should have as a final product: what to mix, how to revise, where we wanted to arrive—that was the road map.

JM: I imagine communication was key.

HAK: Yes, open communication between all parties was essential in getting buy-in from both sides instead of forcing integration from outside by a consultant or by management in isolation.

We communicated endlessly to both organizations every step of the way. We even opened a help desk for anybody who had questions. And I traveled between both companies and communicated about how proud we should be, how we need to work together, and how the struggles of today will shape the success of our integrated company in the future.

At my first joint meeting I showed people the inverted pyramid where the leadership is the slave of the company and the staff are at the top. They remember that pyramid today, because I sat in the lowest, most humble position as CEO. The management serves the workforce. And as a result, everybody's happy. We are now reaping the benefits. We're counting how many millions we gained out of this synergy and it's great.

JM: That's really powerful because most companies are struggling with integration efforts. But cultural transformation is an ongoing process.

HAK: So often people do not recognize that they have to be agile to continue the path forward. However, essential in this map is that you cannot sustain transformation without also showing the results of that transformation.

JM: That's a very good point.

HAK: The celebration of success and celebration of achievement is very important to push the transformation and cultural transformation forward. If it's just lip service without showing the results, you will lose your team's trust. It must be concrete and sincere—you cannot continue talking forever without substance.

JM: Indeed! What is the one thing that you would recommend to other companies to break down siloes?

HAK: The way is to have projects where you put people from different functions together. You need to put people from disparate functions together to form a stronger whole.

I may want finance, marketing, and other people from different units to work together and deliver a good product; this is very helpful. They're then required to cooperate and work together.

Breaking siloes could also be achieved by transferring people from different functions so they can go and see what others are doing and what their challenges are. It creates relationships, building more capacity for people to work collaboratively and help one another.

JM: And you did all that.

HAK: Yes, and as important as it is for people to move around in departments and gain an understanding of their coworkers' struggles, it is equally important as CEO to be visible both to your own staff and to the wider business world. I try my best on this and it consumes a lot of time, but it's important. You cannot favor a certain department, either. This can easily make departments feel isolated and you can lose them.

JM: You can, and keeping them connected to you is not easy, so congratulations. Was there a misstep along the way and do you feel like you managed this effort well?

HAK: I think we've relatively done a good job. There is always more that can be done. For example, now we are struggling a bit with "total alignment." When we align from top to bottom, we don't know whether there's something misaligned unless and until something goes wrong. Then you find out that although you are mostly aligned, there are still weak points in the balance. Perhaps alignment is off because out of 10 people that have to push the agenda, 2 people sit back with the assumption they're not part of it. They may not throw resistance into the process, but they will just sit out as a silence audience while the train keeps moving forward. In that case, you have to go back and try to convince people to move with the plan. To hop on the train, as it were.

So when we integrated, we did not have total alignment. We had alignment, but it was imperfect and needed strengthening along the way. Culture transforms not at once, but over time.

JM: And that's never going to end, it's never going to be perfect. It's an endless and worthy pursuit. I believe that the culture starts with the CEO and the senior team, what are your comments to that?

HAK: I agree with that. The senior team has to be an important and paramount part of the push in the culture.

You do the best you can. You have to revolutionize the way we work.

JM: Absolutely.

HAK: Now, some people would have some doubt on what you do because they accept that status quo is the best way forward. They are relaxed and are scared to change—this is the type you don't want to have around. When you try to change—pulling people out of their comfort zone—some will resist.

But as a CEO, you must move forward with determination and instinct. You listen to your gut feeling and you will find that this is the way to move. You absolutely cannot and should not wait until you have that 100 percent of the staff convinced.

JM: Tell me more about that.

HAK: If I have 60 percent or 70 percent convinced, I move on. Because when I produce good results, the remaining percentage will follow—they'll have no choice except to follow when they see the right way forward.

JM: That is an excellent point. You have to establish momentum.

HAK: Indeed—it's momentum. A process cannot be hijacked by anybody. If you believe in it, you move forward. Today, I try not to create a lot of debate on the things that I believe and the majority of people believe this is the way forward, so that these peripheral noises that come around it and try to kill it all fade in time, because you eventually show them that your vision led to this result.

JM: Absolutely.

HAK: When we are all together, we produce more and more results. Unfortunately Oman is not like the U.S.—it is very difficult to let people go.

JM: Yes, here in the United States, if you have somebody on the senior team who is out of alignment you get rid of them, you really can't do that there right?

HAK: No you cannot—it's very difficult. As a result, we are really enthusiastic about cultural transformation and moving forward and getting your staff on board is even more essential. The challenge inspires even more communication for ultimate success.

JM: Amazing. That's fantastic. Finally Harib, what is the message you want to deliver to the young people regarding what they need to do to become stronger people and stronger leaders, so that they can give more to companies and society?

HAK: There's no one pill to solve all the problems, but the number one issue is don't accept that the status quo is a solution to the world's problems. We need to hold fast to the mind-set that there are better ways of doing things, better ways of leading organizations. We need to recognize these new ways and follow through to produce results. We need to trust our gut feelings as much as we do any theory or book or advice.

JM: Absolutely.

HAK: We need to go to somewhere undiscovered for these hidden gems in your gut feelings and your heart. We sometimes get too relaxed in our success and forget to strive at a higher level. If we could create what we call "chronic unease" in everything we do, we would achieve better results. When we build this into our mind and into the way we work, we can achieve a lot. No complacency! Live and thrive within this chronic unease to achieve more than you are supposed to be achieving because you don't leave any stone unturned! That would be my statement to future and growing leaders.

JM: Excellent.

HAK: If you move on and continue to show the results even in a drip method—a little bit gain here and there—it will encourage people to follow your dream.

JM: This has been unbelievable. I can see why you're so centered, and I can see why you are the person that you are.

HAK: Thank you, I continue to learn and grow every day—that is perhaps the biggest secret to my success. As a child I struggled to obtain life's most basic needs, as a CEO I continue the struggle, not because I have to, but because I want to. Success comes on the shore of struggle.

7

Hap Klopp

Founder, The North Face

Great leaders commit to becoming more capable, committed, and connected today than they were yesterday.

— *John Mattone*

KENNETH "HAP" KLOPP WAS BORN in the idyllic town of Spokane, Washington, which sits west of the Rocky Mountain foothills on the Spokane River. As a boy, Hap quickly realized he was different. Although a colleague would later joke, "Hap's just like everybody else, just shorter," it was clear that something in Hap, even as a boy, set him apart from his peers.

In his early days at school, Hap was what he calls a "disturber," unable to endure the entire day of sitting at a desk. Fortunate to have teachers who recognized his differences, Hap only attended class in the mornings, spending his afternoons on directed reading or athletic pursuits. Even so, he did well academically and excelled at sports. He possessed a kind of inner confidence innate in many natural leaders, never showing a moment of doubt. His success in athletics further emboldened him to follow his own path, even when being different wasn't easy. "All leaders are internally different," says Klopp. Recognizing his difference early on and choosing a path without doubt helped solidify his leadership and entrepreneurial spirit.

When it was time for university, Hap wanted to pursue sports, but his father pushed for MIT. They compromised on Stanford, where Hap would earn both a bachelors and an MBA. In his senior year, Hap's father passed away, and he spent many months flying back and forth from the Bay Area to Spokane, first running and eventually selling the family business. Following the NCAA ("No Clue At All") school of management, Hap quickly developed his fail forward and fail fast style of business, proving himself far ahead of the Silicon Valley curve.

It was during this chaotic year that Hap Klopp hatched his plan to create The North Face. In 1968, the newly minted Stanford MBA decided to give his business plan a practical revenue stream and purchased an already-named North Face duo of stores in the area. The revenue stream from those on-the-ground establishments would fuel the vertical integration of The North Face brand.

As founder, president, and CEO, Hap turned what was a backroom operation that employed 14 people into a global apparel business employing over 1,000 people involved in manufacturing, licensing, retailing, and distributing in 45 countries. At a time when the outdoor market was just emerging, Hap set the standard. He, like many innovators in other industries, saw the proverbial parade and jumped in front of it. The North Face became the baton with which Hap Klopp championed his passion for the land and those who endeavored to experience and protect it. The North Face went on to create the standard for innovation and quality in the outdoor, mountaineering, backpacking, and skiing industries.

Hap sold The North Face in 1988 to establish HK Consulting, a strategic and brand-oriented consulting company in the San Francisco area and now has clients ranging from start-ups to multibillion-dollar corporations. He recently purchased a 100-year-old New Zealand-based company, Canterbury, with offices in New Zealand, Australia, Hong Kong, the United States, Canada, the United Kingdom, South Africa, and Japan.

Hap is a highly sought after international speaker on business, social, and employee issues and travels more than 200,000 miles a year consulting and lecturing. He has spoken at the Young Presidents' Organization, Young Entrepreneurs' Organization, the Heart of Business Conference at Carnegie Hall, the American Apparel Manufacturers' Association, the Western Conference of CPAs, and the sales force of *USA Today*.

Hap lectures at the business schools of Stanford, the University of California, and the University of Montana. He actively mentors and advises students from these institutions. He also serves on a number of boards of directors.

The North Face, Inc., is a U.S. outdoor product company specializing in outerwear, shirts, coats, fleece, footwear, and equipment like sleeping bags, tents, and backpacks. I talked to Hap Klopp about building the legendary U.S. brand and how he continually transformed not just his leadership skills, but his company's direction on the way to the top.

JM: Kenneth, thank you so much for making the time to speak with me.

HK: Absolutely. Please call me Hap.

JM: Will do. Well, let's jump right in with some questions I've asked many of the leaders I interviewed for this book. When you look back at your career and life, what has made you successful? What would be three or four things that have differentiated you as a leader and as a person?

HK: There are three that quickly come to mind. The first one is passion. I have a passion for everything I do and if I don't have a passion for it, I step aside and let somebody else do it. That passion fuels me and is conveyed to other people. It motivates them and draws them in. A second thing is that I do a lot of reading. This helps me to see things from many different perspectives. Reading gives me outside input, which can really help me avoid responding to situations from my own individual vantage point.

The third thing is that I have sort of a higher calling. By higher calling, what I mean is that I've always wanted to make the world better. I've seen the imperfections that exist today. Society is riddled with imperfections, more than when I was growing up. I'm one of those people who asks, if not me, then who? Who's going to change the world? Who's going to improve the situation? I felt called upon to act. I've been pretty lucky. I've felt compelled to share that luck, to have the vision, energy, and commitment to improve the world and make it a better place for all of us.

JM: That's powerful. Asking "If not me then who?" is one important aspect of strong leadership, and it seems that there is a big demand for more and more people to step up and be those kind of people today. I speak all over the world and hear a similar sentiment everywhere: we need stronger leaders. There is a major gap in leadership all over the world, not only in business but in all kinds of institutions in every country. We have a lot of great leaders, no question. But we haven't moved the leadership needle significantly enough to meet our current challenges. What's holding us back do you think?

HK: I think that some of it has to do with being too short-term focused. All the tools we have these days give us such immediate feedback that we end up limiting our view to what's happening now, today, this instant. Both the rewards and penalties that exist in society today are extremely short-term. I think that leadership requires a commitment to and vision for the long term.

JM: Excellent point.

HK: I don't want to be a politician, but I have opinions on where this thinking emanated from, and I see a lot of it tied to our current political landscape. Whether you're a Republican or a Democrat or an Independent, anyone who steps back and looks at Congress has to be disappointed by the decisions or lack thereof that are being made. Why haven't we done anything about issues like climate change or the fact that the national debt we are accumulating is not sustainable? These shouldn't be left versus right issues, or Democrat versus Republican issues. They are societal issues that we all need to solve together. Most elected officials would admit this if you spoke to them off the record, but that doesn't get you elected. So, we do nothing.

Our leaders are becoming too reactive and that doesn't inspire people to follow. A lot of things that we now aspire to are not necessarily great long-term values economically. Making a lot of money for yourself isn't leadership. It certainly isn't motivational. And, I personally doubt if it is sustainable.

JM: I agree with you, yes.

HK: I think real leadership is more holistic. It has to do with understanding the environment, people, and their needs. The issues we face as a society are extremely complex, and that can be confusing and paralyzing to people. Great leaders are those who can distill the complexity down to simplicity. They can communicate these complex issues in a way that is motivational and understandable but still encompasses the totality of the world today. Unfortunately, we tend to elect people who are clever and have quick sound bites, but not necessarily the ability to deal with the complexity of modern society.

One great example of someone who could distill complexity into simplicity is Buckminster Fuller, who I had the good fortune to work with. He is famous for discovering the concepts of geodesic design (think geodesic dome) and created an entirely new kind of math to explain it. As Bucky said, "Our math is inherently illogical because if it was logical, everything would be whole numbers like 1, 2, 3, 4. You wouldn't need numbers like pi (3.1416) to give you the area of a circle or use the number 1.414 to calculate the area under a line in calculus. He turned to nature and found that there is a shape in nature for every whole number that exists. He then developed a new math based entirely on these naturally occurring whole numbers. For example, 1 is a triangle, 2 is a rectangle and so on. He used this simple math to come up with incredibly complex geodesic structures.

Bucky's geodesic structures are unique in that they become stronger as they become more complex. Starting with simple triangles, he added more and more triangles to create geodesic domes, which are the only physical structures we have that get stronger as they gets larger. Alternatively, look at structures like old churches that get weaker as they get larger, requiring buttresses to hold them up.

When I was talking with Bucky I asked if this geodesic concept applies only to architecture or if there is a similar set of principles that apply to political systems or businesses. For example, most large businesses are less productive than small businesses and have less innovation. He said, "Yes, of course. We don't have the structure yet, but there is a way for these social systems to get stronger as they get larger."

I understand that sort of thinking can be difficult to comprehend and a lot of people would much rather put their head in the sand and join the big institutions in pursuit of some elusive security. It seems to me that when politicians dare to say, "I'm going to change the way governments and businesses are structured. I'm going to change the world," they are greeted with cynicism and rejection. We don't seem to embrace the complex and forward-thinking people like Bucky Fuller. Nor do we reward them. What we do is look for the easy, overly simple answers to our complex problems. Sorry that's so negative.

JM: No, I think it's powerful. It reinforces the fact that we love to live in a comfort zone that the Bucky Fullers of the world were outside of.

HK: Absolutely.

JM: But we need to think differently, we need to think big. I remember when Steve Jobs came back to Apple in '97. I love to talk about the speech that he delivered. It was very powerful. It was all about a marketing campaign. Do you remember that?

HK: Yes I do.

JM: It was incredible. We need more leaders like Bucky and Steve who weren't afraid to think differently. I want to ask you about failure. Can you share your thoughts about failure?

HK: Let us start at the high level and then get down to specifics. I teach a course for executives from around the world called "Failure Is the Secret Sauce of Silicon Valley." The point that I make there is that everyone in the Silicon Valley ecosystem embraces and accepts failure. There's an unspoken agreement that it's alright to fail. Maybe even beneficial. This mind-set encourages people to swing for the fences and take big chances. They recognize that even if thinking very big doesn't always work out, it won't ruin your track record. In fact, it makes you more valuable and more prized by VCs, banks, and founders of the new, "swing for the fences" businesses. The people who have failed have also learned things that are invaluable when they start their next business.

JM: Yes.

HK: If you want to scale a business very rapidly, you don't have time for people to recreate the mistakes that others have made. The things they have learned during the process of failing generally aren't repeated. That doesn't mean that everybody can make a failure valuable, nor does it mean you should try to fail, but in Silicon Valley what's important is the insight you gain from failure. There's a great quote from Thomas Edison who said, "I've never failed, I just found 10,000 ways something won't work." That's how we look at things in Silicon Valley.

If you look at the venture capital pools you will see that they plan failure into their portfolios. If a VC had 10 companies in their portfolio, for instance, they would expect two to be home runs, two to be abject failures, and the remainder to be middle-of-the-road companies that are really failures because they are stagnating. The only real successes are the two home runs, which makes for a pretty high failure rate. But the success and wealth that comes from those two are extraordinary enough to make up for all the failure. This encourages everybody to try for the big ideas and the big companies.

You can transplant all the Silicon Valley infrastructure to other parts of the world—things like abundant money, start-up friendly bankers, and even the big pools of venture capital. But if you don't also bring that swing for the fences culture, the acceptance of failure, you will never be able to recreate the vibrant environment that makes Silicon Valley so unique and successful. When I speak to people from New Zealand, Australia, Ireland, Austria, or Egypt they constantly tell me, "You can't fail in our country. You can't admit it or you will become an outcast." These are cultures that don't allow people to try to swing for the fences, which blunts entrepreneurialism. Those few people who dare to break the norm and go big and fail end up with blemishes and stigmas that will preclude them from trying the second time. I believe you should fail fast, fail forward. You should learn from your mistakes and have an obligation to try to do something great. None of the mistakes that I've made have been fatal, but all of them have taught me certain things that I try to pass on to others.

JM: That's great Hap. Can you give me an example of one of your failures and what it taught you?

HK: I would say that the biggest failure I've had was probably the business model we used at The North Face. Nike had a much better business model than we had. The basic difference was that Nike had a lot of vendor financing so they could grow at whatever rate they wanted to grow without diluting the stake of the original owners. With our model, on the other hand, if we wanted to grow we had to add capital, which diluted the stake of the investors. We had a culture of very rapid growth so we were constantly refinancing, which meant bringing in different investors with divergent ideas about how to grow. It resulted in conflicts and sluggishness. Phil Knight at Nike was on a much better path. He used Nisho Iwaii as Nike's principal vendor to fund his growth, which enabled him to singularly decide the direction of his business for many years. Despite our partially flawed business model, from a product, growth, and image standpoint we succeeded. We built a great brand, and we were able to grow rapidly by constantly refinancing. Plus, we were able to make the best product in the market. From a financial reward standpoint, however, none of our investors did nearly as well as Nike's.

When I consult with entrepreneurs, the first thing they often say to me is "we need a lot of new money." My response is, "Let's first step back and ask ourselves how we would operate our business if we didn't have the money." When they are able to come up with a "cash light" solution, then we have created a much better business model to inject all the new money into.

JM: Thanks Hap. That's great. Can you talk to me a little bit about the role of culture in the success or failure of a company?

HK: I've seen a number of other businesses in Silicon Valley that didn't work out the way it was planned. I have a new book coming out in the fall called *ALMOST*, which is about a company that should have been successful but wasn't. It was doing some fantastic research into portable, lightweight energy and had a great product. They had people from Stanford, Carnegie Mellon, the Naval Academy, and two people who were in astronaut training. They also had lots of capital. Yet the company ran out money and never reached its potential. It failed. It is still operating—but only as a slimmed down version of itself running off of government grants. What caused the failure? You'll have to read the book. But it had to do with the company culture—things like greed, conflicting ideas, and the deluded belief that it's easy to be an overnight success in Silicon Valley.

JM: Yes.

HK: A big challenge for the company was the ongoing internal debate between the salespeople who wanted to "make what you can sell" and the engineers who wanted to "sell what you can make." The conflict paralyzed the company. I was unable to reconcile those two cultures for a variety of reasons, which I write about in the book. But from my perspective, even though the company continued to limp along, it was a failure.

JM: Wow, that's powerful. I recently told 1,000 conference attendees that in the end, I want you to be proud of your differentiators. Your products and your services and your brand are important, but in the end if you're not most proud of your culture, eventually you're going to lose your way. I talked about the Jim Collins book, *Good to Great*, which is an amazing book. If you go back to that book, some of the companies he writes about aren't even around anymore.

HK: Yes.

JM: You know? And they lost their way because they tried to grow too quickly or they became very distracted. That happens a lot, right?

HK: Well, they don't know what they stand for.

JM: Yes.

HK: And they started believing what they were reading about themselves or their peers in the *Wall Street Journal*. They started chasing short-term success and losing what's unique about them. And they just bailed out and joined another company.

JM: Absolutely. Absolutely. This is a great Hap. Let me ask you, what would you say would be your two leadership gifts?

HK: I have an innate sense of urgency that I believe is perfectly matched to the times we're in. There's an accelerating pace of change. An exponential rate of change. Many of the people who are leaders now tend to impose restrictions on the growth of their business that are inconsistent with the demands and pace of the marketplace.

JM: Interesting.

HK: And I would say another important aspect is the ability to listen to the marketplace. At The North Face we always joked about the concepts that underpinned our business. We called it the Scotch Principle. It was a bunch of people who were product users, who loved the outdoors, and who got together over drinks and began talking about making our avocation our vocation. We started with the idea of being involved in something we loved and knew a lot about as a business, and before we were finished drinking we were convinced that we were going to create a global company that would dominate the outdoor market. We claimed the conversation was over a bottle of Scotch, but the reality is that at the time, we couldn't afford Scotch so it was probably over a number of six packs of beer. Whichever, that was the origin of our idea for The North Face. We wanted to make products that we would use ourselves and, while doing so, have a lot of fun and laughter. We firmly believed that not a lot of great ideas, great products, and great companies came out of disconnected, hierarchical organizations.

JM: Right.

HK: There is a concept I've tried to put into many of the companies with which I've worked. I call it Possibility Thinking. The concept is that when you have a meeting, during the first half of the meeting, nobody can use the word "no." Rather, I encourage them to let the ideas flow so that people who can't articulate their ideas very well or people who have really novel ideas have a chance to put them out before they hear the negatives from others. Negatives like "we tried that and it will never work," "that is way too expensive," or "that is a stupid idea."

JM: Without question?

HK: Yes. If you allow these ideas to percolate, you may come out with things that are very valuable or novel. At a minimum, you embolden people who are quieter or don't have the corporate position to push their ideas through to completion. Of course, at those meetings you ultimately have to come to some resolution and agreement, but you don't have to do that in the Possibility Thinking phase. Rather than assume everything from the beginning, I advocate for giving an opportunity for people to speak up even if they don't have the gravitas of the C-suite. Remember, they may actually be closer to the market than the people at the top of the company.

JM: Right. Let me ask you this: What are two things that you're always working on in terms of your leadership skills?

HK: Well, everybody's strengths are also their weaknesses.

JM: Yes, sure.

HK: That urgency I spoke about as being a great strength, sometimes I need to have more patience. I have to remember I'm helping people, mentoring people, and have to allow them to make their own mistakes. I can't just let urgency trump everything else. I have to balance that urgency with patience and work with people in a way that will allow them to learn the same way I learned—by trial and error.

The second challenge I face is that I love being around people who have complex and different ideas, but I know in my heart of hearts that the key to success is really executing well. Don't ever confuse planning and strategy with execution. Execution is the most important. Coming up with incredibly brilliant but not easily executed ideas is what I often see from the large consulting companies like McKinsey and Bain. They develop these wonderfully elegant solutions, but they are the only ones brilliant enough to actually execute their strategies.

JM: Absolutely.

HK: Most likely they are generating lifetime jobs for themselves. But for real companies in the real world, I've found that those complex, three-dimensional solutions are just not workable. And so I have to step back from all the complexity to simplify into something that's actually manageable.

JM: That's wonderful. I have a couple of statements I just want you to react to. One of the themes that we're building into the book is that culture starts in the C-suite, it starts with the CEO. Can you give me your perspective on that?

HK: Simply put, if you don't have a culture that everyone can follow, you just have a bunch of managers operating on their own sometimes-conflicting intuitions. Ultimately, the major decisions in a business need to be decided at the top of the company and must all be congruent with the unique culture of that organization. To motivate employees and to speed up decision-making, you want to delegate out as much as you can. But when it comes to the basic tenets and principles of the business—what you stand for, your principles, the qualitative goals that you have for the company—those have to come from the top of the company.

JM: Right, right, right.

HK: And if the whole team does not embrace the culture of the company, then it is just not going to happen. So to me, it's essential that you have a culture in your company and not just a bunch of people operating as individuals. Allowing people to be lone wolves is a form of culture, but it's not a culture for a successful business. The transformation you have to enable is to co-opt people's individual culture into a collective culture. One that is meaningful, positive, competitive, and purposeful.

JM: And if they don't fit the culture, you need to get rid of them, correct?

HK: Yes, or have them step away. We used to do strategic plans every two years at North Face to ensure everyone was on the same page. One of the most important functions of those strategic planning sessions was to bring all the new employees up to speed with our culture. Invariably, at the end of each of those sessions, I would say: "I hope we were so clear at this meeting that some of you leave the company. I don't mean that because you're not valuable and great employees with great ideas, but if you can't agree with the course we've decided to follow then you should take your ideas and find a company that embraces them." To be a successful company we couldn't have a variety of cultures. We could only have one. We couldn't have a variety of directions. We could only have one. I would explain that we would have a meeting in two years and that would become the time we would rethink our direction. Not until then.

JM: I love that. You're really giving them the option to self-select out.

HK: Right. And if they didn't fit in we would actually help them find a place and a company where they would fit. It's not that they're bad people because they didn't agree with us. But you can't run a business going in a lot of different directions.

JM: Absolutely. That's outstanding. The second statement is that you really can't change culture without changing the people and the best way to change people is to change their thinking and beliefs. What's your perspective on this?

HK: I agree with that.

JM: Talk to me about how you have been successful working with people to think differently so that the vision that you have for the organization takes hold. How do you get people to abandon a thinking pattern that they're comfortable with?
How do you get them to move from the A direction to the B direction?

HK: One of the most successful tools I've found is setting up higher levels of goals than just increasing sales and earnings. Most of the people who work in a company cannot actually relate to the bottom line, no matter how much you talk about it. They are only looking at their small subset of the company. But while they can't really relate to many dimensions of the financials, they can relate to the job they have and to the higher-level purpose of the organization. When we were at The North Face, we talked about our company goal as trying to positively change the world. For example, when we developed our geodesic tents we were developing a concept that could create housing all around the world using our design principles but with indigenous materials at the lowest possible cost. Given the global need for affordable housing, everyone in the company could see that we were doing something that was really pretty special. We believed that we could, in fact, solve the world's housing problems with the designs that we created. People could relate to that greater goal.

The second greater goal we embraced at The North Face was our belief in the value of the wilderness. We saw that wilderness and nature were a real antidote to many of the endemic social problems associated with our primarily urban culture. So we believed in trying to save the wilderness, we believed in trying to love the wilderness, and we believed our products created evangelists for our message.

JM: Yes.

HK: We did also have concrete goals. But we also tried to put greater meaning into those as well. For example, when we set a goal to cut our scrap rate, which would allow us to make more profit, we decided to then donate some of those profits to good causes.

JM: That's great. Last question: What suggestions do you have for the younger people reading this book, the leaders of tomorrow?

HK: I think the first one is stop complaining and start doing something. We all know that there are a huge number of problems that exist in the world. Those are not other people's problems, they're our problems. Let's stop quibbling and get on with solving the problems. And so for me a reason to lead is the same reason that I'm doing what I've been doing for so many years. And that is to make a difference in society. There is a great joy in that and there's a benefit for one's self and for society.
I think that is really important.

JM: Yes.

HK: The second thing I'd say is don't worry about failure. Embrace it and accept it because if you're trying to reach great goals and swinging for the fences, you will inevitably have failure. Try to manage it, try to keep the risks down so the costs aren't too high, but don't back away from things because you're afraid you're going to fail. Rather, put your neck on the line, live large; enjoy it because that's where the big ideas are. That's where the big changes are. That's what leadership is about.

Also, allow yourself to be vulnerable. Don't be afraid to be human because most great enterprises need a human element. While it may be effective to have a leader who tells everybody how to do things, it's even better to have somebody as a leader who understands you. A great leader tells you why to do something, not just how to do something, and then gets out of your way.

8

Russ Klein

CEO of the American Marketing Association

Great leaders engage in quiet, daily reflection: *Did I bring
extraordinary value to my family, my team, and my organization?*
And then make the commitment to bring even more value
tomorrow

—*John Mattone*

WHEN ONE DOOR CLOSES, ANOTHER opens. Throughout his life, Russ
Klein weathered closed doors with grace and heeded the opportunity
to walk through open doors with humility, courage, and self-reflection.

Russ Klein grew up in the small town of Middleburg, southwest of
Cleveland. At that time, Middleburg was farmland as far as the eye
could see. His father, grandfather, and great-grandfather worked as
metal smiths. Russ's father owned and led a third-generation metal
engineering and fabricating company in downtown Cleveland.

Building a home from scratch with the help of extended family and
friends, the Kleins settled into their hand-forged home about 30 miles
southwest of the city. It was a childhood out of another time—where
the work of a simple trade and the loyalty of friends and family were

the order of the day. Today, thanks to the suburban sprawl of most Midwestern cities, Middleburg has become connected to the Cleveland metropolitan area and the farmlands are all but gone. But in the memory of the three Klein boys, it lives on.

Russ and his two older brothers were fortunate to grow up on what was known ostensibly as a gentleman's farm (also called a hobby ranch) where they had stables and horses, ducks and ponds, and orchards and forest land on which they were always engaged in what seemed like endless—and possibly pointless—work. Even though they were moving boulders from one end of the property to the other, they loved their life on the farm.

But it wasn't all easy going or typical. Russ's father died when he was just a toddler, leaving a devastated family behind. None of the next generation of Klein boys was old enough to step into the role of leading the family business. In an unexpected twist of fate that would forever impact Russ's work ethic, his mother ended up stepping up to become CEO of an industrial small business in the 1960s.

It was no easy feat for a woman in that time to juggle raising three boys alone with being a female CEO in what was clearly believed at the time to be a "man's business." As a result, the Klein boys grew up to be very self-reliant, self-sufficient, with an all hands on deck kind of mentality to work together and do whatever it takes to be successful.

Along with this growing sense of independence, Russ organically developed a high comfort level regarding working with strong women, a skill that would later serve him well in the advertising business. Mrs. Klein taught Russ and his brothers how to use both their wishbones and their tailbones. Despite losing their father, life on the farm with their courageous mother was the perfect place to grow up. Young Russ had the added bonus of having brothers old enough to step in with mentorship and guidance.

With one brother six years older and the other 11 years older, in some ways they were surrogate fathers. Part a function of the loss of his father and part a function of his commitment to seeking out mentors, Russ had uncles and cousins and family and friends to guide him in his young life. He continued to find mentors even after he went to university.

Russ headed off to college at Ohio State University in Columbus. Joining a social fraternity, Russ threw himself into campus life. He showed an early glimpse into his leadership abilities when he became president of the Acacia fraternity his junior year. And then he did it again senior year, something that had never been done before. It was the perfect opportunity to try out his leadership skills, and he was recognized by the national fraternity body for being an outstanding leader, receiving the Order of Pythagoras award. It was in his role as president that Russ first considered the notion that leadership is about adversity: In the face of a challenge, a leader either manages change or creates change. So it was a time of building his leadership and following his dream: marketing and advertising.

Those were heady, wonderful years for Russ and—displaying his penchant for loyalty—he borrowed the very first $10,000 to give to Ohio State University after reading Woody Hayes' fabled "Paying Forward" commencement speech. He remains connected to the university to this day.

Russ learned early on the value of leading a self-examined life. A natural introvert, Russ's energy source came from within. "My source of energy tends to come from reflecting inward, but I have a need to connect with others. I try to look at even the smallest things in epic terms, because I believe that a little thing could lead to a gigantic thing," Russ says.

With every action comes opportunity.

Like in the old movie *Sliding Doors*, Russ believes the power of a single decision or event can alter one's journey to a great degree, even place one in a different orbit altogether. One single event, one way versus another way can literally change the course of your life.

So when the door opened for Russ Klein to become CEO of the American Marketing Association (AMA), he walked through. By that time a career marketer and advertising executive with more than two decades of experience in marketing management, brand turnarounds, and value creation, Russ started his career on the agency side and went on to occupy senior posts at Leo Burnett and Foote, Cone, and Belding advertising agencies. He worked on accounts like McDonald's, Gatorade, and United Airlines. Later, he switched to the client side, working as the top marketing guy for companies such as Dr. Pepper, 7-Eleven, Burger King, and Arby's, generating record sales performance and profitability.

Russ is frequently invited to speak at industry and academic symposiums, including the lecture series at Harvard Business School. He was once given the nickname "Flamethrower" for his provocative advertising and managerial boldness. A graduate of the Harvard Business School Advanced Management Program, Russ was also presented with the Distinctive Alumni Award from Ohio State University Max M. Fisher College of Business. He has served on a number of boards for charitable foundations, including the Jackie Robinson Foundation and the Jesse Owens Foundation.

As CEO of AMA, Russ carries on the organization's original mission—to serve as a trusted resource for marketing education, training, information, and tools that help advance marketing practice and thought leadership and facilitate sharing of knowledge and networking by connecting like-minded individuals. AMA has grown into one of the largest marketing associations in the world. It is the trusted go-to resource for more than 1.1 million marketers and academics with some 30,000 members in 118 countries across 74 professional chapters and 345 collegiate chapters throughout North America. AMA publishes several handbooks and research monographs including the *Journal of Marketing, Journal of Marketing Research, Journal of Public Policy & Marketing*, and *Marketing News. The Journal of Marketing* and *Journal of Marketing Research* are the number one publications in their respective segments in terms of impact and influence on marketing best practices around the world.

I spoke to Russ about rising above adversity, the serendipity of crossing paths, and knowing how the sliding doors closing and opening at any time in our lives provide opportunities we may never have dreamed we were destined to seize.

JM: Thank you for your contribution to the book, Russ. You're such a humble, introspective, loyal leader. Congratulations on all your success. I imagine it all led to your current position as CEO of the American Marketing Association.

RK: Yes, it did. It's a busy time at the American Marketing Association, but it's a good busy! We're having lot of fun and going through tremendous change at a very rapid rate—it's been a great adventure. I have a very supportive board and that's made for a pleasurable experience, albeit very busy all the way around.

JM: I read the blog post you wrote about curiosity. Essentially, you said that without curiosity, there will be no success.

I love that post, because you are so correct that you know the curiosity factor. You are not going to be successful without the curiosity factor. You have an interesting combination of being self-reflective but also other oriented, which seems to be the secret to your success in your current role.

RK: Yes—it's a highly stakeholder-driven position. The American Marketing Association is complex in terms of all the various constituencies to which we are committed to extending our service and thought leadership. It's part of our strategic platform, of which the first plank is service leadership. We also operate on what we call a "be-do" basis. That means it is more critical to *be* grateful and joyful, curious and courageous, customer-centric and stakeholder-sensitive than it is to *do* anything! Of course people have work to do and they need the skills and competencies to perform those duties, but you cannot be part of the "Next AMA" if you don't first project the *be* values. I know some leaders will differ on this, but I have never met somebody so smart that they could be exempt from living the values of an organization. I would rather take a ragtag group of bad news bears who all shared in a vision, in which they saw themselves playing an epic role and viewed themselves as but one part of a team on which our relationships were more important than our decisions, over any so-called all-star team of intellectually superior but self-centered talent.

JM: Absolutely. How did you come to your passion for marketing?

RK: I have always had a passion for the factors of marketing at work. I was infatuated with advertising long before *Mad Men*, that's for sure! I was infatuated with the field of advertising, and I can still remember projecting myself into Gregory Peck's role in the old movie *The Man in the Grey Flannel Suit.*

After my last horse died while I was in junior high school, we sold most of our land, including our barn, and we planned a barn sale for which I was responsible for designing and constructing the signs and placing the signs everywhere in our trading area. The family made enough money to be able to go to Jamaica for a month during the summer and rent a villa! The full circle of having something that the people might want, making them aware of it in a timely fashion, letting them know where it could be found, and of course pricing it right led to my discovery that, if successful on a larger scale, I could have a better quality of life! That homespun lesson was no doubt my original affirmation that I wanted to be in the field of marketing.

JM: Great. The seeds of leadership are so often planted in our early experiences.

RK: When I graduated from Ohio State, I had several offers from on-campus companies. I actually turned down a job offer from the Leo Burnett Company, as well as offers from Dow Chemical, emerging technology companies, a bank, Federated Department Stores—all because I was hell-bent on getting an advertising job in Cleveland, Ohio. Why? That's where my girlfriend lived! Although my family felt I was being ungrateful and I should have accepted one of those offers, the heart wants what the heart wants, and so my advertising job had to be in Cleveland!

So, when you make a decision like that, you've bought in to a potentially long journey. I volunteered at the American Red Cross where I wrote press releases, and it so happened that a member of the Red Cross board was an executive for Carr Liggett, later changed to Liggett Stashower, an ad agency, a fairly large agency in Cleveland terms. This board member learned of my advertising or bust mission, and he decided to give me a shot. I was working on their regional McDonald's business, so I was in my dream job in my dream city because that's where the love of my life was.

Unfortunately, we broke up, and again through pure serendipity, I received a surreal phone call. To this day, I don't know how it came about, Gene McKeogh was the chief operating officer at Leo Burnett Company. He called up me at my office at the Cleveland ad agency about a year and a half into my stint. Gene said, "Russ, we have an opening on the United Airlines account, and we also think that we're in line to win the McDonald's business nationally, and we've love to have you. If you come here, I'll personally watch out for your career. Call me back tomorrow with a favorable response." Then he hung up. I don't how to put this in perspective but here I am, a 22-year-old kid, and this number two guy at the Leo Burnett Company called me to tell me he wanted me. I went. Unfortunately, he died on an operating table about nine months after I joined Burnett. I still look to the heavens now and then and thank him for his mysterious intervention in my young life.

The job at Burnett and move to Chicago was a life-changing event for me, shaping so much of who I am today. Burnett was in the first *Top 50 Companies to Work For* study and book. Working there, you felt as if Leo Burnett was in a corner office somewhere even though he died 10 years earlier. His principles were still alive and it was very much a purpose-driven agency devoted to being the best ad agency—bar none. We were a team of people who literally felt like we were unstoppable—an amazing culture.

JM: Incredibly powerful. How long were you there?

RK: I was there for about seven years. And in fact, I was 29 when I was made CMO with Dr. Pepper/7 Up. My then-president was concerned about my being 29 as opposed to 30 when I was named the CMO for the public, for the press, for the shareholders. The company was private at that time, but I remember my chairman telling me to say I was 30 when I was still 29. That little white lie got picked up in a securities filing and when my chairman decided to correct the record, I was 30 for two years in a row in that filing!

JM: That's so funny. That's amazing. But you were effective, no matter your age!

RK: We had great success. When I was offered that job, it was at a time when Philip Morris had decided after many failed attempts to become the third player in the soft drink industry versus Coke and Pepsi with their 7 Up brand. They felt they could introduce a product like cola to complete their portfolio but were never able to build up the scale and the brand power to compete. And so 7 Up was having great difficulty from a distribution standpoint, getting squeezed out little by little over time because of distribution and pricing. So Philip Morris put on it the block, and it was purchased by Pepsi. But then the Justice Department blocked the U.S. element of the deal for antitrust reasons.

So, the international element of the sale went through Pepsi. The domestic piece ended up going to a guy who is now famous for owning the Texas Rangers and Dallas Stars, Tom Hicks. Tom Hicks and Bobby Haas put together the Dr. Pepper Company, which they took private and 7 Up instantly became the new third major soft drink company. My opportunity came about when I was presenting on behalf of Leo Burnett to due diligence teams from various suitors seeking to acquire the U.S. operations of the 7 Up Company. Obviously, my objective as the Leo Burnett account supervisor was to keep the 7 Up account at Leo Burnett when the new owners came on board. Little did I know that after the deal was reached, I would receive another mysterious phone call from John Albers. John was the dynamic and charismatic CEO and chairman of Dr. Pepper, originally from Minnesota. For some reason, he took a liking to me and asked me to be his head of marketing. He also said, "I'm going to make you a millionaire." Even then, I was clueless for the first five minutes he was recruiting me. When I finally caught on I said, "John, I'm so flattered, but I love Leo Burnett, and it's great you feel that way about me, but I can be more useful to you by staying here at Burnett."

JM: You said that?

RK: John said, "No, no, you're coming to down to Dallas and we're going to do this thing. After some back and forth, I went down to visit him in St. Louis where 7 Up was based at the time. We ended up flying back to Chicago together because he wanted to keep talking and we ate in some dimly lit restaurant at O'Hare. I finally said, "Okay, I'll do it." I went into the job, running scared—like I do probably with just about everything I do.

JM: That's a good thing! You have to be a little bit afraid: I see that in the coaching that I do with executives. It's in fear that we find our courage. So your admission is very important and you were successful, right? That's the point. You had to fight through the fear.

RK: We were very successful and I was in that job for eight years. Despite having four different presidents over those eight years, John Albers was always behind the scenes watching out for me. Another amazing, inexplicable mentor.

Again, I don't know how to explain the appearance of people in my life out of nowhere, whether Gene McKeogh or John Albers. I can only point to Lady Luck and Lady Providence.

JM: That is a good lesson that we really cannot nor should not underestimate any human being that we meet. So you're there for eight years and then what?

RK: John made good on his promise and the company went public and I gained more money than I thought I would ever see in my lifetime. So after that I wasn't trying to chase the next rung on the corporate ladder. I was just having a lot of fun and now I had some financial security, and so I really thought to myself: *I want to make sure that I keep doing what I enjoy doing.*

So I decided to take the call that came from a small ad agency in Chicago. I loved living in Chicago while employed at Leo Burnett. With this small agency, it was the Gatorade business they had that lured me in. So I joined Bayer, Bess, Vanderwarker as one of their partners. I was the managing director of the Boston Chicken account; later we helped them rename it to Boston Market. I later would end up heading their Gatorade account.

I got married to my wife in 1991. And then about two years into that stint, our agency becomes attractive to True North Advertising, which was the holding company for Foote, Cone & Belding. And so the next thing I know, we got bought out and I am now the managing director of Foote, Cone & Belding in Chicago. I'm right back in a large agency setting! I was particularly connected to the Gatorade account and they were the people with whom I enjoyed working most. My daughter, Chandler, was born in 1994 and a few years after she was born, we discovered a brain cyst doctors felt might have been interfering with her development. It was a stressful time in our family and Chandler had to have two brain surgeries. She was then, and still today, a special needs child—now young adult.

At that point I had two children—Cameron and Chandler, born about 18 months apart. Luckily, I had a supportive management team and board from FCB. They agreed to fund my continued education at Harvard Business School in their Advanced Management Program. When I came back, after this amazing time at HBS and also an important time for self-examination and reflection, I decided to take some time off. This allowed me to be at home with my family and closer to Chandler.

JM: You had to be there.

RK: I was a stay-at-home dad. I was a substitute teacher. I also served on the school board of New Trier School System. I taught gym class at my son's school. I didn't know if I was ever really going to return to an operating role again because I was able to make my way pretty well thanks to owning stock in Dr. Pepper/7 Up as well as BBV. And then in 2002, I started getting very edgy. I missed the social context of business.

That's what I was really craving. Ultimately, I was offered the post as CMO for 7-Eleven North America. So we moved down to Dallas. And about a year later, the Burger King board came calling. Having seen the wealth creation power that a leveraged buyout turnaround with an IPO exit strategy, combined with the chance to really take a big brand with almost a half a billion dollar marketing budget, it was impossible to resist. I believed that the new owners—TPG, Bain, and Goldman Sachs—would grant me the palette to do things my way at Burger King. Burger King was a brand that had been suffering greatly for many, many years. So when our team got there, we were very fortunate to get it turned around 10 months from the day we got there. We then went on a run of six straight years of record-setting sales and profitability not seen before or since. That was another, really dynamic time for me.

JM: Where did you go next?

RK: I took about a year off, then joined the Arby's Restaurant Group, based in Atlanta. At Arby's Restaurant Group we reached numerous milestones that continue to pay dividends for Arby's today. After leaving Arby's, I had several opportunities to return to the restaurant industry, or to try something new at some online brands. But when I was contacted about the CEO post for the American Marketing Association, something inside me lit up instantly.

I knew it wasn't just a privilege, it was a calling.

JM: When you were offered the CEO position, you had been a CMO at large companies but never a CEO. Had you pictured yourself in that role?

RK: A friend of mine at Ohio State would describe me to other people as a "serial CMO." At first I thought, "Is that terrible, man? Is he trying to say that I'm never going to be a CEO?" I think he helped me come to grips myself with the fact that I have always loved the business of marketing, and I've always loved broad gauge marketing jobs. By that, I mean jobs where I always had a large span of control reporting to me. There is no better training to be a CEO than being a broad gauge CMO.

And in the role of CMO, I was the number two guy to the CEO, the guy stepping up to solve problems or write a speech behind closed doors. I enjoyed it. I wasn't counting myself out to be a CEO, but I did wonder if my love for marketing might make life difficult for a CMO working for me.

I thought to myself, "Here's this venerable institution that's been around for more than 75 years, millions of marketers trusted this association and this brand to be a source knowledge and best practices in their craft." It was a little dusty, graying around the edges, in need of modernization.

I thought, "So here's an opportunity as a CEO to not only come in and do important branding work, but it's a chance now to build an esteemed community essential to marketers." I also had one more chip on my shoulder, and it was the concept of culture. The fact of the matter is that even as a powerful CMO, there's only one person who can really set the stage and tone for a values-driven culture. That's the CEO.

JM: There are legacy aspects of the AMA that are powerful and positive that you want to sustain, but I'm sure that there are elements of the culture you want to change. How are you tackling that?

RK: It started with a vision in which people could see themselves as having a starring role. To me, that was an important foundation piece to lay out. So we went through a process of what I call a "stakeholder-built strategic plan." It was the function of lots of listening, lots of input, and ultimately, allowed us to articulate a vision in which people could see their own ideas and their own inputs reflected in it, and they could see how they fit into that vision.

That was job number one.

JM: If you've got alignment, in which people feel connected with the mission and the vision and the purpose, magic can happen. So clearly, that's where you started—pillar number one. What was next?

RK: That was pillar number one and right next to it were two concepts that I told our story about over and over and over again to my internal staff and to our external stakeholders. The AMA culture is hinged on community.

So while we are a big organization, we need to also make sure that we're all pulling in the same direction. And I used this story to try to bring to stark relief how difficult it is to be a leader of change. One story I tell is the Genovese syndrome, and I'm sure you've heard of it. Maybe by other terms, it's called the "bystander effect."

JM: Of course, yes. How have you applied it?

RK: Kitty Genovese is the woman who was murdered in the '60s in New York City when 37 people listened or watched without calling the police. And social scientists who studied that event concluded that the more people present during that murder, the less likely she was to get help because of the human nature to assume that the person next to them is going call for help so they don't need to. As horrific as that story is, I loved it because if someone can lose their life over apathy, you can certainly lose a business over apathy.

JM: I think that's very, very well said, very powerful.

RK: So that's number one. The other story I tell is something I learned in our business school from Michael Beers from HBS. In his algebraic equation, Change = a vision × a process × D, the D stands for dissatisfaction. His point was unless there is universal dissatisfaction, there can be little or no change. The multiplication sign means if dissatisfaction is less than whole, change will be suboptimized. And if a group of people is not universally dissatisfied at all, it means anything times zero is zero. I find that equation irrefutable.

I held a town hall meeting in my first 30 days at AMA, and I asked my leadership team to stand up in front of the balance of the staff and share with them, what it was, they were dissatisfied with about the current AMA.

JM: Amazing.

RK: And then we held workshops from that point on to keep the concept alive as part of our ongoing change management.

JM: I find that so powerful. For cultural change to occur within an organization, two things must be present. One is dissatisfaction. The other is compelling vision.

This is a basic wisdom that young leaders must incorporate if they want to survive the ever-changing climate. You have a lot of young talent at the AMA. What message would you want to deliver to those upcoming leaders, and all leaders?

RK: That's a big question! I might say that leadership is an opportunity to see your principles and values advanced in the world. Therefore, the legacy of your own values and your own principles has a chance to survive and go another generation.

I would also encourage young people to embrace the belief that you're not going to inspire without taking stands. That does not mean being argumentative or combative but that your values and principles are not divisible, to be cut up and split in half or filed off around the edges. You can compromise on lots of other aspects in the business world, but values and principles are not divisible. Leadership is also the opportunity and the responsibility to make sure that those values and principles survive into the next generation.

JM: This has been powerful, Russ. I have some final questions. What aspects of your culture are you most proud of? Why?

RK: Curiosity and gratefulness. All of our values are what we call "be" goals. They are all more important than any "do" goal anyone has. What's unique about curiosity and gratefulness is that they will serve anyone who passes through the American Marketing Association for life. Additionally, they are gateway competencies that open you up to positive possibilities because they are outer-directed.

JM: What aspects of your culture are the ones you need to transform? Why?

RK: The Next AMA culture is freshly minted. There was only a default culture of careerism, individualism, and I would describe the enterprise as rudderless, uninspired, and running at an unhealthy normal of mediocrity. Yet not everyone in the organization wanted this—they were simply unable to change it, because such change has to start at the top. In fairness, my predecessor, aside from sitting on the selection committee that hired me, had led the organization through the Great Recession and achieved other noteworthy milestones in the 75-plus year history of the AMA. But it was time to move from professional management to inspired leadership if the AMA was going to rise again as the preeminent, knowledge-based enterprise devoted to marketing in the world. The one cornerstone that seemed rock solid both inside and around the AMA was a genuine sense of earnestness. I took note of this early on, and my observation has proved correct time and time again. The AMA staff and our thousands of volunteers across the country are involved with the AMA for the right reasons and the positive intent is palpable. And quite directly, I believed then and now it represents an uncommon earnestness among such a large group of individuals. With that to build on, the cultural tenets of the Next AMA are curiosity, courage, gratefulness, joyfulness, customer-centric, and stakeholder-sensitive. Why those and not the full list of Boy Scouts values? Simply, because in my 35 years of experience, 28 of it in the C-suite, they represent the invisible forces that drive a high performance/feedback organization. As CEO, it was my first chance to build a culture on the basis of empirical proof from past cultures: great cultures, default cultures, toxic cultures, all of which I've had the opportunity to see firsthand from multiple vantage points. I have chronicled a case for why each of these *be* goals are fundamental to a high functioning organization, and the message to the team is clear; if you can't *be*, you can't *do*.

JM: What is your strategy for transforming and what kind of progress have you achieved?

RK: Service leadership that translates into an enterprise-wide obsession with not just satisfying, but inspiring our customer; thought leadership via a big tent intellectual agenda that addresses relevant problems in industry; a digital/physical fusion of AMA.org and all of our physical forums into a personalized, connected, and seamless AMA user experience, as part of One AMA Brand. One AMA Community that can leverage scale where advantageous [brand identity, philanthropy] but still provides freedoms within frameworks for agility. Importantly, this constitutes a stakeholder-built strategic plan. It's not my plan. I helped turn what mattered to our customers into the plan as a result of hyperlistening and an understanding of not just what members/customers said, but what they meant. I am a devout believer that it's easy to make decisions when you know your own values.

I believe every leader of a turnaround or a "turn-up" tends to organize their plans in terms of some version of so-called quick wins and long-range plans. I have always loved, and tried to emulate, the fighter pilot mentality of OODA—observe, orient, decide, act. There are lots of opportunities that can be seized simply through decisiveness. I am not talking about reckless abandon, shooting up the town just to prove you're the new sheriff in town. "Command of the glance" however, is a critical quality for a leader especially in a rapidly changing environment. I don't do well with managers who need to build a cathedral of analysis on every project. Voltaire had it right when he said, "Perfect is the enemy of good." If you don't think good enough can be a strategy you haven't been paying attention to China. Don't get me wrong, I am actually a perfectionist, but there is a sweet spot of idealism and a certain pragmatism every leader must find if they are to make progress in a timely fashion.

So at the Next AMA, we had our quick-win plans that we named "Rolling Thunder." We wanted to launch a series of tactical initiatives that would act as proof points to our customers and stakeholders that we were indeed listening to them and that we intended to act accordingly. The most important element among these tactics was *being there.* By this I mean I sent my leadership team on the road. My board was kind enough to hit the road, too. I traveled to over 30 cities in my first six months as CEO. The day I started, I asked my assistant to say yes to everything to which I was invited for the first year. There's a reason why politicians still stump and rock-and-roll bands still crank out concerts despite the brutal travel schedules. Nothing can replace being there. Now I concede that technology has made virtual video-conferencing a great alternative to face-to-face meetings. But we all know, there is something magical about encountering another human being … the handshake … the affirming head nod … the dynamic of live on-the-spot empathy is something that instantly creates something bigger than any one individual. When you take the time and trouble to be there for your constituents, they will always notice it. Whether they say so or not, by going out to them, you have earned a place in their hearts and heads that would otherwise have dissipated the moment your Skype session ended.

While implementing our Rolling Thunder plan over a period of several months, reinforced by frequent if not almost constant travel to oblige every invitation, we also knew that there was a significant skills and competency gap between the AMA and the Next AMA in our ability to pursue our four transformational strategies. Every leader has the challenge of not only identifying their strategic direction, be it transformational in nature or not, but they also have the more stressful challenge of identifying their *enabling strategies*. Enabling strategies are the fuel—finance, talent, technology, knowledge, and alliances. Invariably, every leader needs to find the optimal blend of enabling strategies to power their change efforts [read: transformational strategies]. In our particular case, we had plenty of deficits to manage, but the most critical was talent. As I said earlier, we had a remarkably earnest group of individuals on the AMA staff, but not all were geared for the Next AMA, either because of their inability to be the type of employee we felt was supportive of our cultural aspirations, or because—possibly through no fault of their own—they did not have the skills or competency to do the work of the Next AMA. That is, to perform at a high level, advancing our four transformational strategies in an agile, collaborative, team-first environment. As a result we initiated a "future back" project to redesign the organizational structure of the Next AMA.

Organizational fitness became the major challenge for me. I had to do everything I could, playing the hand I'd been dealt, with the current staff that I knew was capable of doing better work, while an outside consultant was working on the new design of the enterprise. Having identified the opportunity—an opportunity that would later be reaffirmed by the external organizational consultant—to break down silos and create a sense of connectedness between and across both internal and external groups, I admit I stole a page from Allan Mulally's book and announced with corresponding drama, a "merger." I then quickly released the tension from something representing such dramatic change as a merger to confess that "we are going to merge with ourselves!"

We created a virtual suggestion box. I hosted monthly town halls that included "day in the life" sessions wherein an individual shares a day in their work life at the AMA to begin to build empathy for what others do. We created two awards: one for service leadership and one for resourcefulness, both of which stem from inspiring true stories from history. We always reviewed the performance of the enterprise and reviewed our team goals. We celebrated successes no matter how small. I began to write to the organization occasionally, outside of my AMA blog, sharing an article of interest with my take on it and solicited feedback. As a staunch believer in what some call "performative language," I believe that language is literally a predictor of outcomes. That is, the language we use leads to outcomes commensurate with the tone and nature of the words themselves. As one example, I sign every piece of correspondence, "Positively," and I've been doing it for more than 30 years. I am quite certain that cumulatively that sign-off has played a part in creating the many positive outcomes with which I've been associated accordingly! What we say plants ideas in particular ways and I believe in taking great care, through the use of nurturing words, of the ideas I plant. I took an AMA personality test and shared the results with the entire staff and requested them to do the same—only about a quarter of the organization reciprocated; hint, there's more trust to be built. Externally, we spoke of "One AMA Brand. One AMA Community." We tried to paint a picture of the Next AMA in an epic story in which everyone could see themselves as an epic part of it.

I want every person in the AMA, whether they're in my office or some small, rural outpost, to feel that when that sliding door opens, they are ready to step into the starring role.

9

Rohit Mehrotra
Founder & CEO, CPSG Partners

The most powerful leadership truth is that failure almost always precedes success, yet the most powerful leadership irony is that success is often the first step to failure.

—John Mattone

INSPIRED BY HIS FATHER, ROHIT MEHROTRA'S ethics, vision for technology, and passion for mentorship have defined his career and his life.

Rohit grew up in a middle-class family in Lucknow, India. By the young age of 17, he had developed an uncanny ability to find innovative solutions to challenging problems: he could find clarity while others would get lost in the noise. He attended the prestigious Indian Institute for Technology (IIT), where he earned a degree in electrical engineering and then joined a college graduate rotational program at a company that built tractors.

Rohit looked at the tractor engines and said to himself, "If we took this engine and put an electrical winding around it, we could create individual power generators." Rohit recognized the potential to create a profitable, inexpensive generator using parts already at hand. Moreover, he saw an opportunity to provide rural Indian villages with affordable electricity and change lives.

Several preliminary discussions ensued, but ultimately, Rohit voluntarily left the company to pursue other opportunities. Shortly after, the company designed an engine that loosely echoed Rohit's concept and called it the Flywheel Mounted Generator or FMG.

Even though he no longer worked at the company, Rohit had proof of his entrepreneurial insticts — one of his own ideas had hit the market!

Upon reflection about his time in the rotational program, Rohit discovered that while electrical engineering was interesting, it was the software aspect that captivated his attention. He wanted to go to graduate school for computer science. The problem was cost — his middle-class background didn't allow for frivolous spending, never mind an expensive U.S. university degree.

Always a risk taker by nature, Rohit set out with little more than $100 in his pocket for the University of Alabama in the United States, which had promised a full-ride scholarship. Upon arrival, he received his scholarship and found an additional fellowship. It did have one key complication — the fellowship required a 3.8 GPA *within* the graduate program, which, as a new student only a few days on campus, Rohit hadn't yet earned. Even so, the head of the department had such faith in the new graduate student that he was awarded the fellowship on the spot. But the requirement was simple and severe: Make the grade or go home.

Rohit maintained the grades. But unfortunately, the funding fell through. A new fellowship was necessary to remain in the United States, so Rohit applied for and won a prestigious assistantship in the aeronautical department. At once, he found himself in front of a flight simulator with minimal instruction: "These are data stream generators one, two, and three." Endless data flowed through their process that all required advanced coding knowledge. Luckily, Rohit was a quick study and the project succeeded. In no time, Rohit graduated and moved to Miami, Florida, for employment.

Until this point, Rohit had been in the backseat of leadership teams — an intern, a graduate student, a research assistant. But here, things began to change. Rohit's new boss, David Pederson, took the time to teach him a myriad of skills. Recalling his own mentor, David took Rohit under his wing in much the same fashion. It was a direct confirmation of one of Rohit Mehrotra's most fundamental beliefs: In life, people give back what they have received.

David and Rohit would sit down in the evenings and look at business trends. Cracking open leading magazines of the time, the two would sit and discuss. David would ask Rohit to analyze material he had never seen before and push him harder and harder to achieve. "I'm going to drive you like a race car, Rohit, because if I don't, you're going to stutter."

One day, David came to Rohit with a new project. Unsatisfied with the UNIX vi text editor, David asked Rohit to find an editor similar to Brief, one of the most popular and powerful editors on the market at the time. Rohit researched and found a product called Crisp, which was "just laying around" on UUNET. Rohit worked to improve Crisp's functionality and eventually brought it up to speed.

After a few edits, Rohit realized that this was an uncut diamond of a product—with a solid redesign, many others might be able to benefit. Wanting to share his edits and collaborate, Rohit began looking for Crisp's author, Paul Fox. His exhaustive search proved futile, so he moved ahead and created a mailing list for others to use the product for free.

In a matter of weeks, several hundred people enrolled, and the mailing list became a network of connections. One day, a member of the mailing list mentioned that he had Paul Fox's contact information. Rohit immediately called Paul. Rohit learned that Paul was coming to Disney World, so they made plans to meet. When they did, the two agreed that if Paul would build the product to Rohit's specifications, Rohit would focus his efforts on marketing and selling it. They'd split the proceeds evenly. With a firm handshake, a partnership was formed.

Together, they combined codelines to retool the product. Then they sent the new, graphical product to Rohit's original mailing list as a commercial offering. The price was $650. In a matter of minutes, a man from Sweden replied and asked to be the first customer. He also asked a question: "What's the name of your company? I'd like to write a check."

Rohit immediately flipped through the magazine next to his laptop. He scanned photo captions and checked the domain availability for promising-sounding adjectives. Clear? Silver? Vital? Vital! He checked the domain (it was available), paid a few dollars to register, and confidently replied, "Vital Technologies is the company name." Within the week, a check for $1,300 made out to Vital Technologies arrived from Sweden.

With this $1,300 and a new job offer in hand, Rohit moved from Florida to Houston, Texas, with his new wife, Gigi. Without even stopping to see the new house, Rohit and Gigi went straight to the courthouse to register their company and legally begin the new business.

They were a team; Paul coded, Gigi worked to set up the sales operations, and Rohit marketed and sold (all after his day job).

But soon, Vital Technologies took off—so much so that Rohit would often become too busy with customers to deposit his checks! Checks for hundreds of thousands of dollars often sat for weeks in his desk. What started as a simple text editor on UNIX became a leading cross-platform integrated development environment. Rohit's determination and work ethic brought Vital Technologies to a competitive standard within months; within a few years, Vital Technologies was booming.

After working for almost five years concurrently at Sybase, Rohit and a co-worker, Jessie Mann, quit the company to start their own technology services company focused on database and systems management. This company was called Vital Solutions. Utilizing his software sales background, Rohit developed a business model that was very unique to the consulting industry at that time. This business model and Rohit's management style made Vital Solutions the fastest growing IT services firm in southwest United States with an exclusive focus on systems and data management.

Soon, Vital Solutions was acquired by a private equity group and made part of ONE Community, Inc., a national consulting firm focused on demand chain solutions involving customer relationship management, operational strategy, e-business, and architectural design. Rohit and Jessie both accepted positions as senior vice presidents as part of the acquisition.

In January 2002, ONE Community, Inc. went under. Not wanting to lose their best employees, Rohit and Jessie founded Vivare, a systems integration firm. As CEO of Vivare, Rohit was responsible for strategic planning and development of key customer and partner relationships. He focused on providing solutions involving service-oriented architecture, wireless, mobile content delivery, and business intelligence.

At the same time, Rohit and Jessie purchased Paranet Solutions, a struggling professional services provider specializing in network services and enterprise security. Rohit named himself the CEO, worked his magic, and sold a profitable firm to a private equity group in October 2006. (Vivare was acquired by a public company in September 2005.) These successes all set the stage for his crowning achievement and current company: CPSG Partners, LLC.

Rohit's experience stretches well over two decades of building technology companies, mergers and acquisitions, and alternative investments. He currently is the CEO and founder of CPSG Partners.

In addition, he advises business entrepreneurs, provides angel investments to start-up companies, and works as a vice president at a money management group specializing in ultra-high net worth wealth management.

Today, Rohit and Gigi make their home in Plano, Texas. I talked to Rohit Mehrotra about his staggering success and what he has learned along the way.

JM: The first thing I want to do is congratulate you on the incredible success! You are the definition of a serial entrepreneur and you're having amazing success with your current firm, CPSG Partners. CPSG is the fastest-growing privately held IT services company in the United States, is that correct?

RM: Yes, that is correct.

JM: Did you have a particular strategy for exponential growth? Maybe based on the successful model of one of your previous companies?

RM: I have changed opinions on that through the years. When I first started my career as an entrepreneur, I equated growth with objective success. More sales meant more jobs, which meant more profit; at the end of the day, more growth was positive. I was very ambitious at that point, and growth was my main goal.

At that time, in the late 1990s, everybody wanted to start with hundreds and hundreds of employees. And I thought, "That's no way to grow—it's too capital intensive." Instead, I wanted to create a high-quality ecosystem for subcontractors. We needed to find competent, high-end people who could go and represent themselves well: a strong network of consultants to make good on whatever we sold.

First, we focused on just the sales. Then, we created the systems to make the quality stay consistent. We were right about the contractor ecosystem, and the company flourished—right off the charts. A private equity firm came in and acquired us within a year, and we became part of ONE Community, Inc. Things were going well. After Vital Solutions was acquired, my dad called me from India.

JM: What did your dad have to say?

RM: He said, "I am very happy to see you succeed. I hope you are doing everything the right way."

I said, "Yes. Everything is fine."

"I trust you," he said, "but I've never seen this kind of money made so quickly in an honest way. I just want to be able to die with my head held high."

And I said, "Don't worry about it—everything is exactly the way you would expect it to be." And it was.

ONE Community Inc. disintegrated after 9/11. The company abandoned their employees when they shut down—I saw it firsthand. There were people in the hospitals left without medical plans and all sorts of messes.

My business partner, Jessie, and I had to sit down and make a decision to restart this thing from the ground up or to walk away. But I couldn't just leave. I still remember that evening; I called the head of the company and said, "I'm one of your biggest units out here—the one you acquired—and you're shutting this whole thing down? You're hurting people."

And he said, "I'm sorry; I can't do anything."

I said, "Do what you have to do." So Jessie and I sat there that night, and we wrote personal checks to employees for over $2 million total.

JM: Unbelievable.

RM: This is all without knowing what would happen the next day.

I experienced the principle that often dark situations are where you can best show how to step up.

The next day, I assembled our best employees and asked who wanted to stay. Some of them, believe it or not, took the check and left. They didn't want anything to do with a new organization. But with a core group remaining, we went to our largest customer and told them honestly what had happened. They believed in us and gave us an opportunity. We grabbed it, and Vivare was started right then and there. Right from the ashes, Vivare started growing very, very fast.

While at Vivare, we got a call from one of our previous employees, who told us that Sprint was planning on shutting down their e-solutions group, Paranet, and might be interested in selling. Lesson learned here:

Don't lose contact with your employees, and take their opinions seriously. It took another leap of faith to complete that purchase, but it turned out well in the long run.

But although they were all very exciting, none of these mergers or acquisitions were the tipping point for my career. What changed my life and set the tone for the next stage was my dad's passing away in 2005.

Even before my father died, I had been thinking over what he'd said for many years, and had never really understood what he meant by dying "with my head held high." I suppose I understood it, but I didn't get the spirit of it. I went back to India during that year when he was sick, and then he passed away. After the cremation and the services, this postman walked up to me, a man who had been coming to our house for almost 30 years. He hadn't seen me that often because I left home when I was 17, but he knew my father well.

He looked at me and said, "You resemble the man who used to live here—who are you?" I said that I was his son. He looked straight in my eyes and told me, "I hope you are half the man he was."

JM: Wow!

RM: "They don't make men like him anymore."

JM: That's incredible. What a moment.

RM: Even today when I tell that story, I get chills and feel his eyes looking right at me. I then realized what my dad meant. And it changed the way I started looking at clients and business opportunities. It wasn't that there was anything particularly wrong with what was being done before, but it added a compassionate and strong ethical compass to my life that I have striven to follow ever since.

JM: That's very moving and it speaks to why you've done great things. And this was something that hit you as a marker in life—you always had enormous respect and love for your dad, but the real meaning of that came through at this particular point.

I imagine at that point you were able to say, "I'm doing great things now, but I've got to hold myself to a higher standard. I have massive responsibility for my employees, and I've got to make sure that I uphold my most honorable side." Would that be true?

RM: Yes. The experience gave me a different perspective in life. Someday, I hope that somebody will be able to say to my kids or to the people that I work with that I, too was a man to emulate. And to do that, you've got to hold yourself to a higher standard and think longer term. My dad obviously had spent his entire life building that sterling reputation. His lesson gave my life new meaning.

So at this stage I was pretty much done; all my companies had been acquired and I had retired, at least in theory.

JM: Yeah, and how old are you—in your 30s?

RM: I was around 40. So I retired for a while, thinking that I'd spend my time golfing and being with family. But I really wasn't doing much of anything. One day I woke up and I thought about the fact that my son would grow up without ever seeing his dad work.

JM: Another marker.

RM: Yes, absolutely. So, I started job hunting. But I was surprised to find that even with my experience, I couldn't find a company that wanted me. I hit a lot of dead ends. But soon my money management guys called and said, "You're one of our largest customers. Why don't you come and work with us?" I didn't know if this was something that I wanted, but they said to come give it a try, at least. So, not seeing any better option, I did.

It was a very humbling start. Everybody there starts at the bottom. I had been the largest client of this money management group, and I still had to start at the very bottom alongside people more than several years my junior, both in age and work experience. I even made cold calls.

I learned that the money management business really did not like to have the clients interact with each other. Their theory was that someone would always be unhappy if clients were allowed to compare themselves to others. But I found myself in a unique middle ground—a member of both the money management executives and an elite client with my own private wealth. I thought, "What would happen if there was some kind of exclusive group for all these high-profile clients to network and share connections? Would this be something that I would want to join?" I started talking about this and brainstorming, and soon, we started a club for our most elite customers called "The Platinum Group." At the same time, I also insisted on a disciplined way of managing money, and created an asset allocation program to do it.

These two ideas reinvented our group, and we became one of the largest private wealth managers in the city.

I enjoyed the wealth management business, but I missed the world of technology. However, I didn't want to create just another cookie-cutter consulting firm. If I started another business, I wanted something unique.

The idea came when I took my daughter on her first college visit. At Harvard, she asked the question, "How do you earn a merit-based scholarship?"

They answered, "We don't award any merit-based scholarships."

My daughter (and my wallet) asked, "Why is that?"

The admissions officer said, "Because we have no way of choosing; all of our students are meritorious."

And then something clicked in my mind. How has Harvard kept such a phenomenal reputation for so long, that students will come from all over the world? I answered my own question: by accepting only a diverse group of equally meritorious people across the board, bottom to top, no exceptions. So I asked myself, "Can a commercial business be created on the same principle?"

I knew that all organizations—large, small—they're all going to have exceptional people. They're also going to have less than exceptional people, and then they're going to have people who are just fit enough for the job. That's just a fact.

But could an organization be built differently—where everyone is exceptional? Rather than thinking, "Can this person do the job?" I needed to think, "What is this person's potential, and how can I help him soar?"

So I started to study, research, and plan. First, I looked at different companies that could have been based on the same principle. I found Bell Labs and McKinsey, and those were close. But really, the organization that embodies this principle is the United States Navy SEALs special operations force.

I went and spoke with a retired Navy SEAL, and I asked him, "What would I need to make a SEAL business?"

He said, "You need to find a problem set that will attract the brightest minds in the world and then create a culture where they will thrive."

First, I needed a business puzzle to fully engage the minds that I wanted to attract. I found it in Workday. Workday was (and still is) a great piece of software built by great people, but, more important, it was at the epicenter of two areas that were transforming: cloud adoption and human capital management. (Remember, David had taught me to read technology trends long ago.)

Once I found Workday, I was hooked. I asked Jessie to join me and launch a new venture like nothing we'd ever done before. I hired world-class leaders and mentors as my first "commercial SEALs."

The problem was that Workday locks its ecosystem, so it was almost impossible to gain partnership. The first time I went out there to present to Workday for a partnership, they said, "Thank you for coming, but the answer is no." After creatively knocking on the door over and over, we finally became a Workday partner. Believe it or not, we were the last boutique firm that was admitted into Workday's partner ecosystem.

JM: So that's how it started? That's incredible.

RM: Yes. And I stayed at it, and that allowed us to build CPSG. So, going back to your question about growth—growth has never been the main goal of this company. Instead, we focus on quality delivery and quality culture. When we set this ideal for ourselves, it just so happened that we became the fastest-growing tech service company in the country—exponential growth was a byproduct.

The actual number of employees is not an issue—we are never going to compromise on our ability to hire the very best. This is a home for the brightest college grads, industry recruits, second-career entrepreneurs, really anybody as long as he or she is exceptional. This is my masterpiece—my favorite of all the businesses I've started. I genuinely enjoy the company of the people here.

JM: I know you said that the number doesn't really matter, but how many employees do you have?

RM: About 225, and I know each one of them. Believe it or not, I hired many of them right out of elite schools like Harvard, Yale, Princeton, Stanford, and MIT. It's not that students at other schools wouldn't be great, but at Ivy League-caliber schools, someone else has already done the work. I hire uncut diamonds, I shine them up, and they do very well.

JM: And it works?

RM: Yes it does. We do the same thing for industry veterans; we find people at the pinnacle of their careers who are also world-class mentors and leaders themselves. They could be young, they could be up-and-comers, but they need to have a different way of thinking. They have to like collaboration with other brilliant people and enjoy mentorship.

JM: This is wonderful. But have you ever worried about an arrogant superstar who might break the company culture?

RM: I did worry about that. I thought, "I'm hiring all this talent, these young cracker jack students who have done nothing but succeed in their lives. What could stop them from becoming arrogant?" That started bothering me, so I went back and I talked to my friend the retired SEAL. He said that I would never find an arrogant SEAL because "when you surround yourself with world-class people smarter and stronger than yourself, you yourself will become smarter and stronger, and you'll never be arrogant." So far, that has been the case here as well. Our employees consistently say that the people are the best part of working here—and I agree.

JM: I love the social experiment, but I love even more how you started our conversation today, showing gratitude to others. We need more of that, Rohit. Don't you agree?

RM: Yes, I don't think leadership can happen without a lot of people helping you along the way. For me, that was David, my wife Gigi, my partners Paul, Jessie, Steven, and countless others.

JM: When you look back on your career, what are your three most essential leadership strengths?

RM: The first one is that I'm very transparent. People know exactly where I stand. Being successful means staying true to yourself. I teach that to the kids I mentor.

I also take responsibility and do it openly. If there is a failure, instead of worrying about the causes, you can simply identify what role you played. You can't learn from failure without taking ownership of it.

JM: I love that.

RM: My other is that I have a natural affinity and ability to lead and harness the outliers, the exceptions, the people who are good, but don't fit the mold. In my mind, the most powerful act of leadership is to find the outliers and take care of them. Build around them. They are the ones who can imagine greatness.

JM: Amazing. Boston Consulting Group just did some research on culture, and they make the point that 75 percent of organizations that are currently leaders are not being proactive; they're not reading the market variables, they're not being responsive enough, or they're not transforming at all. If you don't transform, and if you're not constantly looking at your organization and looking at your leadership population and asking yourself, what can we do to get better and better and better, you're going to get left behind.

RM: I agree. Innovation is a necessity, even when it's uncomfortable.

JM: I love your thinking. What can you point to as a good example of leading cultural transformation in your organization?

RM: I demand loyalty from every employee—not to me, but to the best within themselves. The employees who work for me will likely at some point move on. All I ask is that they do something great when they do.

JM: I love what you're saying; it's beyond spreadsheets and it's beyond big data. Leadership is asking ourselves, "How do you want your life remembered?"

RM: Yes. Money loses its luster. In the end, the real question is, "Why not create something special?"

JM: What other wisdom do you want to share with the future leaders of our world?

RM: You must find the foundational principle that you believe in, and then bank everything on it. Think of yourself as an orchestra conductor. When you are directing the orchestra, your back is toward the crowd. You are not going to see how the crowd is reacting, but at the end of the day, that symphony is created to your unique satisfaction. If you lead with confidence and get that unique satisfaction, others will follow and find pleasure in your work.

JM: A few final questions. First, what aspects of your culture are you most proud of? Why?

RM: CPSG truly focuses on team success. It starts with the structure—CPSG is a very flat organization. This means from the staff consultant level all the way to the C-suite, the client will hear from all, and employees can walk into any upper management office—including mine—and talk over problems or ideas. I have given explicit instructions to others in management that if a junior employee has a request, their default answer should be yes. If the answer is no, I need to hear about it.

This company tradition of saying, "Yes! And how can I help you do it?" fosters collaboration and mentorship. At the end of the day, this model gives us an unfair advantage as a company: exceptional relationships. When this advantage is best used, we can outperform much larger consulting partners in the same market, and the company flourishes.

I am most proud of CPSG's culture of open communication, collaboration, and mentorship. We take care of each other, just like the SEALs.

JM: What is your vision for the future?

RM: I expect us to be a market defining cloud-enablement and cloud services firm. Ideally, I would also like to see some firms started by our current CPSG employees. Hopefully, I will have had a chance to invest in them. I believe that nothing pleases an entrepreneur more than seeing another one succeed.

CPSG is in the business of assisting customers with innovation adoption. And when your job is to help companies embrace what the industry refers to as "leading edge," you have to make innovation part of your own DNA. Otherwise you'll simply burden new innovation with old tired methods. That's not who we are. Although I can't tell you exactly what or how we'll innovate in the future, I know that we'll be never stop reaching to be better than we were yesterday and preparing to be even greater tomorrow. In the end, every move I make is governed by what the postman said to me after my father passed away, and I know, as long as I am being the good man he was, I will succeed.

> In my mind, the most powerful act of leadership is to find the outliers and take care of them. Build around them. They are the ones who can imagine greatness.
>
> — *Rohit Mehrotra*

10

Irv Rothman

CEO of HP Financial Services

You have the choice to either accept or reject feedback; however, if you reject feedback you also reject the choice of acting in a way that may very well bring you abundant success and happiness.

—John Mattone

THE INTERNATIONAL BUSINESS WORLD IS chock-full of CEOs who have established their place in the business world as a kind of legacy—they are the sons and daughters of educated, upper- or upper-middle-class families, afforded private secondary educations and gained entry to the best universities. Irv Rothman is not that kind of CEO. Raised in the gritty, hardscrabble town of Bayonne, New Jersey, Rothman created his own success from a combination of hard work, determination, and an unwavering commitment to building a successful life.

The son of a WWII veteran father and stay-at-home mom, young Irv was like many kids in the cramped city of Bayonne. Just across the river from Manhattan, yet a world away, Bayonne was a small city with 85,000 people of varied ethnicities but a common blue-collar existence. Like most boys, Irv loved to play sports. From school teams to Jewish city leagues, there wasn't a sport Irv didn't like. Not that he was brilliant in them, but he enjoyed the thrill of competition, the collaboration of being on a team, and the satisfaction of dedicating one's self to the art of the game.

It was a simple life, with all the necessities met. A roof over the family's head, food on the table, clean clothes tucked neatly in dresser drawers. In many ways, it was the good life many American children in the 1960s enjoyed. Irv and his brother were happy, satisfied with their lot. It was what they knew.

But along with sports, Irv had another passion—reading—which offered him a glimpse into the wider world. Instead of the trailer parks of Bayonne with a view of Port Newark, the pages of books detailed foreign settings both far away and near. When Irv was 14, he jumped at an opportunity to experience a completely foreign setting—a sleepaway camp for wealthy children located in the Pocono Mountains of Pennsylvania. The children who were there weren't working as delivery boys in their grandfather's liquor store, as young Irv did. Their parents weren't blue collar. It was in that first storied summer teaching the children of the wealthy to swim that Irv got his first glimpse into another culture. With keen observation skills, he was introduced to another way of life. In two summers as a waiter and later work as a waterfront counselor for the campers there, Irv observed a different way of living, a different group of people who conducted their lives far from the streets of Bayonne.

Irv combined his strong powers of observation with his love of reading and became the sports editor for his high school newspaper. Even after winning a National Scholastic Press Association prize for sports writing his senior year, his future career as a journalist was far from set. Indeed, Irv's mother implored that the life of a journalist was not the right path for a "nice Jewish boy." With dreams of pricey Division 3 schools out of reach, Irv set out for Rutgers, the state university of New Jersey in nearby Newark.

It was there that Irv's upbringing among hard-working people became relevant. Determined to pay his own way and graduate debt free, Irv balanced life as a full-time university student with not just one but four part-time jobs. From working in the middlebrow men's clothing store Charles Menswear to tackling a territory for class ring and favor company L. G. Balfour, Irv was busy selling favors for events like homecoming or other special weekends while many of his classmates simply attended those events. Squeezing a full load of classes into a three-day-a-week schedule, Irv worked as a substitute teacher the other two days each week. Sure enough, Irv achieved his goal, graduating from Rutgers completely debt free.

The United States was at war in Vietnam. Irv, joined and served six years in the U.S. Army Reserve, which included six months of active duty, with two weeks every summer dedicated to being a full-time soldier. It was with the determination and discipline of a soldier that Irv arrived at his first job on Wall Street as a trainee.

Today, Irv Rothman is president and CEO of HP Financial Services (HPFS), a wholly owned subsidiary of Hewlett-Packard Company. At HPFS, Irv leads more than 1,500 employees, overseeing $12.5 billion in assets by championing a culture of trust, collaboration, autonomy, and ethical behavior. Irv brings his personal values and code of ethics engrained in him on the streets of Bayonne to the streets of Wall Street and beyond.

Before joining HPFS, Irv was president and CEO of Compaq Financial Services (CFS). He led the company's 1997 start up and built it into a global business spanning 43 countries. In 2002, Irv was instrumental in the HP/Compaq merger. Marrying Compaq's global reach with HP's technological prowess, the deal culminated in a state-of-the-art finance and leasing company that has more than $12.5 billion in assets and produces more than $3.5 billion in annual revenue.

Never losing sight of his journalistic leanings, Irv authored a book, *Out-Executing the Competition: Building and Growing a Financial Services Company in Any Economy*, a memoir-leadership hybrid volume that at once shares Irv's road to success with his well-earned wisdom about being an effective leader in today's global marketplace. I talked to Irv Rothman about his rise to the top of American business, and the qualities that embody a successful leader.

JM: Thank you for talking with me, and congratulations on your many great successes. I understand that you went straight from the U.S. Army Reserve to Wall Street. Can you give me a sense of how your career progressed from that stage?

IR: Yes, I worked in Wall Street for a few years. I was young and new and what was interesting was that I really did look like a baby. When my daughter was born, I actually grew a mustache so I would look a little older. I didn't fool anybody! Wall Street was interesting at the time—the economic climate in the early '70s was on the vulnerable side. I was pleased to be on Wall Street, but didn't feel I was making a lot of progress there. It was coming along slowly and I was still young. Unlike some, I didn't have any family contacts. Ultimately it was totally the wrong thing for me—though I did learn a lot in training and earned points for paying my dues. One day I bumped into a friend of mine, who was a recruiter. He said, "I have this company I want you to look into." At the time I didn't know much, but I went to work for them, starting out as a territory salesman. I was in my 20s at the time, and found it new and fascinating. I did very well, so well that when I hit my early 30s the company came to me and offered to move me to the home office in San Francisco.

JM: Wonderful.

IR: So I packed up the family—my wife and two young children—and moved to the City by the Bay. And it was just two years later that I took on my first P&L responsibility. I have always felt that P&L responsibility is what separates the adults and the kids.

I don't care if you're running General Motors or you're running a six-person team, as I was. At the end of the day, making money is not easy. Competing, making money, getting people to buy in to your point on strategic direction—all of these are the leadership lessons I started to learn and internalize in my early 30s in San Francisco.

JM: That is a pivotal point for a growing leader.

IR: Yes, it was great for a young man. I was a sponge back in those days, picking up stuff from the leadership there at U.S. Leasing. It was a small office, with my office just a couple of doors down from the executives. So while I was attending school part time to earn a master's degree, I also benefited from being in close proximity to these executives down the hall.

JM: You attended Pepperdine for graduate school?

IR: Yes, I attended school part time to get my master's degree at the same time I had a demanding job and a growing family. People were amazed that I could handle so many large responsibilities in my life at once. It was very difficult, but I persevered because it was as essential as it was challenging. I didn't have glass of wine with dinner for two years because I was too busy spending every spare waking moment studying for that graduate degree.

JM: It sounds as if you had a great deal of dedication and focus.

IR: Yes. Being accountable for a P&L is an entirely different level of responsibility.

JM: I agree. In fact, for 14 years from age 40 to 54, I not only held a variety positions but had my own business as well. I lead a couple of consulting firms and was a senior vice president of sales. It was the first operating position I held and I learned so much. When executives ask me where I learned my philosophy, I tell them I didn't learn from a book. Do you know where I learned it? I learned it from that operating position.

IR: That is what it's all about. It always starts with leadership.

JM: The CEOs I speak with are all saying the same thing: Operating experience is essential. You learn from it, you soak in wisdom from your mentor, and it is there you become a leader. Having P&L responsibility at a young age is a pivotal point in the trajectory of a leader.

IR: It was certainly a pivotal point for me. The experience was enlightening and not without challenges. For example, I had an assignment just before they gave me my first leadership responsibility working as a structured finance guy doing complicated deals. The company needed help in an Australia subsidiary.

The CEO of Unites States Leasing International, or U.S. Leasing, calls me into his office. Ned Mundell was an extremely smart guy—very sarcastic. His one-on-one interaction style was highly effective.

So he called me and said, "you know, we really like it in Australia and we would like you to do this and that, and so on." It was confusing, so I asked directly: "What am I going to be doing?"

And his answer made clear that I would be doing much as I'd been doing up to that point, or, in other words, a lateral move at best.

JM: That's excellent. It's a turning point.

IR: But I said, "Okay, I'll think about it." I planned to evaluate the opportunity and come back to him.

JM: And what did you ultimately decide?

IR: I came back to him in a few days and said, "I don't think I really want to go to Australia. Although it sounds like a great adventure, I'm 34 years old and I don't think this is the time to be adventuring in my career. I'm trying to build something here and I would like to stay and see it through. What I want is a bigger P&L responsibility. I'm saying yes to P&L but, with no disrespect, no to the Australian opportunity."

So unaccustomed to being told no, he almost fell off his chair at my response.

JM: Was there any hesitancy in your mind? You're a young guy making your way in a company, did you pause before declining the opportunity?

IR: First of all, it took a couple of days because I needed to run it by my family, to ask if they were ready to move to Australia. Even though they said yes, I continued to think and think about it. I said to myself, "You know something? This isn't the right professional opportunity for a guy who is in the early stages of his career when the department has finally taken a fairly strong step. P&L is what separates the adults from the children." My most pressing concern was that I would damage my strong relationship with Ned. Ned was a guy who could make or break your career. I had only been in San Francisco a couple years, I didn't know him well. So did I have second thoughts about saying no to the boss? You bet your sweet life, I did.

JM: But you did it.

IR: It worked for me. I worried if I was going to be blackballed for life, but ultimately decided I needed to be true to myself.

JM: Absolutely, that is essential.

IR: I had to make what I felt was the right decision, so I walked into his office and said no. Even though I was scared, I knew it was what I had to do.

JM: You married your cognitive analysis with your instincts. You knew that this guy was very critical, that the relationship was very important and you needed to cultivate it, but you had what sounds like a gut feeling that this was not the right direction for you.

IR: This was a really good example of me playing what I called "guts ball."

JM: Tell me about that theory.

IR: So guts ball is a not a term commonly used in the American lexicon. My definition of guts ball is having the ability to set aside anxiety or apprehension and take action.

JM: Excellent! An essential leadership skill.

IR: Secondarily, it's the ability to take action without fear while acknowledging the potential consequence.

JM: Wonderful—I love that. We need to teach all executives that principle, don't we?

IR: Absolutely. Guts ball is a primary tenet of my book, because it comes into play at so many levels. My decision to say no was an early example of my willingness to trust my instinct and move forward with a kind of intrinsic courage.

JM: Yes, and it's an effective example because it worked. How much time progressed before you knew it was, in fact, the right decision?

IR: My immediate boss put me up for senior vice president a year later.

JM: There you go; that's unbelievably powerful. And I assume that was another pivotal point for you.

IR: Yes, I was subsidiary SVP.

JM: Good for you, that's outstanding. Allow me to fast forward a little bit. So, after making strong progress in your 30s, what comes next?

IR: What happens then is that after I was in San Francisco for 11 years, I received another recruiter call, offering a position with a Wall Street investment-banking firm, that had similar culture and goals to my current work at the time. The only hitch? The job is in New York.

JM: Back to your original stomping grounds.

IR: Yes, but living in San Francisco was nirvana.

JM: It is, indeed, beautiful.

IR: It's nirvana. We lived in beautiful Marin County; the kids were thriving. Everybody loved the outdoor life.

But at the same time, relocating back to New York would mean a return to family and old friends. It was a chance to be in charge of something, running my own show, tackling a larger P&L—it sounded pretty good to me. So we returned New York. I was on Wall Street for a short period of time when my old boss at U.S. Leasing, who had been recruited by AT&T and was now in New Jersey, called me and asked me to be his CFO.

Actually, he didn't ask me right away. He asked about New Jersey real estate. He was the same guy he always was! I finally had to ask him what he was calling for, because I knew it wasn't real estate!

JM: And that's when he offered you the position?

IR: Yes, he did. I joined him at AT&T Capital in 1985.

JM: Wonderful.

IR: I was CFO. And while I love my job now, being CFO in those days was a tremendous amount of fun. I loved it.

JM: It's so essential to enjoy your work.

IR: Everything we were accomplishing was brand new. We had an opportunity to work directly with the best and brightest minds on Wall Street and the legal community. We had a fantastic opportunity in the AT&T world because we were providing financing for big and small switches. We made a lot of money; we did a lot of great stuff. There's no other way to say it but that I was working 8 days a week, 30 hours a day, having the time of my life. I couldn't get enough.

We were exploding: acquiring companies, growing organically, and making money. Near the end of 1988, my boss comes to me once again and says, "We're going to do something here, my friend. We are going to think about maybe acquiring some companies, which we will then organize. I want you to work with me on what the things should look like going forward. I am going to step up to more of a strategic M&A role, and I want you to take on the role of president and COO of our largest, most profitable subsidiary." And I said, "I got a lot of stuff that I'm doing here and I really don't feel like doing that." It was as if history repeated itself.

We argued over that for a solid year because I just didn't want to leave the job I was doing. I was having too much fun. One day we were both in San Francisco on business and he calls me on the phone and he says, "Come up to my suite and have breakfast with me." I said, "Okay, give me 15 minutes to change, I'll be right up." And as soon as I get there he starts in on me that he really wants me to do this. He has endless reasons and it's clear he's not giving up. Finally, he got so frustrated with me that he said, "Damn it, do it because I'm asking you to do it." My reply was, "why the hell did you say no in the first place?"

JM: That's great.

IR: It was great, and effective! So in 1990, I took on very senior leadership responsibility at AT&T Capital. In those days, the subsidiary was called AT&T Credit Corporation and was the original captive finance company and primary profit generator. I was responsible, in all, for better than 50 percent of the revenue and profitability, and it was a fascinating experience. I had been developing some young talent along the way, and I brought them all on board with me at AT&T Credit.

JM: It's wonderful to be able to build a team.

IR: Yes, and they all started growing into their roles extremely well, which was a mesmerizing experience. And as AT&T Capital continued to grow, I took on more responsibility. I became a group president. So, we broke the company into two groups, each led by a senior guy. I was now responsible for about 85 percent of the revenue and profitability as well as global operations.

JM: Amazing, amazing. Wow!

IR: Yes, that was pretty good! But then AT&T had a brain cramp. They were worried that we were growing too big and too fast, that we might restrict access to the capital market. The predivestiture guys who are still running AT&T, they were all worried that AT&T Capital was getting too big and that we would lose our identity as a phone company.

JM: Growing pains and resistance to change.

IR: Indeed, but I told them we have to do something different regarding the ownership structure. We took the company public in the summer of 1993. AT&T retained an 8 percent ownership. We established our stock, went public, and were now a publicly held company. With that comes doing the roadshows, investor relations—a whole new world opens up.

JM: You now have to deal with governance, right?

IR: Yes, you have to deal with all that stuff—sell-side equity analyst issues we never had to deal with before. So that was fascinating because now you're into—they've got their model and they run your model say, "gee your EPS [earnings per share] sort of look like this."

That was a fascinating experience, which also allowed me to step back and consider the balance sheet and operating ratios in a way we had not previously.

JM: Of course.

IR: So we needed to look at our operating efficiency in a way we never had to look at it before. We needed to look at our return, our capital, in a way we never looked at it before, we needed to look at our strategy in a way we never had before, because we have to explain it and make it simple enough for people to understand. Because if they don't understand it, they'll just write something bad about you.

JM: Exactly. And it's essential for the culture as well.

IR: Absolutely fantastic. We took the company public in a year and a half or so, after an almost three-year lead up. It was a great, interesting experience. At the same time, to avoid distraction, we developed an operating philosophy about how we wanted to run the company: building a collaborative organization, building an organization where people respected and counted on each other, minimizing levels, maximizing team performance, giving people the opportunity to feel empowered to make decisions on behalf of the customer, and ensure that they had insight to the P&L based on what they do on a daily basis. Sometimes when you have too big of a company, people lose sight of how they can contribute. When we walk out at night we don't much care what happens.

Let me tell you story I use in public speaking to illustrate this point. I'm a sports car enthusiast, right? I drive a little German sports car—you can figure out yourself which one that is. But you know if you work for Ford, you get to the factory in the morning, you take your place on the assembly line after you punch in, and for eight hours you do the same thing again and again. You never see the raw material at the beginning of the process and you never see a shiny red convertible rolling off at the end of the process. It's almost impossible, then, to feel ownership and recognize your compelling contribution to the company success. So we believe in ownership, we believed in it then and we carry it through today. We believe that making people feel like owners of the business is the only way you get your workforce committed emotionally as well as intellectually.

JM: That is absolutely true.

IR: If you go to the factory of the little German car where I had the privilege a few years ago of taking a private tour, you learn that the first stop on the tour is where they build the engine. How many guys do you think it takes to build the Porsche engine?

JM: Oh, I have no idea.

IR: One.

JM: It takes only one—wow.

IR: One guy builds the engine and he walks this thing around down the assembly line from start to finish and at every stop, he puts on a little something, or connects something, or adjusts something, and that is *his* engine.

JM: Yes, that's ownership indeed.

IR: That's his engine. But the interesting thing is when they finish building the engine they subject the engine to this ridiculous speed test. It's something the equivalent of driving 150,000 miles at an average speed of 180 miles an hour constantly. So we observed the speed test. So I said to my tour guide, "That's a really tough job." He said, "Yes, it is." I said, "Do you have any engines fail?" He said, "Less than 1 percent, but it has happened on occasion." One guy built that engine all by himself and it failed—what happened to him? He said, "We just give him a little training." That's a $135,000 car.

JM: Training.

IR: Yes, he says they simply give him a little more training.

JM: Amazing.

IR: That was really eye opening. And then the other thing that was eye opening was that before they put these cars into the distribution channel they put them through an actual road test. All the highest rated factory guys every month get to be road testers. So they grade these guys and those who get the best grades each month get to be road testers the following month.

And I will tell you something, the expression on these guys' faces is absolutely priceless.

JM: It becomes a huge reward.

IR: You can't even imagine how huge, because I don't think any of these guys are buying a new Porsche any time soon.

JM: No, not at all. It's amazing.

IR: So this whole idea of ownership was very much part of the philosophy at AT&T Capital and I think we got distracted from it a little bit, preparing for the IPO. But then in the fall of 1995, AT&T suddenly divested itself of its hardware business and they no longer needed a capive finance company, so they decide to sell an 81 percent interest in the finance company.

JM: I see.

IR: And they said to the leadership of the finance company, "you guys go sell yourself—we can't be bothered."

JM: Incredible.

IR: Which is a fascinating process; it took us a year. And at the end of the time, we finally just sell it. I didn't particularly care for the operating philosophy of the new owners. This was a private equity group and they wanted to use a securitization, so they could get their money out up front. They securitized about 25 percent, 27 percent of the assets on the books. There is no way you get those assets back on the books fast enough, so it was clear to me that the earnings are going to be under pressure for long time.

So I have an opportunity to think about whether or not I wanted to continue there. They offered me a lot of money and other incentives. But considering all the factors, I said to myself, "Well, I can take my marbles and go home."

JM: Yes.

IR: Because I didn't want to witness the tearing down of what I'd given my blood, sweat, and tears to build. So I decided that was the end of that chapter for me.

JM: And how old were you at that time, Irv?

IR: Forty-nine. I walked out with not quite eight figures in my pocket. And I said to myself, "Okay, I have no idea what I'm going to go do now but I've been working like a dog since I was a camp counselor at 14 years old—I think I'm going to take a year off."

JM: Fascinating.

IR: I play a little golf. I'm going to read some of the books that are piling up on my desk. Smoke a few cigars, enjoy some of the wine in my cellar and I'm going to work on my short game, which desperately needed it.

JM: Sounds reasonable!

IR: Well, that was the fall of 1996. The weather patterns from October and November of that year, the end of golf season, it rained every day.

JM: You're still in New Jersey, right?

IR: Yes. It took about three weeks for me to start climbing the walls. Then I got a call from a headhunter who said, "A company is looking to start a captive finance company—would you be interested in talking to him?" But I said, "You know, not really. I'm working on my short game. I'm smoking cigars, et cetera, et cetera." So I hung up the phone and thought, *Well that was stupid.* When the guy called me back a week later and asked, "Are you sure?"

JM: You said, "I'm interested."

IR: I went to talk to them and I said, "Well, we're going to sell the paper and you're going to have 12 people. You'll sell the paper and get all kinds of forwarding fees." And I said, "That's no way to run a captive finance company." And they said, "Oh, what's your model?" So I told them my model and they liked it. And so I started, the only employee for the first four months.

JM: Amazing, absolutely amazing story.

IR: When I walked out at AT&T Capital, I had no non-solicit, no non-compete. So of course, I immediately recruited my entire team.

JM: Of course, isn't that amazing?

IR: Because I talked Compaq into letting me locate in New Jersey, "Where do you want to put the company?" I said, "Because Houston is not a financial services is town." So we really have to put the company in New York or San Francisco. I said, "Which one?" even though I was trying to say San Francisco, I knew that my team was New Jersey based. So I recruited all my team.

JM: Amazing story, wow.

IR: The start of Compaq Financial Services was a clean sheet of paper. And at the time of the Compaq/HP deal, which was five years later, we'd grown the company $3.5 billion in assets and a billion of revenue. We were operating in 40 some countries around the world.

JM: What an amazing success story.

IR: So then comes the merger. Bob Wayman called me on the phone and said, "I'm Bob Wayman. I'm the CFO of HP." He said, "I understand you're running Compaq Financial Services. In the next couple of weeks why don't you come and talk to me?" And I did, and our scheduled one-hour meeting lasted three hours.

I was still thinking more of my short game. But a couple weeks after the meeting, Bob calls me up and he says, "We'd like you to run a combined finance company—and merge the two (HP Tech Finance and Compaq Financial Services) into one finance company."

JM: Incredible.

IR: So I said, "Okay, but I'm not moving to California and I want to keep my team and our model and our operative philosophy around ownership and teams being empowered to do work on their own." So he said, "Of course, go do what you want." So I said, "Okay."

JM: And how many years ago was that, Irv?

IR: That was 2002.

JM: Thirteen years ago.

IR: So here I am, 68 years old and I'm still going strong, and I've been tempted to think about maybe I have climbed the mountain. But every time I think that, there is always new stuff to do. I'm still having fun. Most of my teams are still with me. My number two has been with me for 30 years. There are five others as well, and we have stayed together through three different companies. So I kept the leadership team more or less intact.

JM: It's talent, right?

IR: It's about talent and leadership. We've all bought into the operative philosophy and the principles. We run a unique organization. We run an organization that people want to work for. Our annual turnover rate is very, very low.

JM: You have a strong culture. Can you expand upon your perspective on merging and building cultures? I believe culture starts with the CEO, the C-suite. Companies need to be proud of the products and services and branding but if you're not most proud, in the end, of your culture, you're going to lose your way.

IR: I feel sure we're in violent agreement about culture. I think the reason mergers and acquisitions fail is because CEOs don't pay enough attention to the fact that you have worker A and worker B, and both have fear and doubt about the other guy because they used to compete against each other, tried to beat each other's brains out. Now they're sitting next to each other and they are supposed to team up and be fruitful and multiply.

I think culture is absolutely the CEO's job. I spent the first 180 business days in 2002 traveling around the world, talking to the people from both former organizations. All I talked about was our operating philosophy and our business model, not about customers, not about strategy, not about how we're going to do things. Instead, I focused on: this is who we are. This is what you can expect from your leadership. This is why we think this is a good way to go, why we think you're going to happy working here.

JM: Excellent.

IR: And why it's going to be personally and professionally enriching and a rewarding experience for you. That's how I felt about it at the time. It's how I feel about it now.

JM: Great.

IR: We don't hire people unless they fit. They could be the smartest person in the world. If they're not a team guy, if they're not a consensus-building guy, if they're not a people development guy, they're not going to work here. And when I interview somebody, by the time they get to me, I know they've got the technical stuff down pat. I don't even talk about that.

JM: Absolutely.

IR: I wonder who they are. We're still using the same operating model and business philosophy and set of operating principles we had at AT&T Capital. I think we improved it at Compaq and brought it to a fine art at HP Financial Services. We have an extraordinarily low attrition rate. Our annual turnover is about 6 percent, and that includes salespeople, by the way.

JM: That's amazing.

IR: People want to work here and I want to work here because of the type of organization we built.

JM: What do you want to share with the younger generation of incredible talent all over the world? It's unfortunate a lot of the young people are shying away from leadership roles.

IR: Some of the advice may sound a little generic but I'll tell you what I tell people in response to that question all the time. First, nothing is guaranteed in life. You must make sure that you're working harder than the next guy.

JM: Absolutely.

IR: Secondly, try to work for somebody who you can learn something from.

JM: Yes.

IR: And third, don't be wedded to a career path, don't even be wedded to a geographical location. This is a very mobile world. It's a very global world.

JM: Absolutely.

IR: If you're going to be wedded to a career path or geographic location, you're probably going to be stuck and you're not going to realize your potential. Be willing to take on an assignment that is outside of your comfort zone. That's the only way you're going to learn. That's a little bit of guts ball there. Recognize that the world doesn't exist in your little circle. It exists everywhere around the world. My son is learning this now.

JM: Wonderful.

IR: I'm very close to all my children. My son and I have a special bond because I schlepped him around in the car every weekend for his whole life growing up from soccer tournament to tennis tournament, from the baseball tournament to the swim meet.

JM: We did the same.

IR: So now he's headed off to London. I hate to see him go.

JM: He's going to grow tremendously.

IR: He's taking on a responsibility to build some expertise that he's demonstrated. But he's headed out of the home field. This could be a grab for the brass ring and he could fall flat on his face, and either way he's going for it.

JM: Guts ball.

IR: Guts ball. The final lesson is don't be afraid to play guts ball because the sun still comes up tomorrow and then you figure it out.

JM: That's simply an amazing philosophy. I have a few final questions for you. First, what aspects of your culture are you most proud of? Why?

IR: The aspect of culture I am proud of is that we did really well in creating a worldwide company. It's a difficult task, because everybody operates in different locations and with different cultures involved. At

HP Financial Services we have been stressing this now for 12 to 14 years: having one company on worldwide basis enables us to serve the needs of our global customers.

JM: What aspects of your culture need to be transformed? Why?

IR: We need to get our people to exercise the authority that's vested in them by virtue of our schedule of authorizations. People are sometimes reluctant and fall back on the rule book. We need to be more responsive, more nimble, more flexible in responding to the customers' needs and that's why we set them up in self-managed teams to be able to just that. Our strategy for transforming is that we have done a couple of things: first, we have liberalized the schedule of authorizations in giving people greater levels of authority and stressed to them that we expect them to exercise it; second, we established an escalation protocol in which we try to respond to our customers' needs within a 24-hour period of time.

JM: You play guts ball for the customer.

IR: I play guts ball for the customer, for my son, for the people on my team, for the entire company. Because culture doesn't happen in stasis, it happens when we're willing to move ahead on instinct, regardless of risk, with the intent to succeed.

11

Juan Carlos Archila Cabal
CEO of Claro (Colombia)

Your presence is determined by your reputation; your reputation can spiral up or down based on your "wow" factor—do you fall short or just meet people's expectations . . . or, do you wow the people in your life?

—John Mattone

JUAN CARLOS ARCHILA CABAL WAS born in Bogata, Colombia, where he auspiciously attended a U.S. school run by the Benedictines. It would be the first of many times in which internationalism forged his values and paved his path. It was Juan Carlos's father, a Colombian physician who spent three years in the United States in his medical school residency, who insisted on an education that offered a wider worldview.

The senior Archila Cabal's vision became a reality not just for young Juan Carlos, but also for his brother, six years his senior. After high school and completing a Bachelor of Science degree in engineering at a top-tier Colombian university, Juan Carlos followed in his brother's academic footsteps by attending the University of South Carolina where— like his brother before him—he earned a master's degree in international business. A primary factor in choosing that program was an internship abroad program. Juan Carlos knew instinctively that international experience would serve him well in his career.

He was right.

At the completion of his master's degree, Juan Carlos, already married and longing to return to his homeland, was hired by Motorola into their Cade 2000 Plus Program. With 18 months of on-the-job training that would send him back to Colombia, it was the perfect opportunity to meet Juan Carlos' needs. He said yes, a fateful decision that would inform his entire future.

One of the main tenants of Cade 2000 Plus was employee development. Ironically, as Juan Carlos began to build leadership teams across the globe in developing countries in Asia, Eastern Europe, and Latin America, he was also developing his own leadership skills. True to his penchant for international business, Juan Carlos bounced back and forth between Colombia and Mexico in his time with Motorola. From the Cade 2000 Plus program he became president of Motorola Mexico, eventually becoming CEO of Motorola in Latin America.

Motorola offered Juan Carlos the opportunity few leaders get: experiencing the arc of a company's initial rise and eventual fall. After 14 years, Juan Carlos moved on to become president of Brightstar Corp. Latin America. Finally, he moved to his current position as CEO of Claro.

Under Juan Carlos's leadership, Claro has become Colombia's leading communication services provider. He brought cell phone and Internet services to the remotest corners of the country, areas other companies were not interested in investing in due to security concerns and low revenue potential. But Juan Carlos was driven by his mission to improve the quality of Colombian people's lives. He offered the lowest possible prices so that the maximum number of people could use the services. He continues on the path of this mission, with cell phone and Internet access playing a critical role in the future and security of the country. Being able to communicate means being able to attain security, ultimately improving one's quality of life.

Claro has achieved astounding success in its mission with the number of Internet connections in Colombia tripling in the last two and a half years to 6.2 million. Claro has succeeded in getting 3G technology to almost 100 percent of Colombia's municipalities—a feat that hasn't been achieved anywhere else in Latin America.

To his role of CEO, Juan Carlos brings the knowledge that like no person, no company is immortal. Just as individuals pass away, so too can companies. Although Motorola met a stunning demise, the legacy of Juan Carlos's impact lives on in his commitment to Claro. I spoke to

Juan Carlos Archila Cabal about the rise and fall of great corporations and the legacy leaders forge in their many positions over the course of a long, successful career.

JM: Thanks for your contribution, Juan Carlos. You have such a fascinating story. Particularly your time with Motorola—you were there through the whole arc of the company's rise and fall.

JCAC: It is a fantastic story, both from a legacy and a leadership perspective.

JM: It must have been huge in your personal leadership development.

JCAC: Motorola was an incredible powerhouse in terms of creativity and innovation. But amidst it all, they were not allowed to move forward, not allowed to transform.

JM: Yes, and that's why I'm focusing on cultural transformation. It's a huge issue that affects companies in profound ways. Often by the time organizations realize transformation is essential, it's too late. People don't realize the company is dying.

JCAC: Motorola is the quintessential example: a huge U.S. flagship that faltered and died. It went from 140,000 employees to what it is today. So it becomes a relevant story for me in that I lived through it and I saw it happen.

JM: It most certainly had an impact on what you're doing and your legacy. You know this, but I'm not sure everyone does; just like people die, companies die. Any company, no matter its current success, could die. Including Claro. Do you think about this in your position, having witnessed the demise of Motorola?

JCAC: Yes, of course. Claro absolutely could die. The mission then becomes to ensure the company's sustainability. Claro's parent is America Movil. In a span of 20 years the company has become a $60 billion-plus organization.

JM: It's amazing.

JCAC: It has grown very fast, but right now it's essential that we transform ourselves so we can effectively move on to the next phase.

JM: That's your current challenge, then?

JCAC: It truly resonates and defines what I do today and every day moving forward.

JM: When you were in grad school in South Carolina, did you ever imagine you'd be in a role like this?

JCAC: No, I did not.

JM: But the opportunities kept arising and you kept meeting them: growing, developing, enjoying every minute.

JCAC: That's a key reality. I was getting to know the world and to see how things were done in different places. That was something I enjoyed. I grew into my love and expertise for technology. There is no other industry today that changes so rapidly. If you don't have your eyes open things can change in an instant and you'll be finished. I've seen that happen with Motorola, with Nokia, with BlackBerry, with pretty much everyone.

This industry is relentless. In this fast pace, you have to be constantly on top of your game. If you're not atop of it, you really end up in a very bad place in a few short years.

JM: Absolutely. Timing is critical. Only 25 percent of market leaders possess the capability to transform to meet the needs of their organizations. That leaves 75 percent who are not up to the task. You may be way ahead of the curve, but you cannot rest on your laurels.

JCAC: We recognize at this point in time that even when you're a market leader, you have an incredible challenge within the changing technology. Very quickly you recognize how the competent companies are challenging the carriers in the rear.

We need to adapt and transform our business models. It is also a very young company.

JM: Talk to me about the greater journey that led you to where you are today. After Motorola, what was next?

JCAC: After 14 years at Motorola, I went to Brightstar. Brightstar is a service provider to the technology industry, mainly distribution services. I spent three years as president of their Latin America operation, which was a great experience. They are a very entrepreneurial company founded by a visionary Bolivian guy who built it from the ground up to a $10 billion organization.

Eventually, the Japanese corporation SoftBank bought Brightstar. The founder of Brightstar became the CEO of Sprint.

JM: Your entrepreneurial CEO position with Brightstar combined with your leadership experiences at Motorola became pivotal developmental experiences for what you are doing today.

JCAC: Yes, absolutely. When I became vice president at Motorola—the youngest vice president ever to be named a vice president at Motorola—the role gave me the opportunity to lead the device business for Latin America. I built relationships and connections and one of those was to America Movil. From there I went to Brightstar as president of Latin American, which was about 70 percent of their business.

JM: How old were you at that time?

JCAC: I was 44.

JM: At some point in your 30s did a lightbulb go off and allow you to say, "I've got what it takes to run a big company?"

JCAC: I think I grew into it, like many leaders do. It's a gradual process. I wanted to make sure I was always progressing—that was my preoccupation. That, and finding the balance of being always challenged while also maintaining a reasonable personal life. Unfortunately, I ended up at one point being out of balance.

JM: Most people do.

JCAC: It was a time period of great growth and experience, but I would not want to repeat it. I was making my way in the world, just as the economic crisis of 2008 hit, plunging the company under water. Suddenly I had an enormous amount of pressure on my shoulders.

JM: And you had a family to think about as well, I assume.

JCAC: I had responsibility to my family and to the founder of the organization at once. Just like I wanted to provide for my family, the people working for us depended on me to keep the company afloat so they could provide for their families. The responsibility is great and highly intertwined. We are not just dealing with the success of organizations, we are dealing with the livelihood of families. The great responsibility ultimately took a toll on my health. It was a significant toll that reinforced the notion that balance is not just an idea, it's essential to continued success as a father, a leader, a person.

JM: Sounds like it was an inner transformation.

JCAC: It was a transformative learning experience. I bring it to how I lead at Claro today.

JM: How did you arrive at Claro?

JCAC: There was a management change and, having worked with them for so many years, they called me up and asked me to come aboard. They needed a Colombian national that knew the business and would be willing to come back to take the position.

Coming back to Colombia had been my dream.

JM: You eventually achieved the dream.

JCAC: Yes, and it's been six years now. I came in as president and CEO of the mobile operation, and since 2012 I have been president and CEO of the entire operation.

JM: Looking back on all your years of development as a leader what would be your proudest accomplishment or moment?

JCAC: If I had to single out my proudest moment it would probably not be the most important to my career but it was where it all started. It was when I was selected for the Cade 2000 Plus program at Motorola.

It was a very key moment that laid the foundation for my entire career. Of course I didn't know that at the time. We see the significance of these moments only when we can look back. It's an important lesson for young leaders that what can seem fairly insignificant can eventually change the course of your entire trajectory. Being chosen for that program changed mine.

JM: And it's not about the money and the prestige for you, it's about the lifestyle and the people with whom you travel this road. Your altruistic nature compels you to give back to Colombia, to your employees, to your family.

JCAC: Altruistic seems too big a word for what I do. I simply view it as something that allows me to feel complete, to have an authentic reward for the work I do. I try to help people when I can, just as others helped me. That way, we grow together. One day I will not be here and what will remain is the legacy of these relationships forged.

JM: That's what leadership is—it's about your legacy. If you were to pinpoint two or three leadership strengths or gifts that contribute to your legacy, what would they be?

JCAC: Integrity. Integrity is the name of the game in business.

It's just a matter of creating your own unique quality of life, which becomes your personal equation, nobody else's. I see today as the start of my career. Every day is a new beginning, built on the foundation you've forged over the course of your career. It is with this experience that I lead a major transformational effort to sustain our company. This is the beginning of my next 25 years.

JM: So integrity is first. What's next?

JCAC: Discipline with passion.

JM: What do you need to improve?

JCAC: The main thing is my ability to work with others and delegate.

JM: You're holding things too close to the vest.

JCAC: Yes, I am. Partly because I have such high expectations, which can be an issue and a strength.

JM: That's exactly right.

JCAC: I am definitely an enemy of mediocrity. I'm very passionate about execution and making sure that even when our execution is good, we can always improve. Execution is the name of the game for large companies to behave as small companies. It makes all the difference.

JM: It will make the difference. As CEO of this company, what's your biggest challenge currently?

JCAC: I have a commitment to our employees, to our people. As a leader, I value experience over newness. It's important to have a stable environment of people that are committed to giving their all for the company they're loyal to. Once you have that, then you can bring a lot of bright minds to create short-term value.

JM: I have a lot of respect for what you're saying—many new CEOs clean house.

JCAC: At Claro, the average age is 40. These people have grown up within the organization, have developed themselves in the organization, have grown from within. That's part of our policy.

JM: Excellent. Let's talk a little bit about culture. When I say cultural transformation, what does that mean to you?

JCAC: It starts with having the right mind-set. Currently we are transforming the company mind-set to a more customer-centric vision. Not only customer service, customer advocacy. That is our current road map.

JM: It's excellent. In your mind, what does the need to "think different, think big" mean to you as a CEO?

JCAC: The people who work with me never thought about the possibility of a company this large in Colombia.

It's a $5 billion company. But they have experienced, just as I did at Motorola, the whole process. They have executed it as a team.

JM: Tell me about transforming Claro into a customer-centric company.

JCAC: I only recently introduced to them the concept of advocacy. I don't know if I'm pushing too hard; advocacy is a tough thing to sell.

JM: Your question in your mind is, "Am I pushing too hard?"

JCAC: Yes. But there is no way to know. That's where courage and decisiveness comes in. As a leader, we must move forward with what we feel is the right transformative direction, without knowing if it's right. That is the only way to get to the other side.

JM: What would be your message to future leaders?

JCAC: There is one very simple tip that I give to everybody:

Make sure you spend at least 20 uncomfortable minutes a day. Twenty minutes in which your stomach aches, as it were.

When you have that feeling, you know you are thinking deeply about what needs to change and what you need to do differently.

JM: Excellent. Those 20 minutes are a marker.

JCAC: Yes, you pick your battles and gather up the whole of your experience and you do it.

12

Nabil Al Alawi

CEO, AlMansoori Specialized Engineering,
UAE

Go forward every day committed to worthy achievement, being
altruistic, and building rewarding relationships with the people in
your life.

—John Mattone

NABIL AL ALAWI SPENT HIS childhood on the island country of
Singapore. Like many others in Singapore, he was the son of Hadhramis
who arrived on Singapore's shore when forced to leave their homeland
in order to eek out a living in a faraway land. Young Nabil's great
grandfather, grandfather, and father were all born in Hadhramaut in
southern Yemen, where the land was so sparse and unforgiving that
the people who called it home were required to have not just a deep
adherence to their religion but a legendary fastidiousness. The Al
Alawi family brought these values with them when they arrived in
Singapore. In fact, the great majority of the Arabs in Singapore are
Hadhramis. These fierce immigrants made major contributions to Islam
throughout the East. In Singapore, they created a microcosm of their
own culture, centered on Arab Street, which was alive with Arab life,
culture, food, art, goods, and the voices of multiple generations.

It was a good life, where young Nabil went to a Catholic school, learning to pray every morning, "Our Father, who art in Heaven, hallowed be thy name." Being an Arab attending a Catholic school in a land far away from his origins began to forge the religious tolerance and worldview that would later serve him well.

But when the oil boom hit, many in the Arab community left to return to the Arabian Peninsula, including 12-year-old Nabil's father. So the Al Alawi family left Singapore behind, though its lasting impact would be etched into his attitude and values for a lifetime.

Cairo in the 1950s was the center of the Arab world, where powerful Egyptians mingled with wealthy Europeans on holiday. Nicknamed the "Mother of the World," Cairo was a world-class city bursting with opportunity. The family thrived and young Nabil excelled in school. Eventually, when Nabil reached high school age, his father—who dreamed of his son becoming a doctor—sent him off to boarding school in Kuwait, where the educational system was superior.

Again young Nabil thrived. Alone at a four-year boarding school, Nabil took up the sport of tennis. Soon, he was winning all the school matches, then district matches, and finally he became a full-blown tennis star. At the age of 16, Nabil won the Kuwait Open championship. The next year, he won again.

Upon graduation, the Kuwait government offered Nabil a scholarship to Lebanon University. To his father's dismay, he declined. He had his sights on farther shores: the United States. Namely, Louisiana State University. This time, it was his father's turn to decline, declaring the endeavor far too expensive for the family to afford.

But Nabil, with the classic teenage characteristics of both confidence and a hardheaded singular vision, vowed to raise the money and go on his own, no matter what. He spent the next year working for the British Bank of the Middle East. Much to his surprise, his father succeeded in that year in securing a scholarship to LSU. But LSU was not his only choice—no less than four colleges offered admittance to Nabil. Nabil wanted a culture that ate rice and a town with warm, balmy nights. LSU fit both bills.

Upon arrival, Nabil approached the tennis coach. The team was already full and the coach had no idea who he was. After he introduced himself as champion of tennis in Kuwait, he was allowed to join the team, securing a second scholarship. His determination was already serving him well. Nabil adjusted to life at LSU, and began to fulfill his father's expectation that he become a doctor by taking mostly pre-med science classes. Even so, he had a nagging thought in the back of his mind: not medicine, but engineering.

That first year, during the holiday season in Kuwait, Nabil expressed his desire and misgivings about being a doctor. A cousin who was already studying medicine offered to help solidify his final choice.

It would be an enlightenment that would change everything.

Without telling him where they were going, his cousin took them to a great hall at the local university where he was studying medicine. With high ceilings and a stark coolness, the room was lined with endless metal drawers. Without explanation, Nabil's cousin suggested he pull open one of the drawers. As he slowly slid the metal drawer out of the wall, he immediately came face to face with a shocking vision: a head, mostly decomposed, all dry hair and protruding teeth. He staggered back with the fright and shock, pissing himself. And it was in that card catalog of both human despair and man's triumph over science and medicine that young Nabil Al Alawi made a choice: He would be an engineer.

He returned, after the holiday, to LSU with a renewed commitment to engineering. Oddly, it was his prowess on the tennis court that first put the thought in his mind. As a teen tennis champ, he was invited to a camp run by BP and Smith Chevron. Camp is a misnomer: the Brits and Americans had constructed typical townships, each a microcosm of American and British life. Young Nabil was so impressed not only with the way these towns were built—with perfect roads and fine buildings—but with the standard of life they offered. It was then it dawned on him: This was a feat of engineering made possible only by the monied world of oil.

Today, Nabil Alawi is the CEO and managing director of AlMansoori Specialized Engineering, a wholly owned private company in the oil and gas services business. True to form, Nabil graduated with a degree in petroleum engineering from Louisiana State University and started his career with Otis Engineering Corp. in 1965. He worked for Louisiana-based Otis Engineering for 13 years in multiple countries before founding—with Abdulla Nasser and Hilal AlMansoori—AlMansoori Specialized Engineering in 1977. Since launching his oil services empire, Nabil has overcome many challenges and witnessed the ever-changing fortunes of an industry that is intrinsically linked to political instability. The company has a global presence stretching across 24 countries in the Middle East, Europe, Africa, and Asia.

While there is a lot of hype about depleting oil supplies, Nabil remains undeterred in his belief that the industry can survive for generations to come: "I'm an optimist and have to stay that way to go on with my life," he says. I talked to Nabil Al Alawi about how his unrelenting values were forged by both success and challenges in life.

JM: You have lived a remarkable life, Nabil. You're a man who built a wildly successful career by anyone's standard. What are the three or four attributes that contributed to your success?

NAA: Number one: never, ever give up about anything that happens, personal or business. Always be optimistic that on the worst rainy day, sunshine is coming.

JM: Yes.

NAA: This philosophy is the number one wisdom I have leaned on in life. When I started my company, I recall many, many, many, many examples. One must have faith that whatever happens, the sun will come up and solve all my problems.

JM: Your first product—the wire—was amazing. How did that come to be?

NAA: That was the one. Had I not had the wire, I don't know whether this company would even exist.

JM: Isn't that something? And it came through late, did it not?

NAA: It was a challenge. Every day, I would wake up in the morning and think, "we're never going to get this." There were two British guys who had just opened a brand-new plant in the U.K., making this wire. Previously they used rope wire—the wire they use for building bridges and cranes and the like. They were then making what we call "slickline" wire—very, very thin, at 0.092 inches.

JM: Amazing.

NAA: They had just finished that, and were going around the world trying to promote it. They heard about this little brand-new company called AlMansoori Specialized Engineering that was in the slickline business.

JM: Fascinating.

NAA: So one morning, they walk into my place and say, "We are promoting wires." I replied, "Really?" And despite my heart leaping, I look at them with a poker face and said, casually, "I don't know whether I'm going to like your wire or not." And that's that day that these men set out promoting me and giving me a trial. They were offering these things for free. And that was how it happened.

JM: Never give up! What else would you say? Give me two more, beyond never give up.

NAA: The other one that I always stress is that to be successful, never assume. Assumption is the biggest disaster in doing work. Don't assume, because the minute you do, it's the beginning of the end. To be perfect, you must never assume anything. Assumptions play key roles in the decisions that forge our projects, and false assumptions invite disaster. With my wire, even, I never assumed it wouldn't break. I never assumed it was going to work. That's why I succeeded. Because I always assumed it wouldn't work; therefore, I must have a backup.

JM: Yes, you've got a healthy perfectionism. Perfectionism is similar to good cholesterol and bad cholesterol: there's good perfectionism and bad perfectionism. What you're saying is you are very, very good at making sure that the facts are correct.

As a result, you're going to double and triple check everything. And you coach your executives to do the same, hoping that they'll coach their people to do the same. Is that correct?

NAA: That's correct. But the most important part of running our business is that when they come and join our organization, I tell them, "We're not going to look at the numbers." I tell everyone this: my managers, my partners. From day one at this company I tell my partners, "Our objective is not to make money. Our objective is to satisfy our customers."

JM: Wonderful—that is so important.

NAA: We must fulfill the expectation, rather than the contractual obligation. If we satisfy our customers' expectation, the money will come automatically.

JM: It's beautiful.

NAA: And we'll make tons of money!

JM: No, it's beautiful and so true. When I see too much focus on money and profits instead of on bringing value to the world, it's not sustainable. It just doesn't work that way.

Do you have a passion to bring value to the world? What is the most important lesson that you've learned through setbacks, whether it's personal or professional?

NAA: First let's talk about business setbacks. Every setback I've had in my business was the result of underestimating that at the end of the day, the client is stronger than me. Every failure I had was because I assumed I was in the driver's seat and I forgot about the customer.

JM: It's all too easy to do.

NAA: I'll give you an example. I had this fantastic four-year contract in Syria for Shell Oil. I worked hard on it and built a very, very good service business. And then they decided not to renew the contract, giving it to a company from Egypt whom I was aware was completely substandard in everything they did.

I knew there was wrongdoing and likely corruption.

So I felt very vengeful, after having done such excellent work for them in the last four years. Clearly I wouldn't mind giving the job to another company that I respect. But to give it to such a poor company, there is something unethical about it.

So I said to myself, "I'm going to teach these guys a lesson." However, I forgot at this stage that "these guys" to whom I plan to teach a lesson? They're Shell Oil.

JM: They're not small.

NAA: They're Shell Oil! I'm a little hole in the wall, as far as Shell Oil is concerned. But I was young and conceited and I thought, "I'm the best of the best." And they wanted an extension because the company they were going to give the work to failed to mobilize on time.

At the time, there was no other company in all of Syria who could tackle the job. So they asked me to give them a three-month extension. So I checked around and asked my people, "Are you sure? Is nobody here that could replace us?" They all said no. So I went to the CEO of Shell Oil in Damascus, Syria and I said, "You want three months? I will give you three months. But here is my condition." And I started to dictate my conditions.

One condition was we have no contract prices, which is the one we bid for. In that agreement, I could have a piece of equipment in eight months doing nothing and they might need it for one week. I can charge for one week what I normally charge for a much longer time frame. So I charge, for example, 100 percent of the rate that I charge for contract.

So I said to him, "If you want it for three months, it will be all callout rates. Plus, I want you to give an extension of one year from my back contract price."

And they started say, "No, that's not fair."

I said, "This and this is not negotiable. Take it or leave it."

The minute I uttered those words, I realized—too late—who's the boss in the negotiation.

JM: You knew immediately you made a mistake.

NAA: Immediately. They guy stood up and said, "I'm going to blacklist you. You'll never—neither you nor your company—set foot on these premises again.

JM: You had to have been devastated.

NAA: Yes, because when I was awarded this contract in 1991, America was attacking Iraq. The whole of Syria and Iraq was, therefore, a no-fly zone. I had to track everything I needed all the way to Turkey and into Syria to get my job done.

They were hard on me because they were completely against me getting this contract, which was run by an American company called Shelton Baker from Houston. When I was awarded the contract, Shelton Baker negotiated with AlMansoori and said if they give you the contract, you'll be the subcontract.

They basically called me and I said, "No, thank you. I'm capable of doing this job." So when all that happened, Shelton was so happy. They wanted to do everything possible to make me feel welcome and appreciated. I had a problem in that the Americans who were working for me all left when their country invaded. They all left the job site, and went to the American Embassy and said, "We're not going back."

So I had no alternative but to fly in there myself. I stayed with my guys. We did every job, including city jobs, including opening the well, going with the wire, taking the bottle, and coming back. We did this every day. I was with my boys. When we finished and I went to pick up luggage, there were no flights from Damascus. I had to drive to Beirut, catch a flight to London, then from London to Abu Dhabi.

And so this was the situation when I was negotiating. When I said, "Take it or leave it," they kicked me out of the camp. Blacklisted me. They were able to half-rate every bit of equipment and support the contract. They brought in experts and the contractor they chose become a very good contractor who eventually competed with me for years.

JM: Stunning setback. Huge blow.

NAA: It's like the slogan, "Customer is king: They help us pay our bills." I learned that the customer never makes a mistake. My people have to understand that as well. I do seminars to teach everybody in my company the lessons I learned the hard way.

JM: That is a powerful story. So here you were, AlMansoori has grown tremendously since you formed it in 1977. You have in excess of 3,000 employees in more than 25 countries. That kind of success does not arrive without growing pains. I believe the culture of any organization starts with the CEO.

The culture is a reflection of the character, values, habits, and thinking patterns of the CEO. If the CEO is strong and vibrant and positive, the culture reflects that.

NAA: It's interesting, I'm not sure my philosophy is the same. My role model is not the western companies, but Tata in India.

The main reason they're my role model is because my business is about people.

Unfortunately, many big American corporations and some European corporations have a culture in which the value of a human being doesn't exist anymore. Everybody is a number and everybody is dispensable. I look at it the other way around: Every individual that joins me at the senior level is indispensable. When I look at my managers, they're indispensible. The minute I look at a manager as indispensible, I not only care for him, I respect him. Because I value him, I do not want him to leave.

JM: Absolutely.

NAA: My whole mind-set is totally different than that of some American companies.

JM: You make an excellent point. The latest research shows that companies that have CEOs and senior executives who understand it's about people and talent will far outperform companies focused on numbers. But that mind-set it too rare; we've got a problem. We have to get back to basics. It has and always will be about people. You're not going to be successful unless you optimize your talent; you're not going to be successful unless you get the right people in the door; you're not going to be successful unless you give people great opportunities.

NAA: Absolutely. It's all about people and when guys stay with you, after a while, they become like you. I sit down sometimes with people who would have been with me for 25 or 30 years, and see an echo of my character.

JM: That's beautiful. It's incredibly powerful to have that kind of long-term relationship. What's next for AlMansoori? You've transformed the organization. It's a strong organization. You've made it a culture of glue where people stick together and it's a family. And yet there will always be challenges.

NAA: There will always be professional and personal challenges. Just when you think you have everything figured out, a completely unexpected challenge will arise. For me, it was being diagnosed with cancer 12 years ago.

Although it was a personal setback, it also brought professional insights I never imagined. Immediately I knew after my diagnosis that I would reject the American way of treating cancer. I embraced a completely unconventional healing methodology, defying anyone who chided me, "If you don't embrace conventional treatment, within months you'll be in bed and likely pass away." But I rejected that. And 12 years later, I am healthy and stronger than I was prior to my diagnosis. And my cancer diagnosis made me realize the value of health in the workplace. And I realize that if I hire someone at 20 and that employee learns about health, he will be as vibrant and alive when he is 40. And if at 40 years old he has the same waistline and health standards and no diseases? What a fantastic management team I'm going to have. I decided that would be my number one focus and mission for my employees and hopefully, it's going to eventually reach a point where I can extend it to create that effect in the community around me.

JM: That is a core part of your culture — the health of your people.

NAA: Shell oil, BP, Exxon are also beginning to make changes in how they look at health. They must, because they keep saying to the world that our health and the environment is an essential value of how they run their businesses.

JM: I talk to so many CEOs about how they must really care for their teams. Your commitment to the people who work for you is powerful. You probably don't lose many people. Is that true?

NAA: No, I don't. The majority of the time the guys who do leave do so over money. And when they come back, they do so with the realization that money isn't everything. It's the culture and lifestyle and loyalty that matters more.

JM: What is your advice, as a CEO and a coach and a man of great wisdom, to the younger talent developing their leadership skills? What message do you want to deliver to the future leaders of the world about what they need to do to become the best leaders they can be to move this world forward?

NAA: First, to become a good leader one must believe that what you're doing is correct—that your values are uncompromising.

JM: That is key, indeed.

NAA: You do not compromise on values; everything else is flexible.

JM: Amazing.

NAA: You may become very successful, but the only thing that you shouldn't be flexible on is your values. If you compromise your values it's unsustainable in your personal life and your business life alike.

JM: What aspects of your culture are you most proud of? Why?

NAA: In AlMansoori, we have a strong sense of belonging, a sense of being together, of working together for a common goal.

A culture of a family. We feel bonded and united. Most of the people working for me come from the Arab world and Asia.

They are far away from their home countries and their families. There is a big social gap.

AlMansoori welcomes them warmly and gives them a sense of belonging, and they feel at home, with a familial feeling.

So going to work becomes a desire—not the feeling of "having to" work. With time, the bond continues to grow.

JM: What aspects of your culture need to transform? Why?

NAA: Although the embedded sense of belonging is an overwhelming positive, it can be a double-edged sword. Some start to get too comfortable in the recognition that the company policy is not to terminate. They therefore develop a kind of "take it easy" attitude I call "the Basha Syndrome." That is the real challenge I have: How to motivate my workforce to get that fire in their belly, to be aggressive and have a never die attitude. That is my biggest challenge.

JM: What is your strategy for transforming culture within your organization? What have been your successes?

NAA: The real challenge is to change the workforce attitude. Setting key performance indicators and deadlines and rewards for achievements are written rules that we put in black and white for each employee. But it does not help to foster change.

I meet with my key managers weekly to talk about not being complacent and not taking our success for granted. We have been very successful for 37 years. It is a dangerous trend for us to forget where we come from. We have to remind ourselves that our success was due to the team working aggressively and offering to our clients a service that is second to none. I ask myself often, "am I successful?" The answer is yes and no, and that answer encapsulates why I continue to see the sun rise every day in both my personal and business life.

13

Cathy Benko

Vice Chairman and Managing Principal, Deloitte Consulting, LLP

If you want others to be happy be courteous, compassionate, and altruistic; if you want to be happy, be courteous, compassionate, and altruistic.

—*John Mattone*

CATHLEEN BENKO IS ONE OF five girls brought up by a mother who did the best she could on her own. Growing up in New Jersey, she was raised with no sense of expectation or urgency to go to college and succeed in the world of business. Luckily, young Cathy didn't adhere to lack of expectations. When the randomness of life presented opportunities, Cathy embraced them utterly and entirely.

An honor roll but not stellar student, Cathy was extremely active in her high school, engaged in myriad activities. She might not have been on the path to university, but she was highly engaged in school and community. So much so that, toward the end of her senior year, a letter arrived one day from the local Lion's Club. Opening it up, Cathy read the line: Congratulations and in recognition of your civic contributions we would like to award you with a scholarship contributing to the first year of the college of your choice.

There was just one problem: Cathy had no plans to go to college. So while it was flattering, she simply left it on the kitchen counter and forgot about it. Forgot, that is, until her mother picked it up and said, "you need to put this award toward some good use!"

So Cathy registered for a one-year, advanced secretarial school program, and soon, soaring through classes, landed a job as an executive secretary in Manhattan immediately upon graduation. She was one of the secretaries, just like in the movies, whose desk was perched outside the mahogany-lined executive offices. Both stylish in her three-piece gabardine suits and undoubtedly appreciated for her sharpness and intellect, at the age of 19 Cathy felt like she had "made it." But within months she began to have a gnawing feeling: *Maybe I aimed a bit too low.* Cathy determined she wanted more and enrolled in evening and weekend classes at Ramapo College of New Jersey.

The part-time, matriculating bachelors program at Ramapo did not attract your average student body. Many of its students, as well as instructors, were atypical, including men and women like Cathy who had never planned to go to college at all, single moms trying to better their lot, and older, displaced workers. Lecturers, for the most part, were local community leaders and business role models who wanted to give back to the community in which they flourished. Continuing to commute to New York City full-time while squeezing in classes evenings and on weekends three semesters each year, Cathy graduated with a bachelor's degree in five years.

It was all related. The company Cathy worked for offered tuition reimbursement—once again, Cathy saw an opportunity and acted on it, changing the course of her destiny. During these years she was promoted out of the secretarial ranks and into the personnel department (what HR was called at the time). Not long after, she moved into the unchartered waters of computer software when her company placed her in a program to learn coding and information systems management.

In time, Cathy felt that pull of wanting something more so she leveraged her personnel and computer skills and moved to a HR and Payroll software company. Here, too, she flourished quickly working her way up to both a product manager and senior project manager. She then parlayed these experiences and relationships by starting her own company, and was soon helping major businesses implement their corporate systems.

By the age of 26, her business was flourishing. But she couldn't ignore the urge to experience university-life, as Cathy puts it, "like normal people do" and started to dream about getting an MBA. About this time a Fortune 100 brokerage company client of hers offered Cathy a vice president's position. It sounded attractive but she was concerned that it might derail her MBA aspirations. So she made a deal: She would accept the offer of employment and, after a year or two, would apply to Harvard. If she got in, she would leave. If not, the company would sponsor her through Columbia's or Wharton's executive MBA program while continuing to work full-time.

How she keyed in on Harvard Business School (HBS) is somewhat a testament to her moxie but also to her pragmatism. Without the experience of ever sitting through an SAT exam, she thought, how would she ever excel in taking the GMAT. At the time, HBS had everything Cathy was looking for: world-class learning at a name-brand academic institution, that was away from home and had no GMAT requirement. Three years later, Cathy graduated from Harvard Business School.

Most students on campus interviewed for jobs with the biggest names in business and Cathy was no exception. So what was it about Touche Ross (who merged with Deloitte, Haskins and Sells the following year), at the time ranked near the bottom of the Big 8, that swayed Cathy to say yes? It was not only their aggressive search for great talent, but Cathy's nature to trust her instinct and take a leap of faith.

And in the 25 years since, Cathy Benko remains at Deloitte LLP and its subsidiaries. She has helped transform the company from its lagging position to top of the heap. Currently a vice chairman and managing principal of Deloitte Consulting LLP, her previous roles include chief talent officer; global e-business leader; high-technology industry sector leader; managing principal of brand, communications and digital; lead client service partner; and national managing director of Deloitte's award-winning Women's Initiative.

Cathy is also a U.S. patent holder and best-selling author of three books each published by Harvard Press: *The Corporate Lattice: Achieving High Performance in the Changing World of Work; Mass Career Customization: Aligning the Workplace with Today's Nontraditional Workforce;* and *Connecting the Dots: Aligning Projects and Objectives in Unpredictable Times.*

Cathy has received numerous distinctions including *Consulting Magazine*'s "25 Most Influential Consultants" and its inaugural "Leadership Achievement Award" for women leaders in consulting. She has been honored by the Harvard Business School Alumni Association, Women in Technology International (WITI), and the *San Francisco Business*

Times, which inducted her into its Forever Influential Honor Roll for exceptional women leaders. And perhaps most notably, she was inducted to her hometown's Hall of Fame.

At each step of the way, Cathy has not only recognized but seized opportunity in her path. For someone who didn't have much of a path to begin with, Cathy has forged an inspiring leadership legacy. I talked to Cathy Benko about her uncommon drive, her resilience, and why leadership is a not a destination but a journey.

JM: Your story is amazing, Cathy. Congratulations. So how long have you been with Deloitte, after joining them straight out of your Harvard MBA program?

CB: We just celebrated our 25th MBA reunion, so it's been that long.

JM: That is truly remarkable.

CB: But when you boil it down, I have been fortunate to have had many different roles—just with the *same* company.

JM: That's actually a good thing. I want to ask you about your growth within Deloitte because I know that you've embodied many different roles. Can you give me a sense of the
trajectory from when you joined Deloitte and through the various roles you've been through, eventually landing in
your present role.

CB: It took me between five or six years (depending how you count maternity leave) to be admitted into the partnership, which is relatively quickly. Subsequently, I was appointed Deloitte Consulting LLP's first global e-business leader—in fact, I was on maternity leave with my daughter (our second child) at the time and received a phone call from our CEO who said (paraphrasing), "Hey, you know there's this whole movement around e-business? We need to get on it—we need to be relevant in it, and we'd like to appoint you as our global e-business leader."

JM: Fantastic.

CB: I believe at the time I was a second-year principal and on maternity leave! My response was "okay, that sounds like a good idea to take on when I get back from leave" and then didn't think that much about it. But when I actually looked at it, I realized the enormity of the task. I live in Silicon Valley and all of a sudden, it seemed, e-business was evident everywhere. There was not a billboard in sight, for example, that didn't advertise pets.com or cfo.com or you fill-in-the-blank.com.

JM: Absolutely. It was a new era.

CB: I recall, after studying the space for a while, going back to our CEO and saying, "Look, I had a hormonal imbalance when I thought this was a good idea, but this is bigger than I ever anticipated." I told him, "The world will never be the same. We'll never interact the same way. We'll never transact the same way. Commerce will never be the same. Nothing will ever be the same." His response, to his credit, was "maybe you didn't know what you were doing, but I did. Get back to work."

JM: The fact that you grasped the enormity of the transition was likely confirmation he had the right person for the job.

CB: It was very much a case of "get to work." That was my first major leadership role. It was a big effort in and around e-business globally with seats on both the global operating and executive committees. Somewhere toward the end of the internet bubble is where my first book (with co-author F. Warren McFarlan) came from: *Connecting the Dots: Aligning Projects and Objectives in Unpredictable Times.*

JM: Wonderful.

CB: The book was not my idea. I actually didn't want to take on a project like that. It was my boss who kept insisting. And I kept saying, "I'm not going to write a book. I hate to write, have a day job and brilliant concepts for a book are hard-earned.

JM: And so what happened?

CB: I teamed up with one of my HBS professors, Warren McFarlan, a brilliant mind and wonderfully gracious man who was a trailblazer in the area of using technology for competitive advantage. *Connecting the Dots* was published a year later.

JM: Sounds like the perfect co-author.

CB: From there the firm asked me to become our high tech industry leader.

JM: Wow!

CB: Not long after that appointment, I was asked to also take on the role of managing principal of Initiative for the Retention and

Advancement of Women (WIN). This was a very visible extracurricular role which also gave me a seat on the firm's executive committee.

And then from there it was on to lead talent as the firm's first chief talent officer across all of our businesses. That is where the next two books came from: *Mass Career Customization: Aligning the Workplace with Today's Nontraditional Workforce* (with Anne Weisberg), and *The Corporate Lattice: Achieving High Performance in the Changing World of Work* (with Molly Anderson).

JM: Excellent titles, excellent books. Your books continue to do very well, correct?

CB: Yes. Several wound up being best sellers and all seem to have staying power, which is nice to see. But more importantly, we accomplished what we set out to, which was to position Deloitte's talent agenda for the future. Along the way I had the benefit of great sponsorship including my boss, our CEO, and the chairman of our board.

Because if you really want to make big change happen, you need to give people time to go on that journey, to internalize the change and impetus behind it; you need to give them permission — mental permission. And that's really what *Lattice* did. Because when you're unconsciously stuck in the mental model of a one-size-fits-all corporate ladder, it's difficult to see other possibilities. One point I communicated regularly was that our research showed how many assumed that everyone else's careers were zooming straight up the ladder, while theirs took more of a meandering approach. So while many think their careers are aberrations, but the fact that we could show how fewer and fewer careers today climb straight up was comforting to many.

I was appointed to the role of chief talent officer (akin to chief strategy officer or chief financial officer. My role was to cultivate a market for talent. While the transactional side of HR was important, the charge — to create a world-class value proposition for talent — was significantly greater than that.

JM: Absolutely. Tell me about your roles since then.

CB: Our succeeding CEO (when my boss became our global CEO) had asked me to take over brand, reputation, communications, digital, and our citizenship efforts. It was a way to parlay some of what we were able to achieve in the talent marketplace and scale that across our brand in a broader way. I spent nearly four years doing that and now am bringing all this back into the marketplace from talent and product branding perspectives. I'm also leading elements of the emerging tech side of our practice.

JM: That is excellent. And how are you making that a reality?

CB: While there are a few public companies of great scale that are natively digital, the majority need to go through a process of translation from traditional to digital business models and work practices. This taps well into my experiences—the common thread across the various roles I've traversed across over the course of my careers is transformative change.

JM: Absolutely.

CB: If you think about e-business, there is no way to go back, right? And there's an old adage: You're only done with change when you can't go back.

JM: That's a great saying. In fact, there are few companies that want to actively change. That's not the mentality. The mentality is that it's not about wanting to change, it's about having to change. And companies that are not transforming every single day may not be around long. We have to drive greatness differently today and many or most market leaders today are not transforming themselves from a position of leadership or strength.

Very, very few are. I love to cite the Jim Collins book, *Good to Great*. Some of those companies don't even exist anymore. So that's what you're talking about right? Really, you can't go back. That's not an option anymore.

CB: There are two things. One, you can't go back. And two, if you want to continue to be relevant, you don't really have a choice.

JM: True. These are very powerful insights. What you've achieved is phenomenal, and I imagine you look at yourself in the mirror and probably pinch yourself every now and then say, "this is incredible. I kind of grew up in kind of humble beginnings. And I have achieved really incredible success." I sense a lot of gratitude in you. I sense in your language a tremendous sense of humility, tempered with a great sense of belief in yourself, clearly. Otherwise you wouldn't be doing what you're doing. But there's a huge humility aspect to you, which is a character element that is just beautiful. What are the three things that you would say have led to your success?

CB: I don't view myself as successful, but rather a continual work in process who's been very fortunate with the opportunities that have come her way.

JM: We all are, aren't we?

CB: When people say to me "you're so successful," I think that it's a transient declaration and not really what it's all about. One thing I've learned is simply not to overthink things. I wasn't smart enough to know that it's unusual at times to venture into the waters I've jumped into, and fortunately, those times have worked out. Applying to HBS was one example.

JM: And how's that?

CB: The application can easily take more than 100 hours. It was due in early January as I recall, so I was late getting to Christmas dinner because I was working on it—not "missed dinner" late but later than expected. When I walked in, my mother was in the kitchen stirring the gravy. She looked at me—you know how mothers give u that disapproving look—still stirring the gravy and said: "You're late." And I say, "Yeah, I know, but I'm applying to business school and was working on my Harvard Business School application." I'll never forget the look in her eye. She put the spoon down, looked straight at me and said, "What are you thinking? That's not for people like us. That's not for our kind."

JM: Really? Why do you think that was her reaction?

CB: She went on to express that I was just setting myself up to fall. Her belief was that people with roots like ours don't belong nor would be welcomed in places like that. Until that moment that actually had never occurred to me. And honestly if I hadn't pretty much already completed the application, I wouldn't have forged ahead.

JM: Is that so? That's fascinating. So you would have stopped.

CB: For sure. I was like, "oh, I didn't think of that." I refer to it as "too stupid." Sometimes the trick is not thinking things through so much that you talk yourself out of it.

JM: Absolutely, that is so true.

JM: Yeah, absolutely. There's an impulse to you.

CB: Perhaps an impulse, but I'm not impulsive.

JM: And a persistence.

CB: I am more in the "planned spontaneity" camp.

JM: I see what you mean. You set your sights on going to Harvard and you didn't follow the impulse to buy into the thought that "people like us don't attend schools like that."

CB: Yes. I think "why not?" before I think "why," which has turned out to be a benefit.

JM: That is a great example of an imperative question leaders should ask. Instead of *why me* or *why us* they should ask *why not me* or *why not us?* It opens up significantly more opportunity. What is interesting is that if you had never advanced that far in that application through your persistence and your why not attitude, you would have never gone to Harvard.

CB: Likely not. I wouldn't have had the opportunity to do that. I've certainly been very well served by the school and give back as well. Since graduation I've held holding various leadership and board level positions for the school's local and global alumni associations, support its research agenda, and lecture and present on campus when invited on campus to do so. I support the School's mission to educate leaders who make a difference in the world just as I believe it credentialed me in a way that helped me help others.

JM: That is wonderful. It's all interconnected.

CB: Certainly—interconnected across family, extended family, friends, colleagues, acquaintances, and acquaintances of acquaintances. It might be something as simple as a request to lend a hand or open a door. And that is meaningful, because where I come from, there aren't a lot of people that can answer that request by saying, "Sure, let me see what I can do."

JM: Talk to me about leadership, Cathy. I know you've done so much work in leadership both through teaching and mentoring others. Looking at your style of leadership, what are the two or three aspects of your leadership style that you believe are powerful, strong traits that you are most proud of? Obviously you are smart and strong, have a sense of purpose and a commitment to creativity, your values are geared toward trust and loyalty, and you seem particularly inclined toward innovation.

CB: I'm a little uncomfortable to hear those observations or get that feedback. I don't really think about it that way. At the end of the day I'd say there's a hint of moxie, and an inspirational leadership style. It's like, "we are going to take that hill, we are going to own it."

JM: That resonates with me—there is massive gap in that whole area of inspirational leadership and we need more of that. We also need to embrace humility as leaders, and in my work I find the best leaders are never satisfied to rest on their laurels. Are there things that you're working on and if so, what are they?

CB: Oh my yes! I feel I'm a continual working in progress, and never actually get there—wherever there might be. I really have a lot of time for people who are open and willing to grow. I find time for people who want to engage, who want to improve, who are curious and lean in. I go way out of my way to enable lots of different things, I'm really good at that, I'm committed to that. I tell my kids that all the time—I'll enable you but *not* entitle you.

JM: Yeah, yes, that is imperative.

CB: It's a fine line sometimes.

JM: It is, indeed. What would you say is your greatest professional accomplishment?

CB: That's easy, although you may argue what category it belongs in, but I have two kids. I have a son who just turned 21 and a daughter who is 16. My son is in college and when he came home last Christmas, he made a comment that stopped me in my tracks. In that moment, I turned to look at him (technically looked *up* at him—he's got more than a foot of height over me). What he said showed so much maturity, was so caring, and had such insight I was simply amazed. My thought was, "this kid is fully baked and what a terrific person he's turned out to be." My daughter is great as well, but nearly five years younger, is still a work in process. She is my spitfire. High energy, willful and spirited, along with bright, articulate, and highly engaging. I can see advocacy of some sort in her future.

So, when I think about what I've accomplished professionally—best-selling author, patent holder, things I've done in the firm, titles I've held and the like—it's interesting, but I will look at these two kids and see my best accomplishment. For the past decade, my husband has been disabled with a progressive disease so child-rearing wasn't the tag team would envisioned it would be. I would argue, though, that his daily challenges are among what has influenced them most. Their learning is that you either run from adversity or you meet it head on, and handle it with distinction. I believe it certainly made me a stronger professional—and person.

JM: Absolutely. That's a very heartwarming story and I think it tells me so much about you. And I'm very sorry about your husband—that's very, very tough.

CB: You could wallow in it or you could handle it. That's what we've done. We might be a little rickety wherever we roam, but our motto is no man left behind!

JM: Wonderful, and good for you Cathy, definitely a role model, very powerful stuff and I'm very moved by all of this. I can see the essence of who you are.

CB: We all just do what we can do.

JM: That's what building a legacy is all about. And that's also the true essence of leadership. Talk to me a little bit about the challenges of growth and transformation as Deloitte has transformed, and continues to transform itself in the professional services industry. You're a senior leader in the organization. What are some of the challenges around transformation and making sure that Deloitte continues to be the incredible strong brand name that it is, that your consultants continue to do the great work that they do?

CB: First, with great success comes great responsibility. I think we've done a really good job on that front. But also with success, it gets harder and harder to scale because the proportions keep getting larger. So you have to continually have in your crosshairs how to you keep the essence of who you are, your purpose, and your culture as you continue to grow, to ensure that you're as relevant tomorrow as you were today.

JM: Absolutely. What aspects of the Deloitte culture are you most proud of?

CB: It's in the people—it always sorts to that. And there is something about being a private partnership. While it presents its challenges, a partnership capital structure also has many benefits. There's a sibling-like component to it, and family, well, is family. There is an expression our former CEO used to say, "if we want to go fast, go it alone, if we want to go far, go as a team."

JM: Interesting.

CB: For example, when we decided to build Deloitte University, we had to determine how do you make a $300 million decision in a partnership with no retained earnings to invest in something that will, for the most part, be accretive to the people who come after us?

It took a few years to do, but we went on the journey together. We had town halls, discussed it for more than a year with the board, held a great D-bate on the topic, garnered all kinds of owners input along with the input of our professionals and staff across generations. We took a long-term view now chronicled in an HBS case study. Once its doors opened, all 109 acres of Deloitte University quickly became a crown jewel and source of great pride.

JM: Absolutely. Are there any other elements of leadership you'd like to bring up?

CB: Yes. Resilience. A famous boxer once said something to the effect of: Everybody has a plan until you're punched in the face. There's a lot of truth to that. I believe resilience is a key, though underplayed, leadership dimension whether applied to organizational, professional, or personal life.

JM: That's so true. You must have courage and a lot of people mess up and confuse fearlessness and courage. But courage is really the guts to be tough, to make tough decisions and be resilient. I agree that resilience is underplayed, as well as undernoticed.

CB: Yes, I was talking to the editor of a business periodical about innovation and the observation that innovation is so often narrowly focused on startups and young disruptors.

JM: That's a very good point.

CB: The fact is, there are a lot of long-standing companies that I would argue are innovative—and I can prove it.

JM: How?

CB: Because they're still here, still relevant, still well-serving their stakeholders.

JM: People define leadership in a myriad of ways.

CB: They certainly do. For example, someone mentioned leadership the other day through the lens of team dynamics. I thought to myself, *really?* I can get behind that but leadership is so much more. For example, think of the interconnection between

leadership and engagement. At its highest level,
you can consider leadership a *currency*—a medium for
exchange of value.

JM: I think you're absolutely correct. I love the term currency. And
there is a currency of change. Talk to me about how companies
transform themselves. What are the key things that have to be in place?

CB: In short-hand, there are two key components to a transformation:
left brain and right brain. In neuroscience, left-brain refers to logical
thinking and processing of information in a tangible, measureable
fashion while right brain pertains to intangibles such as feelings,
intuition, and creativity. We use left brain to refer to the capabilities
and work practices a company aspires to develop, and right brain as a
reference to the mindset and behavioral change requirements. As lyrics
in a song Frank Sinatra popularized, "you can't have one without the
other."

JM: Yes, so true.

CB: Too often, though, right brain efforts are insufficiently tended to.

JM: Absolutely.

CB: So many things a company does—from management
commuications to operational activities to project-based efforts—can
be vehicles to help enable the transformation.
If you're clear and can well-articulate the cultural norms, behaviors,
and traits that you are trying to evolve to, you have a much greater
chance of achieving those aims.

> Those who don't create the future, live in a world not of their making.
>
> *— Cathy Benko*

14

Deva Bharathi
CEO of Fluid Systems Corporation (Oman)

Nobody sees your "inner core" except you, if you choose to see it;
if you do choose to see it, however, this becomes the key to
unlocking your true greatness.

—John Mattone

GROWING UP IN MUSCAT, OMAN, Deva Bharathi was exposed to business management early on. With both a father and uncle deeply involved in the business world, young Deva developed an early fascination for management.

When he finished his twelfth year of school, he was faced with the decision many young men of the time struggled with: engineering or medicine. The two professions were the fashion of the day, and though both were surely noble, only one path spoke to Deva's passion: commerce.

After completing an MBA, Deva went to work with his early mentors, his father and uncle. It was a full circle moment, but one that would be short lived. Though it was fulfilling to work for the family business, Deva soon discovered that not only was the business stagnant, but his father and uncle had no interest nor intention of upsetting the status quo through transformation.

It was time to move on.

In his next position with a publishing house, Deva was charged with revitalizing a struggling business in danger of going under. Discovering a natural talent for turning around companies, Deva rose to the task with ease and vision. It would be his first venture in a lifetime career leaning heavily on his turnaround skills.

Today, Deva is a visionary and entrepreneurial C-level executive with more than 18 years of rich and diverse experience in strategic management. Currently he is CEO of Fluid Systems Corporation, LLC, Oman. Deva has a proven track record of capitalizing on new opportunities, maximizing stakeholder relationships, leveraging third-party partnerships, and engaging cross-cultural teams to boost business performance, customer satisfaction, and efficiency.

Deva has met with groundbreaking success in leading and turning around start-ups and business houses into full-blown, revenue-generating organizations. He played a significant role in making Fluid Systems a strong contender in pipeline and piping projects in the oil and gas industry in Oman. Under his leadership, the company's oil and gas division achieved a 150 percent increase in profit since 2010. Deva has managed revenues ranging from $20 million to $160 million, with up to $25 million in gross contribution.

He has also diversified the business by setting up an events management and senior executive training company called Synerggie Eventz, which organizes conferences with business gurus including Jack Canfield, Robin Sharma, Dave Ulrich, Robert Kaplan, and John Mattone among others. Deva has positioned Synerggie Eventz in the film marketing and screening industry space with the objective of becoming the nation's only provider of such services. He has led Synerggie through nearly 250 percent growth in profits since 2010.

Fluid Systems has been in the oil and gas industry in Oman for the last 25 years. It can supply products and services to major projects in the fields of oil and gas exploration, power generation, mining, and general industrial sectors. Its clients are spread across various industrial sectors all over the Middle East, India, and Europe. The company represents some of the best names in their respective product areas including Petroleum Development Oman, Vallourec & Mannesmann USA Corp., KSB, Weir, Larsen & Toubro Oman, and Essar Steel. Fluid Systems' current focus is to actively take part in the in-country value initiatives of the Government of Oman and venture into areas that would aid in the economic and social development of the country. I talked to Deva Bharathi about his groundbreaking success in his field and what it takes to be a leader when transformation means the survival of an organization.

JM: Thank you for your contribution to the book. What a fascinating career you've had. Looking back, what has been the most meaningful?

DB: I love turning around organizations. Actually, it is turning around people, as organizations are nothing but a group of people. When you turn around people, it is turning around the culture and this is the biggest challenge always. However, I have realized that understanding what someone needs or wants comes from self-knowledge, which is knowing what I need or want. This has been a great journey on the path of self-discovery, which makes you much more equipped to discovering others. This is the biggest aid of all in cultural transformation.

JM: Yes.

DB: The biggest constraint is the culture in the GCC [Gulf Cooperation Council] area itself. Whether you take it from the point of view of the employee or the consumer, the culture tends to influence every level. The biggest learning curve is in how one works within constraints and is successful at the same. A concept like the theory of constraints can find a very comfortable home in the geographical area of GCC. One of the things I really wanted to do was expand across the region and go into other Asian countries. However, the challenges have been so much that the move to other markets is only happening now, after almost seven years.

JM: Transformation is not an overnight affair.

DB: Exactly. It doesn't fit in with any of the models we learn doing case studies at Harvard. The case studies do not explain these challenges in the Middle East because they are so subtle. So that was one of the biggest challenges I've gone through. Then the issue of devising strategies and not being able to execute them, as these strategies tend to be created in silos not involving the executors of strategy. I know that this is a common phenomenon around the world, as I read in an article in *Harvard Business Review* that more than 70 percent of strategies fail because of no connection or involvement in middle or lower management. In the Asian context, the main block comes from the fixation on superior and subordinate relationships. The saying goes that strategy is for the top management only and the rest only follow. Where is the question of flexibility then? What of the ground realities? How do you then respond to sudden market changes? We live in a world where the entire market for a particular product or service could be wiped out overnight. Take, for example, the launch of the "iPod"? and how that affected the Walkman market.

JM: Talk to me about your current business. How is Fluid Systems doing?

DB: Fluid Systems has been a great journey. Taking it from a company that was almost dead to one of the premier providers of piping and pipeline solutions for the oil and gas industry has been satisfying. The job is not over yet, as the challenge is still there. I have discovered that memory is short in this part of the world. Some things that you believe are tried and tested as successful will still get challenged, perhaps over something as trivial as somebody mentioning it in a casual meeting.

The challenge is even steeper with the decline of the oil prices. It may have been sailing at $100, $110 a barrel. Suddenly it comes down to $60 or $45. We're learning to understand how things should not be taken for granted—it pays to have a dynamic strategy in place with efficient resources that can implement the strategy at a short notice.

In a way it is an excuse to make everything more efficient, to cut down the excess and then focus on the core activities. That's what I've been doing. In 2013 and 2014 there was this relaxed mind-set that oil prices are going to be stable and not come down; however, I had heard of the shale gas boom in the United States and how is it going to tilt the balance. No one would hear of it; they all said that nothing would happen in the next 10 years. But I believed that the alternative energy movement was gaining strength in Europe and other parts of the world. I would mention that the present ruler of Oman, His Majesty Sultan Qaboos Bin Said, is a great supporter of preserving the environment and even in Oman small but steady support has been gaining for alternative energy sources, especially solar. We started working with the local authority on identifying the possibility of a solar power plant as sunlight is available in abundance in this part of the world. So this thought is helping us tremendously—the strategy of focusing on other energy sources is bearing fruit.

The future dependence on oil is going to be really difficult, as we have less than our oil-rich neighbors. I was looking at the story from Germany where the windmill is a big source of energy. The Middle East is one of the most sun intense areas and solar energy could be fantastic source of energy.

JM: Absolutely, that seems to be practical but yet very original thinking.

DB: This is a classic example of having a flexible strategy that could be implemented at short notice. As mentioned before, we started working with the ministry of environment here to start talking about solar power plants as an alternative to gas power plants, which they use now. Now there is a huge development happening in Oman and Saudi Arabia for making solar power plants.

So we're basically going through a tough time in terms of new projects or increased spending in oil and gas projects, but I'm not so pessimistic as far as the outcome is concerned. The alternate source of energy thing is giving me a lot of motivation for the next three or four years.

JM: That's great. You have a great reputation as a turnaround specialist. What led you to be successful in turning around organizations and transforming them? What would be three or four things that you would want to recommend to other CEOs all over the world?

DB: I think the first step is basically to have the right message in place such as what outcome is expected and what do we need to achieve the outcome. I mean the big picture.

And of course the right message has to go from the top. The big picture has to be in place and should be clearly explained to the board that this is what needs to be achieved and should be ensured that it is understand clearly.

JM: Agreed 100 percent.

DB: To have a strong management team is the first thing in place, and to ensure the management team is in sync with what is expected of this particular organization. The next step is to have the second level of people because most of the time I see the strategy and execution are worlds apart.

There is a huge habit in the Middle East where strategy is done at exotic locales and you know you come out with some grand ideas of plans. And then the operational team does not have a clue about what is expected.

JM: That's not going to work.

DB: This is the same story in most of the places, I think.

DB: The biggest problem that I'm seeing is the master/slave mentality. This is something that runs in the blood of many of the people here. I mean even those expatriates that come down get a share of this mentality. Even Americans start thinking they are the master and everybody else has to follow. It becomes easier when you discuss the various possibilities with at least two levels down the management chain and the kind of ideas that can be generated would be fabulous, but only if you try.

I think having the right people in the right place is the key. This includes the management as well as the middle level—even at the lower level. The lower level may be done slowly, but then the middle level should have the best people because they are the ones who drive the strategy.

JM: Absolutely. This is so true, Deva.

DB: So that's one step. And the second thing is basically coherence. I mean coherence in the sense that the management team may have beautiful plans but their actions do not match with what they have said. They talk the talk, but they need to walk the talk first.

JM: Good point.

DB: You've got to be walking, breathing, living what you talk about. You've got to be the prime example of it. So the coherence is in your message, the coherence is in your actions—that's a huge turnaround factor.

JM: Excellent. What else?

DB: The third thing I've seen is the plan to action, the speed to implement. What you see is that people get stuck in the planning stage. They spend so much effort planning and then become paralyzed and can't implement action.

JM: Excellent.

DB: The thing is that you create the big picture and then the means to achieve will happen a lot easier when the big picture is in place firmly in the organization.

You must do this, however, without micromanaging people, because micromanagement leads to small thought. I believe that everybody has an inherent talent. And your purpose as a senior leader of the company is basically to develop the talent and give them the space to work. My policy is to create an environment where an employee can use his personal agency and unleash the creativity within, but you define the boundaries and limitations. I believe no turnaround will be achieved fully without an empowered workforce. However, I must admit that I've been surprised many times when I talk to employees who feel that they are in an internal jail where they have been taught to follow and not lead. How can you ever call yourself a leader when you can't create leaders?

The only way you can respect others is to respect yourself first. Everything has to come from within. You create things inside out and not outside in. If you really want to manifest creative people in your organization, then start respecting yourself and the infinite intelligence the universe has showered on each and every one of us. Many of the greatest thinkers and visionaries did not have any labels such as MBA or Ph.D., but we follow them. Why? Because all of these great people were connected to the intelligence within.

JM: Excellent point. What else do you think is critical from your experience?

DB: Follow up! This is something a lot of people lose sight of. You must be willing to follow up and change plans, because strategy is not static. It has to be dynamic to be successful. There are conditions that are not in our control and there can be sudden and unexpected changes, especially in this part of the world, in legal and other regulations, so you need to be having a flexible strategy in place. So you need to have Plan A and Plan B in place at the same time.

JM: Yes. That's an excellent point. I'm interested in what messages experienced executives like you want to share with the younger people so that they can become the great leaders that we need. And we do have just an incredible gap all over the world, both leadership and culture. What would be the message that you would want to deliver?

DB: One of the things that has really driven me all the time is this passion to do something different: be childlike. When your inner child is awake within, you are curious about everything. This is also something that can supercharge your creativity. There is nothing wrong in being labeled a weirdo if you think what others would think of your lack of maturity as we say in the material world. In the end, think what would people say when your plans bear fruit and you are a great success. Above all, don't try to prove to the world; prove to yourself. That is the first and most important step.

JM: I love that.

DB: It's much easier. You tend to get to a lot of structure in the planning processes. When you go to company boards and company meetings, you lose the creativity. One of the things I always tell my staff is to start dreaming.

Every organization is driven by a passion for something. You look at Apple, you look at Microsoft, you look at any of the bigger companies: It all starts from a passion. And that passion comes from a dream. I see a lot of people who have completely lost the will to dream. When you talk to them it's all about a nine-to-five job, settling down, having kids, and then you die and vanish. To every young person out there, can you imagine yourself living a life of rules and vanishing without doing anything that you love?

JM: True.

DB: You will see a lot of this type, they'll just lose hope. Most of the big blue chip companies have begun recruiting liberal arts graduates instead of MBAs, because they need some creativity in place. Why? Basically it is because you will not be taught to follow a certain model and get stuck to the moral, so it's like a means to an end to rather than the end itself. I have realized that if you are stuck on the means always, the end will never be reached. We all talk about hard work but the hardest working people in the physical sense are the thousands of construction workers you see in building sites, and they are poor. Laborers in the Middle East and Asia earn less than $200 a month. Most of them have lost a will to dream because life is too hard for them. If you are also someone who thinks life is hard and you are reading this, then you seriously need to be touch with yourself as the dreamer in you is waiting to be awakened.

JM: I love what you just said. I think that's just great advice. And actually being childlike is freeing and unleashing and we do need more of that. You have to find your passion and sadly, some people never find their passion.

DB: Yes, you have to find your passion within your working life. I believe that is how you find satisfaction and balance. This used to be a difficult issue for me till a few months ago, as I used to view personal and professional matters separately and it used to be a real challenge. However, from the moment I started diving within to understand the real purpose for which I was here or, rather, we are all here, things seem to be much simpler. The constant struggle we all go through within to understand what is right or wrong boils down to our connection with the inner core. If you are connected with the inner core, the rest follows.

JM: How do you work through challenges which, when presented, appear overwhelming?

DB: I have always believed in improvising and this is specially focused on the execution of a plan. If a strategy could not be implemented, then it is of no use. If a strategy cannot be dynamic, then don't use it. So I have always believed in creating a strategy that is both dynamic and executable, which has helped me a great deal in navigating stressful situations.

JM: What has made you successful? How do you define success?

DB: Success and failure are two sides of the same coin. The whole idea is to go beyond these states. To have an expectation is good, but to get attached to this expectation causes a lot of imbalance physically, mentally, and emotionally. My definition of success is now the successful completion of any activity you undertake to the best of your capability at that given time, whether it has made you a billion dollars or nothing at all. This can be a bit philosophical but this is the reality. If you go through any mega deals that have succeeded in either creating a new market or new customer base, you will realize that the reason for this came from things that were never planned in the first place.

JM: How about failure. Have you failed? Can you share and what did you learn that made you stronger?

DB: As I said in my response to the previous question, success and failure are two sides of the same coin. As a probability, both these states occur in our life and both teach us with certain learning. Yes, I have gladly failed multiple numbers of times and as I have said previously, I never attach myself to success or a failure. More often than not, I have realized that failures occur to let you know that the strategy you adopted could be tweaked further to move from failure to success.

JM: Describe your typical day?

DB: A typical day starts with 15 minutes of complete silence when I am in the office. This is a great teacher surprisingly, as you tend to connect to yourself and help develop intuition. I recommend this to any leader who would like to gather powerful energy from within. Then there is the meeting with the team followed by a meeting with any particular department that has been scheduled as per demand of the projects we are working on or bidding on. Usually I try to connect with some of my partners in the industry to understand more about the new projects that are being planned by the government. I tend to limit my working day to just six hours in a day. I also dedicate two hours every day to myself where I read books on different subjects, and my current interest is quantum physics and how it is shaping our realities. Then I make it a point to sit down with my wife and discuss anything under the sun she decides to discuss. Luckily, she is also attracted to metaphysics and quantum physics.

JM: What other roles have you held in this or previous organizations?

DB: From 2004, I have moved from being business development head to CEO and have held this role pretty much the same way all this time. I tend to call myself a CTO—chief turnaround officer—as most of my roles in the past have been to help sinking ships. Maybe this is something that I always like—turning around organizations that sink because of a failed culture. This is pretty much the biggest problem—having a culture that does not drive performance. Culture shifts take time and it needs a strong leader who drives down this culture. This is what I like to do. I am amazed when I analyze organizations (some big names, too) that couldn't be turned around as the culture was completely lacking.

JM: What are the biggest challenges you face in your current leadership role?

DB: Culture has to be driven from top to bottom to have any meaning in the first place. What if your top management (in this case the board) is the impediment in changing the culture? This is a challenge I am facing now. For a problem to be solved, you first have to accept that there is a problem. This acceptance itself leads to the solution. However, if you act like there is no problem, then it is a dangerous situation. This is what I am facing now and it has taken longer for me to convince them that there is an issue that needs to be tackled.

JM: What are you two strongest leadership strengths? Why?

DB: I like to call myself a transformational leader, and I can spot a way of doing things differently pretty easy. Further, I am also empathetic and can easily understand how a person would feel about the ideas I am having. I am also patient enough to understand that change will be gradual and can be risky if the right resources are not on board. This fits in line with my focus on culture transformations wherever I go.

JM: What are your two leadership areas most in need of development? Why?

DB: While I am patient enough, I cannot stand mediocrity. I do understand that everyone is in a particular stage of development; I believe that I need to be a bit more patient when it comes to people's development, especially in this part of the world where this can be a challenge. Second area is the need to focus on the task while maintaining human relationships. I talk about this because I can be very demanding when it comes to implementation, and many who work with me cannot understand this face of me and tend to get into a fear zone. I need to be a bit more compassionate when it comes to these two areas.

JM: What is your greatest professional accomplishment? Why?

DB: Every turnaround whether it is First Publishing or Fluid Systems is a great accomplishment. I haven't got to the point where I could call something the greatest. These were great accomplishments as I had developed in changing the culture mind-set of these organizations. The rest is easy.

JM: Toughest challenges facing your organization? What are you and your senior team doing to tackle these challenges? Is there an imperative to transform?

DB: Culture is to be driven from top to bottom. When the top itself doesn't believe in this fully, how can the transformation take place? It is well accepted within the organization that the transformation is needed and it is the only way. The first is to accept that there is a problem, and this is being done with the board, as some of the members would like to believe that there is no problem and the problem is with the market. We are in the final leg of the phase and the change is taking place.

JM: When I say culture transformation what does this mean to you?

DB: For any organization to succeed, I believe they need to have a vibrant culture that is value driven, mission focused, and vision guided. First, this ensures alignment, creates a performance driven organization, and naturally attracts talented employees. For this transformation to take place you need strong leadership who would drive this down and practice value-based leadership, which naturally ensures the well-being of employees and achieves the mission.

JM: I believe that culture starts in the C-suite. Culture—the values, character, norms, behavior of your organization—rolls downhill. If you have senior leaders who possess both a strong and vibrant inner core and outer core, you have a much better chance of creating a mature culture. Comments?

DB: I believe this is exactly the same belief I have. Inner and outer core are again two sides of the same coin and cannot exist without each other. This has been my leadership mantra from the beginning, and I practice this wherever I go.

JM: Reference Six-Step Cultural Transformational Model—Thinking Differently/Thinking Big, Vulnerability, Compelling Future, Changing Mindsets, Pushing Talent Levers, Measure and Course Correct. What would be the best example of how you and your senior team led a successful transformation of culture? How did you succeed? What were the critical steps you took to implement? Sustain?

DB: In my latest role, the culture was more reactive than responsive or proactive. In the oil and gas downstream business, a number of activities complement as well as supplement each other. I decided to look at the big picture of creating an organization that becomes a one-stop shop for all pipeline and piping requirements instead of looking at only fluid control solutions. The reason was that focusing only on fluid control gave you a limited market with many Asian players with whom you couldn't compete price-wise. However, to move from this to the big picture, you needed a set of new resources, and the existing resources that resisted the change had to go. I believe the biggest push in the direction came when you introduced new resources that saw the possibility of achievement in the new direction and am glad to say that it has gone very well. Now we are in a different situation as the declining oil prices tighten the budget of the operators and this would mean that there is a different strategy that needs to be adopted and implemented. As it was in 2008, I am having the same challenges of changing course that would mean that some resources would go and new ones would come in. As I have always maintained, any strategy that is not dynamic and executable has to go.

JM: What would be a bad example or failure of attempting to transform culture? Lessons learned?

DB: In the beginning of my career, I liked to be a messiah of the people meaning taking all along even if they had outlived their usefulness to the mission you set out to achieve. To transform culture, you need strong measures and that involves pretty strong and hard decisions, which can involve a lot of emotional hardship. However, what would you do to save a sinking ship? I think I never attempted to transform culture without having the heart to make hard decisions, and I was fortunate enough to understand this before embarking on the culture transformation journey.

JM: What are your words of wisdom for the leaders and the future leaders who will be reading this book?

DB: A strong inner core is a must for any leader, as a strong inner core naturally reflects on your outer core and you become a much stronger individual physically, emotionally, mentally, as well as spiritually. A strong inner core also leads you to identify your true self. How can one lead without knowing who they are in the first place?

Every leader starts somewhere. Early on they may have family members or friends who inspire them the way my father and uncle inspired me. They should listen to that inner voice, but be willing to change course when the situation requires it and believe that greater things are on the horizon. And by all means, have a little fun along the way.

15

NV "Tiger" Tyagarajan

President and CEO, Genpact

The best predictor of your future is not past performance; it is the combination of your past, your willingness to accept your gifts and deficiencies, your willingness to commit to a plan in which you leverage your gifts and address your deficiencies, your willingness to execute your plan, your willingness to be vigilant to the results you achieve, and most importantly your willingness to course correct continuously.

—John Mattone

NV "TIGER" TYAGARAJAN GREW UP in the culturally diverse city of Bombay, India, where more citizens were from "somewhere else" than in any other Indian city. From his early days in school to his college life, this would become important as it informed his life in a profound way. A small family of five, the Tyagarajans were close knit and committed to education.

Luckily, a good education was attainable at only one dollar a month. And not only was Bombay full with people of all nationalities, but it was rich with various religions as well, a true metropolitan city. In classes of up to 60 students in the local Catholic school, sometimes 10 languages were spoken. There were Catholic students, Muslim students, Hindu students, and Jewish students, all speaking English. Tiger didn't know it at the time, but it was a tiny microcosm of his future life in New York City.

After these formative educational years, Tiger did his undergraduate studies at the Indian Institute of Technology in Bombay, studying mechanical engineering. Tiger was a natural, excelling at the logic-driven approach an engineering degree required, and yet he felt a mild dissatisfaction with mechanical engineering. Like many future leaders, the gut instinct would be an insight into his future. Tiger realized very early on that his passion lay not in machines, but people.

To earn a master's degree in marketing and finance, Tiger attended the prestigious Indian Institute of Management, spending two idyllic years in what seemed to be the perfect fit. He was able to use his love of numbers for finance combined with his passion for people to drive the marketing needed to bring people to the products they needed.

A sweet spot was found.

Straight out of grad school, Tiger started working for the Indian subsidiary of U.S.-based Chesebrough-Ponds, selling, of all things, cosmetics! After just seven years with the organization, which had been recently acquired by Unilever, Tiger's sales management responsibilities included the country's largest region, accounting for a whopping 40 percent of Chesebrough-Ponds' sales.

Those years proved to be heady and intense—a great training ground for single product marketing. But it was time for a change in course, so Tiger set out to enter the world of financial services. When offered a position with Citibank's retail mortgage lending business, he accepted. In six different jobs in three years at Citibank, Tiger was almost instantly tagged as the "cleanup guy," the person designated to clean up various messes, often very serious. His most effective strategy for doing so? Attracting then developing a team of A players.

Around the same time, GE Capital announced plans to set up a financial services company in India. Tiger, a fan of Jack Welch, knew that he could build a career in a company as big as GE, where he could move from one company to another within the organization over the course of his professional life. He joined GE Capital India as one of only five employees in India, head of risk for consumer lending.

As planned, Tiger stuck with GE, eventually relocating to New York in 2002 as global head of operations and Six Sigma for GE's commercial lending business. Finally, Tiger joined Gecis, which is now Genpact.

Based in New York, Tiger is credited as one of the industry leaders who pioneered a new global business model and transformed a division of GE (formerly GE Capital International Services) into Genpact, a leading business process management and technology services company with $2.28 billion in annual revenues in 2014. With nearly 68,000 employees across 25 countries, Genpact designs, transforms, and runs intelligent business operations, including those that are complex and specific to a set of chosen industries. The company generates impact for more than 800 clients, including more than one-fourth of the Fortune Global 500 representing key vertical industries. Based on the company's GE heritage and Lean Six Sigma DNA, Tiger spearheaded the development of Genpact's Smart Enterprise Processes (SEPSM) proprietary framework for making business processes more effective and driving transformation for global enterprises. Genpact is publicly listed on the NYSE under the symbol "G." Tiger is a Genpact executive officer and serves on the company's board of directors.

Tiger frequently writes and speaks about global talent issues, continuous skill development, and the importance of building a strong corporate culture. He is also passionate about diversity and serves as one of the founding supporters of the U.S. chapter of the 30% Club, an organization of CXOs focused on achieving better gender balance at U.S. companies. Tiger is also a member of *The Wall Street Journal* CEO Council. I talked to Tiger (Skype) while we were each seated at our respective desks, both littered with far too many electronic devices.

JM: Thank you for speaking with me, Tiger. I'm so pleased to have you participating. We have CEOs from all over the world in this book, and it sounds as if that is an issue that is important to you.

NVT: It resonates completely with the way I view my job. I'll often answer the question, "what is the one thing that keeps you awake at night?" It's a standard question that people ask CEOs and my answer has always been, "first of all, I sleep well at night. I sleep actually for a very short time because I believe sleep is a waste of time."

JM: It's fascinating.

NVT: I love saying this.

At the age of 90, when I'm on my deathbed and I'm beginning to say good-bye to the world, I'll sit back and think about how I've spent those years. Do I want to say that 30 years of my life, I slept? No. I'm scratching my head and saying how bizarre is that?

Particularly if you also have the view that even on the last day of my ninetieth year, I'm still learning. And I think, why should I waste time sleeping? Of course, my wife has a big problem with that discussion.

JM: How many hours do you sleep at night?

NVT: Often it's four. But you know, more like five is what it ends up being because there are times when my wife comes into my room and says, "okay, it's time for you to go to sleep."

JM: Well, we're alike. I sleep about five hours a night, too.

NVT: Yeah. I'm also a very, very early morning person. The second part is that I sleep really well; nothing worries me. The only thing I wonder is how do I wake up in the morning and know that the culture of this place is maintained. We pride ourselves on our ability to change and morph as the world changes. And I worry a lot about how I maintain it as the company becomes bigger. To me, that's the single biggest question that I grapple with.

JM: This is good.

NVT: So if I go to the C-suite of my clients and I ask them, "Tell me the one or two things that are different about us, that you like about us versus many other things." They'll have a long list of things that they don't like about us. But they say the one thing we love about you guys is your culture. Then they would go on to explain what the differences are.

JM: Tell me about your early markers. What were some of the things that propelled you in the direction that you have gone in?

NVT: I'm a big believer that history and experiences determine who you are and that applies to individuals, businesses, institutions, countries, everything. So I grew up in the city of Bombay all my life until I went to college. I spent all of that time in Bombay. We were a small family, my parents and a younger brother who was two years younger than me and a sister who is 10 years younger than me, just the five of us.

And as you may know or may not know, Bombay is probably— more so in the days I used to be there growing up in the '70s—much more of a metropolitan, cosmopolitan city than any other city in India. I think today a few other cities are, halfway, 80 percent there, Bangalore, for example, and Delhi, but in those days it was only Bombay. So Bombay had a mixture of people coming from all parts of India, so there's not one group.

And it had probably a larger population of people from outside of India than any other city in India. Again, today probably Bangalore has a good number and so does Delhi. But in those days, Bombay had the most. So why is that important? It's important because from the time I went to school, I dealt with people who came from extremely different backgrounds.

JM: Amazing—clearly that early experience served you well. So after your MBA, what was your first job?

NVT: My first job was to be the sales trainee in a company called Chesebrough-Pond's, which then subsequently, two years into my employment, was acquired by Unilever. In my seven years in that company, I joined sales. The power center of the company was sales. And I joined the sales team as a management trainee. And again, I thought that was great learning. To me, the single biggest learning when joining a team, you come in—you're 22 years old and you're given a territory and you have 10 sales reps who are part of your team and you are the sales leader.

JM: And you're young.

NVT: The sales leader, at the age of 22 or 23, you're a complete rookie. You've never worked in your life. And you have a team of 10 people ranging in age from 35 to 59.

JM: It's tough.

NVT: Very. So you've got to start by finding a way to build a relationship that cannot start by saying, "I'm your boss" because if you do that, it's game over.

JM: Yeah, absolutely.

NVT: And I've realized that—you know, very quickly I realized within the first couple of days talking to people that there's just one person in that group of 10 who is 59 years old, who was considered to be the absolute godfather of the company—he has mentored everyone in the company, ranging from the big guys to the little sales guys and he was extremely experienced and was highly opinionative and was an ultimate egoist.

Within the first 48 hours I walked up to him and I said, "You know, I really need to learn a lot. I don't know anything. I know that I'm supposed to be your boss, but you know this and I know this that I can't do anything unless you teach me. Are you willing to teach me?"

JM: What a critical step in your development as a human being, right? That is a future CEO; that was pivotal.

NVT: I did not know it would make that big a difference. I thought I had no option. He was chopped off his wits. So he actually took me under his wing and said I was like his son. "And I'm going to make you successful."

JM: I love the story. This is so powerful. Talk to me about the work that you've done as a CEO. It's my belief that culture in any organization starts in the C-suite, starts with the CEO and the C-suite. What do you think?

NVT: No question. Zero chance of it being any other way. With a couple of exceptions, I suspect, you know most corporations, businesses, particularly in the western world, I think that's a given. The CEO and the C-suite is where it starts. They are the culture keepers.

JM: Talk to me about the culture at Genpact. Tell me about what you've done along with the C-suite team to create and nourish the culture.

NVT: I'd start by saying that we were extremely fortunate to be born as a subsidiary and as an extension of GE. I consider it to be one of the best corporations to have ever existed, particularly from a leadership and a culture perspective.

Even though we were an outpost in India, much of what we did was Jack's doing. I learned a lot from his example. At some point in time when we were four years into that journey running financial services for GE Capital in India, we decided to set up this business, which is to provide services to GE Capital businesses in the U.S. and globally and, over time, services to all the GE businesses. This was the business we set up.

And very early in that journey, a lot of the culture that we embodied was the GE culture. So what was that? An intense focus on process, which means that if you have a problem that you're trying to solve or if you have an opportunity that you're trying to attack, one of the best ways to go after it is to deconstruct it—deconstruct the process that gets you to the answer, the from and the to and then get down to the deconstructed, granular layout of that process.

And then check out what's working, what's not working, how to improve it. It coincided very nicely with my engineering background and engineering thinking.

JM: Perfect, absolutely.

NVT: One of the tools that we picked up early in that journey was Lean Six Sigma. Jack had launched it in the mid-1990s. We were green, starting from scratch. So our ability to actually inculcate Lean Six Sigma culture within an organization that we grew organically was so much easier than trying incorporating it into an existing culture.

We had the easy job of building an organization from scratch and immersing them in process thinking, metric student thinking, in order to drive improvement using things like Lean Six Sigma.

The other part of our culture would be a culture that says everything can be continuously improved, it never ends.

And so the culture of continuous improvement again, correlates to curiosity. The word that we use and we've now used it for 15-plus years to describe our customer focus is *maniacal* focus on the client.

JM: Love that, Tiger!

NVT: I actually tell people that what it really means is that when it comes to the client, we have to get mad about it.

We have to behave irrationally. Rational decision-making, when it comes to client, is actually not a good thing.

JM: I love this! This is great. You're outside the comfort zone. You're pushing people outside the comfort zone to think differently and act differently.

NVT: And the third one that intersects both these is an incredible metrics-driven culture. When it comes to maniacal focus on the client, we picked up a metric, net promoter score, and we've used it now for 15-plus years to measure client satisfaction.

JM: Tell me about how you view talent in the equation of driving the kind of culture that you've created and you must sustain. Talk to me about how you view talent in the equation.

NVT: It's a great question, John. For us, talent is the nature of our business. At the lower levels of the organization, it's important to look for skills and knowledge in certain specific areas when we hire people.

However, I think deep in the organization, we would all still argue that given a choice, it's better to find a person who is hungry to learn and capable of learning versus someone who may not be very good on those two dimensions, but knows exactly what needs to be done in that space.

Our belief is that what you know today is guaranteed to be irrelevant tomorrow. So what qualities are imperative? One is willingness and the other is the capability. And are you passionate about it? For us, that becomes important. And that correlates well with curiosity, with inquisitiveness, with complete humility.

I'm really looking for inquisitiveness, curiosity, learning, desire, passion, and all of that. And obviously you know, all of that, the ability to work with a broader group of people in order to be able to drive that.

JM: I love that. Give me a sense of when you look at your younger leaders, because I know that you've got a lot of young talent in the organization, what are some things that you're doing to strengthen your leadership skills to ready them for the Genpact of the future, you know, the next 5 to 10 years. What are you doing to help them?

NVT: I am fortunate to have grown up in the world of GE, where leadership development and talent development is one of the key things that they do well.

We learned a bunch of methodologies, tools, and programs from them in the first seven years of our existence as a part of GE. And the last 11 years, we've been an independent company. We have a strong hierarchy of programs that we run starting with very young team leaders. How do you coach them and train them, both in and out of a classroom setting? It's all about experiential learning from each other.

So 50 people in the room go through a two-week program that arms them with the methodology and the truth that hone their skills to be able to manage teams better.

We spend a lot of time bringing people together into these programs. We have a pretty significant investment in these programs. Our leaders spend time teaching the program.

JM: Yes, wonderful. I think that's great. It makes them stronger leaders.

NVT: One of the behaviors that we search for—and a lot of behaviors surface in these programs—is someone who can say, "I just found an answer to something and I tried doing it and I found that it works and I love it. And I'm going to tell everyone about it. And I'm going to teach people about it. And I'm going to share and I'm going to invite them to come and ask me and my team and they can connect and learn and go away." They have a generosity of spirit for the greater good of the organization.

So that's one behavior that we love, which is share your wins and losses continuously so that everyone can learn.

JM: I want to go back to your point about cultural transformation. The stronger the culture, the more difficult it is to change. Give your perspective on your experiences with Genpact and transforming this big company every day. How are you doing this? How are you navigating this?

NVT: Cultural change is continuous. There are times when it has to accelerate because of a series of events, the way the world is changing. I think the world is in the middle of one of those big changes. You can attribute that to technology. You can also attribute it to one of the beliefs that I have which is the world is extremely volatile and uncertain. And that's the nature of the world of today and tomorrow. It's not going to change.

Part of the reason it's so volatile and uncertain is actually technology, because the moment you have cycles of change being so short in terms of new things, the new destroys the old. By definition you have volatility.

But if you go back to one of our tenets of our culture, it's process, it's discipline, it's execution, it's say-do ratio—when I promise something, I deliver it. That is a way to address the chaos. There are no questions asked. That's the culture we have. And our clients love that culture.

And then you combine that with a culture maniacally focused on clients. The client is often right. And therefore, listen carefully to the client and find a way to execute to it. That's the culture we have.

But here is the problem with that culture in today's world that I'm trying to change: Our clients are beginning to say, "you should tell me when what I'm asking you is completely wrong. You should tell me when I'm an idiot. You should tell me when you are unwilling to accept what I'm asking you to do."

This is a shift. Now the clients are not saying, "I'm the expert," the clients are saying, "You are the expert." That's a big cultural change and our teams are grappling with the combination of both. It doesn't mean you give up the say-do ratio, it doesn't mean you give up the client focus and promise, but it does mean you have to figure out how to incorporate the change.

JM: In your mind Tiger, what's causing the client shift, because that's a big shift. What's causing that?

NVT: It's mostly evolution, but it's also partly that patience is limited. The clients are on a path of change that is far more rapid than it used to be. For them, two years is too long. They don't want to go through a two-year process.

So, that's one culture change. The other culture change is a shift in vision: people want to be presented with the dream. They want to be sold on the next most beautiful, best thing. It doesn't matter if that thing doesn't yet exist, they're willing to get in line. And that's a big shift. Selling an aspiration, a dream.

JM: This has been amazing. What do you want to say to the younger people about them getting on a pathway where they unlock greatness in themselves? What are some of the things that you've learned that you want to share with the world?

NVT: One is that I don't believe that you have to follow your passion.

JM: No? That's certainly unconventional wisdom.

NVT: So often young leaders are so paralyzed by choosing the right job, the right industry, the right position. The truth is, you don't know. The only way you'll know what's right is by doing. Once you're out there, you're going to figure out where your passion is.

And the other thing that I tell them is do not choose based on short-term material numbers, because there's going to come a time when you actually realize it has not advanced you to where you need to be, to where you want to get to.

Compounding long-term makes a huge difference. Step functions make a huge difference. And therefore, if you chart your career over 30 years and if your goal is be something big, to create wealth, then do not necessarily jump into the one that's the highest paying today, because that may not be the best path.

You must follow the path and the passion and then be flexible and nimble and move in different directions.

The last thing is start by saying you don't know anything. The end of your college is not the end of your learning. I do think that one of the dangers in society today (and I think the United States probably has the biggest danger of this) is people think about lives as 20 years of learning; 40 years of contribution, both to companies and society and to oneself; and then 20, 30, 40 years of so-called retired life.

That thinking creates a situation wherein we have a stagnant workforce that's unprepared for the new world.

We live in a dynamic, changing world. The only way to thrive is to be willing to learn anew every day, to have a childlike curiosity and sense of wonder, to approach adversity with humility, and to never waste a moment.

16

Anthony Wedo
Former CEO of Ovation Brands

Success has nothing to do with money, titles, and possessions;
success is only about committing—every day—to becoming the
absolute best you can be.

—John Mattone

ANTHONY WEDO IS FAMOUSLY KNOWN as the "Corporate Turnaround
CEO" because in the past 30 years he has led the turnaround for
companies such as Ovation Brands, once thought to be a lost cause.
Transformation isn't easy. What does it take to do it right? The seeds to
Anthony Wedo's success were sewn very early on, in a modest childhood
in the small town of Shippensburg, Pennsylvania. The values of every
leader are formed early in life, and Anthony Wedo learned three things
early on: work hard, keep a laser focus, and serve others.

The Wedo household, in which Anthony was the youngest of three
children, was a busy one. Anthony's father labored tirelessly sometimes
at three jobs—certainly never fewer than two. And his mother managed to seamlessly run the home and family and work to help make
ends meet. Their dedication was astounding. Even with relentlessly gru-
eling hours and surely tiring days piling up on each other, Anthony never
once heard his parents complain. This was important; it crystallized in his

mind the value of a good work ethic. Although they had little, and in fact struggled to make ends meet, Anthony learned that a strong work ethic was essential. Absent of all other advantages—be it intellect, privilege, or opportunity—an unwavering dedication is imperative.

Without a strong work ethic one has nothing.

Anthony lived his childhood in an almost mirror image of his parent's day-to-day living. While his father worked three jobs, Anthony worked three jobs as well: school, athletics, and work. His days unfolded the same: awake, chores, school, athletics, working with his dad in the back-room of their restaurant, homework, bed. It was in the restaurant that Anthony began to grasp the importance of putting others before your-self, an essential early lesson that would later give Anthony the leader-ship advantage. But when he was a kid, it was simply what he did each day. And then the next day would unfold in exactly the same manner, and another, and the weeks turned into months turned into years until, one day, it was time to head to college. His father expected him to take the Wedo values with him, saying, "work is like weight lifting for one's char-acter." That is, if you choose to have an unproductive life, it will impact who you are as a person.

Anthony Wedo lifted a lot of weight, early.

At Ovation Brands, Wedo took a company that was in dire straits (having filed for bankruptcy twice in five years) and revived it. He kept serving the families who depended on it for their livelihoods at the front of the mission. He succeeded.

Today, Anthony Wedo is a successful entrepreneur and sought-after adviser in the restaurant and hospitality industries, having developed over 500 new restaurants in every major U.S. market.

Wedo began his career at PepsiCo. He went on to become the vice president and general manager of the southeast division of Kentucky Fried Chicken, where he was responsible for more than 1,200 restau-rants, 7,000 employees, and $1 billion in revenue. Moving on, Anthony founded Mid-Atlantic Restaurant Systems and grew the company to 160 restaurants in four years, with $250 million in annualized sales. After Mid-Atlantic Restaurant Systems was acquired by Boston Market, Anthony became the chairman, president, and CEO of New World Restaurant Group and successfully turned around the com-pany in three years. Later he served as the CEO of Mainline Capital Advisors, LLC, which provided merger and acquisition assistance, turnaround management, advisory, and executive management con-sulting services to debt investors and private equity sponsors in the restaurant industry.

Among his many awards, Anthony was named Entrepreneur of the Year; U.S. Small Business Administration's Home Business Advocate of the Year; U.S. Restaurant Industry's Area Developer of the Year; and named to the *Philadelphia Business Journal*'s 40 Under 40 List.

Anthony Wedo is a highly sought-after speaker and has developed a leadership guide, *Leadership — The 12 Commandments*. Featured in publications such as the *Wall Street Journal* and *Nation's Restaurant News*, Anthony also appeared in an episode of the hit CBS TV series *Undercover Boss* wearing a long blond wig, a moustache, and tattoos to work in several of his restaurants as dishwasher, cashier, and server.

Anthony holds a bachelor of science degree in business from Penn State University, an MBA from Cornell University, and an International MBA from Queen's University in Kingston, Ontario Canada. He is also a retired officer in the U.S. Navy Reserve. I talked to Anthony Wedo about how his early life shaped his leadership ethics, and how his singular leadership skills led to his unofficial title of Corporate Turnaround CEO.

JM: Thank you for speaking with me, Tony. Congratulations on your exemplary career. You have turned around a staggering amount of companies, something that is a challenge for even the most skilled leader. How do you tackle such high-stakes transformation?

AW: I do handle a lot and deal with a large amount of stress. From the outside looking in, it may look like too much. But I'm doing it for the purpose of taking care of the 18,000 families that rely on me, so I feel it's a just cause.

JM: I have a great appreciation also for your perspective that you don't even really think about it too much. It's more about the fact that every day you get to deliver that stability to the families who rely on you. What are some other traits that allow you to be an effective CEO of a Fortune 50 company?

AW: If it's not in your heart, you can't lead.

AW: If you don't fundamentally love people you can't lead. If you're frightened and have a lack of courage, you can't lead. There are some fundamental characteristics that one must possess. That doesn't mean people can't cultivate those qualities and thus migrate to a role of leader. They can.

JM: Absolutely, I agree with you.

AW: They need a laser focus. When I say "laser focus" people often do not understand what that means. I'll tell a story, however, about when I was a little kid going out to hunt upland game with my father — hunting quails. So upland game is basically small bird hunting. I mean basically.

And when you hunt quail, they're usually on the ground in a group that's called a covey. So when they flush, it's not uncommon for 10, 15, or even 20 birds to flush at a time.

Now, if you shoot into the group I guarantee you will 100 percent not hit a bird. You have to be able, in a split second, to pick out the bird you're going to drop, to block out any other confusion occurring around you at the time.

JM: Excellent analogy—I like that.

AW: Yes, because within that moment there is a lot of noise, birds scattering and branches falling down and brush moving and other hunters moving and you must block that commotion—all of it—out.

You have to only see the one target. Because the immature impulse, the impulse of a child is to think, there's a bunch of birds I can shoot with shotgun, because a shotgun is a bunch of spray and spray powder.

But gunshot doesn't work that way. The ideal way to achieve success is to practice that laser focus, blocking out all distractions and getting to the heart of the matter. You must be able to not be distracted during situations in which many other people would likely be highly distracted.

JM: I think that's a great point.

AW: You're inside of the target. That's probably my biggest ally, my work ethic by a factor of connects. The younger generation doesn't seem to embrace the never quit philosophy and practice like my generation did. Of course everybody wants to quit—that's another distraction you must fight, the urge to give up. If you could instead keep the knowledge in you that you can fight through the pain, approaching challenges like a marathon not a sprint, you will achieve many things you thought impossible.

JM: I totally agree with you. The point about distraction is an excellent one. What I have seen is that not only do leaders derail when distraction comes into play, but—unbelievably—companies derail when distracted too. It's exactly what you said—the company also gets distracted and they get away from their netting, from their differentiators, and then all of a sudden they become very diluted in their focus and when that happens it is the beginning of the end.

AW: When we talk about leaders today, we can do it in reverse. What's missing? The flaw is in this idea that everything should be decided by poll—if not by poll, then by a combination of some opinions. If your whole life is processing research and using that as your compass, you'll be like a spinning top going out of control, right off the edge of the table.

You have to have a compass, and know where true north is, and you have to stay on it no matter how many things distract you. Being politically correct, for example, is extremely distracting.

JM: That's a very good point. When you were at Ovation Brands, did you see some of your up-and-coming fall prey to a failure to maintain focus?

AW: Yes, we had to be very clear—to the point of repetitiveness—some people think I'm boring because I say the same things over and over again. But I want it to stick. When I want it to stick I use colorful stories and direct language. People will quickly spin off the focus and you must constantly remind them of the mission we're on. At Ovation Brands, it was the reminder that we are here to serve families. And this isn't just an Ovations Brands issue, it's a national issue.

Everybody wants to be trendy and politically correct. But the speed in which things are transitioning in the United States is astronomically fast. And being a slave to trends is a losing game. The impulse to meet the fashion, taste, style, and impulse of the day distract from the mission.

JM: Yes. Essentially you must hold firm to your own values, and lead from your personal code of ethics.

AW: Yes, exactly. A good example of this is Billy Graham—one of my heroes. No matter what was the politically correct sentiment of the day, no matter what some group was countering or championing, he never lost sight of his own vision of right and wrong and achieving his mission. He did it in such a thoughtful way. He was a very dynamic guy when he was in his prime. He had the skill to tell you you're wrong but still make you feel great about it.

That's a problem today. People don't want to tell people they're wrong—so in that reality everybody's right. Every politician thinks they have to say yes to everybody and everything to get reelected. This kind of thinking forbids you from judging people. In the end, you always have to say no to somebody.

JM: That's one of your commandments.

AW: Yes, it is. You just have to be willing to put it out there because the best feedback I've ever received in my life has been at once favorable but incredibly honest. As coaches and leaders we do an enormous disservice to the United States by not telling it like it is.

JM: I absolutely agree. What was your biggest challenge in running Ovation Brands?

AW: I like to frame ii in context. I'm the reinvention CEO—the expert at turnarounds, right? That detail makes all the difference. If you think about CEOs across the country and around the world, a CEO will often say they're a turnaround person when in reality what they do is go into an enterprise and hack out all the costs. In most cases, you'll see many of them hack out too much cost. They overdo it.

In the short term they provide their investors—and the market if it's a public company—with the impression that they're making progress; however, all they did is create a short-term destruction of the enterprise by in essence creating an ever bigger gap between revenue and cost. Reinvention is a far cry from that kind of short-term solution.

Yes, you have to be efficient—you must begin to carefully and thoughtfully remove cost, all the while with eyes looking forward so you don't damage the enterprise while you're re-inventing. At my very first board meeting, the first slide I presented was an image of the Grand Canyon.

JM: Love it!

AW: I said, "We're here and we need to get over there on the other side." All board members' jaws dropped. They all said, "Wow, this is the first time we've ever seen a CEO deliver this slide combined with this kind of drama."

But herein lay the secret: it's not drama. It's the assignment, it's the mission, it is a vision for the goal on which we're embarking and I'm asking for your support.

JM: I think that visual is powerful. As is that it was your first slide at your first board meeting. Because reinvention takes great vision. And that's what this book is all about. Cultural transformation takes vision and focus and courage as well. Talk to me about your philosophy of reinventing an organization. I believe that culture starts with the CEO, what are your thoughts about that?

AW: Without question—every day the CEO reinforces the culture. They have stated what they want the culture to be and so that becomes what you bank on. It's like a checking account: you add money to it every day or you withdraw money from it every day. You want to make sure you don't withdraw too much, or your culture will suffer.

The problem I see with a lot of my co-CEOs out there is they don't realize that that's what's happened until it's too late.

They must realize that any action they take is an addition or a depletion of their stated culture. Oftentimes it's a failure of vision: I've seen a lot of CEOs state that they want culture X but in reality what wanted was culture Y. That's when having the maturity to correct and admit the mission is going in the wrong direction becomes crucial.

I was a Navy officer. That's a long commitment, one that keeps your situational leadership well oiled. If you are on the battlefield and bullets are whizzing by your head, you have a different command control of behavior than if you work in the Pentagon.

JM: Absolutely, absolutely.

AW: Some CEOs don't get that. They think you should use one set of tried and tested tools. But of course that doesn't work, because situations will always arise in which you have to mine the toolbox for something new, different, where you must be nimble, flexible, and have use everything you have in your toolbox. Oftentimes tools you haven't picked up in years or perhaps tools you never used. You're in battle? Do you hesitate? Say no? Of course not. You determine what's required and you forge ahead.

It's a reinvention of a franchise. The trick is to not let the front of your army get too far ahead of the rear of your army.

JM: Absolutely.

AW: The rear of your army is the old business, the front of your army is the new business, and you can't allow one to stray too far in distance from the other.

JM: I have been speaking to CEOs for this book about the notion of humility. You seem to have it in particular abundance. I wonder if this is one of the main secrets of your success.

With all the skills in your toolbox, you have to counterbalance them with—I believe—a deep sense of humility. Talk to me about your philosophy regarding being both a strong CEO and a humble individual, and how the two inform one another.

AW: First, self-importance is the enemy of leadership. The United States is incredibly narcissistic today. Much more so than when I was a kid growing up. Everything's about, "me, me, me, me, me, me." Think of the selfie phenomenon. A person is essentially saying, "I want to take a picture of myself and put it out to a million people." Think about that fundamental act.

JM: Absolutely selfish.

AW: My father suffered a stroke and can't speak, but if he could, he'd say, "Selfies are nuts."

So in order to ensure that self-importance doesn't creep in, I stress the notion of service. There is nothing narcissistic about true service when you're doing it out of a deep sense of obligation and responsibility, not to show the world what a great person you are.

If you have a passion to serve others, you'll be a long-standing part of my organization. If you have a compulsion to serve yourself, you'll likely be sniffed out early and not last long.

If you don't fit the method, you don't fit the culture. This is nonnegotiable; you don't negotiate over elements of behavior.

JM: Yes, I love that. That idea is a must in leadership.

AW: It is a must. You have to have it—I'm not accusing you of being a bad person if you don't. I'm just saying you cannot be in my enterprise. And that doesn't fit in in a lot of ways with the United States today.

JM: No, it doesn't, it doesn't.

AW: We have become a land of entitlement.

JM: Talk to me about talent. I believe that the differentiator in any organization is talent. How do you identify high potential leaders that can, in the case of Ovation Brands, both go and run these restaurants and then proceed up the ladder?

AW: I am often asked if I would choose somebody who's talented or somebody who's got enormous work ethic and appetite for work.

I always choose the latter not the former.

JM: Interesting.

AW: To me, talent means somebody who's confident in IT. Perhaps they write code, for example. I call that a skill, not a talent.

Writing code is a skill, so you can replace the code writer. The need for talent directly correlates with the needs of an organization. Yes, you must have the skills you were hired to execute, but you must also have the agility to step out of your skill set to meet the needs of the organization.

JM: Excellent point—you must be versatile and nimble. Talk to me about reinvention. What are the things in your mind that must execute in order to be successful in reinvention efforts?

AW: The biggest enemy to reinvention is being incremental.

JM: Talk to me a little more about that.

AW: Everyone acknowledges that there is a problem, and they likely also have a typical way in which to deal with that problem.
Many managers and leaders, for example, will bring in consultants to help address that problem. Then they will create a testing solution, and then they'll do an alpha test, and then they'll do a beta test. Then they'll go back and they'll
retweak that and then will go out and do a small market
test, and then they'll retweak and move along to a regional test, and then they'll retweak and then they'll go on to an actual watch and that process takes two years roughly. It's a series of, "then, then, then."

And that is absolutely a safe way to deal with a challenge: Everybody keeps their job, nobody gets fired, and you have an abundance of data to back up your decisions.

But I don't have that luxury. To reinvent, one must embrace rapid innovation. One must be willing to take risks, to not be incremental in your behavior.

JM: I see, I love this philosophy.

AW: It's not about nudging. You don't nudge when you reinvent. Consumers don't even see the nudges. Inside the company people think you're introducing a huge change, while the consumer doesn't even recognize there's a change.

So companies, because of their lack of courage from the leader of that company, will be incremental in their reinvention because it's safe.

JM: There's a lot out there, wouldn't you say Tony?

AW: Yes, it's true. Ninety-plus percent of CEOs, in my humble opinion, are more interested in personal self-preservation than they are interested in the well-being of the families who depend on the health and welfare of the organization to make a living. The must have a commitment to that higher cause.

When you talk about what reinvention is, it is the fundamental move away from the cause of self-preservation. It's using your business judgment to move the organization faster because saving the organization is more important than you being right as the CEO.

JM: How do you move people to embrace a new direction?

AW: Let me give an example. Take a junior manager—she is looking to you for a comment. She might want more confirmation on the direction. It is a really important moment as a CEO. You communicate the rules of the game. You get an A-plus with a star for making the correct decision. But you get an A-minus for making the wrong decision. You get an F for no decision. So if you say by making no decision you're going to save your bacon and you're going to save my team? That means you don't get to be on the team. And that's what we practice.

JM: That's great.

AW: If you look at any CEO's track record, they might have made two decisions in six years—they become mere stewards of the machine that's already running.

JM: Exactly. It brings to mind the recent study done by PricewaterhouseCoopers about culture. What PricewaterhouseCoopers looked at is companies that were market leaders in their various areas. What they
recognized was only 25 percent of companies that are market leaders are reinventing in a way that you've been talking about here today. In other words, they recognize that reinvention is a daily fact. You have to be out in front and aware of what's going on in the market. Seventy-five percent of companies that are currently doing very, very well are not reinventing from a position of leadership—either they're too slow or they're not making decisions at all. Those are the companies that are not going to last.

AW: The safest thing for a CEO in modern America is: "don't make a decision."

JM: Absolutely.

AW: And failing to make a decision is often more damaging than making one. In not making any decision, CEOs are depleting their cultural checkbooks every day. They don't realize it, but they are.

And it will catch up to them eventually. It may happen so slowly that they don't know what happened. But I can tell you what happened—they were physically in their chairs but they weren't engaged, they weren't leading.

JM: Absolutely. And it has to be the whole senior team.

I have one more question, Tony. What would be some messages for the young leaders who have the potential to be future CEOs? Leadership is a noble profession if you practice it well. How would you advise those who want to be exceptional leaders?

AW: I can only speak from my base of knowledge. And my philosophy and knowledge is completely expressed in my 12 Commandments. I ask people to read them not just once, but again and again and one more time. When you read something three times it sets off a trigger in your brain that will allow you to understand what the words really mean as opposed to just reading words. So I would ask them to read the 12 Commandments because it's my gift to them as young leaders.

JM: Wonderful. We will include them in this chapter (see Figure 16.1).

AW: Yes, I love to share that essential knowledge. Because it's not about serving yourself without serving others. That's a real struggle for young people. I want to be a boss, I don't have to do anything. The thought, "I want to be boss so people take care of me and serve me," is 180 degrees from what one needs to be thinking.

I really am concerned about the direction of this country. It is no longer cool to be seen as a young person striving to achieve and to serve others.

Take politicians—they receive a lot of media attention. So our children are seeing these individuals and they assume they are a good role model. One of my missions is to figure out a way to increase the size of my megaphone in order to get the right message out for these kids because they are our future.

JM: Well, I am grateful for your contribution to this book and to this conversation. The CEOs in this book are the best of the best people, moving the world in the right direction. You are one of those leaders.

AW: Thank you for including me. Cultural transformation is not just a theory, it's an essential reality in today's business world.

PASSION
A Leader must have an overwhelming passion to serve… to work is a privilege and to serve others is an honor!

CARING
Leadership is that magical blend of the head and the heart… no one cares how much you know until they know how much you care!

EARNED
A Leader is never entitled.

PERSISTENCE
Leadership is a marathon, not a sprint.

RESULTS
A Leader is nimble, flexible and has a desire do whatever it takes.

TEAM
The needs of the organization and those being led far outweigh the needs of the Leader.

JUDGMENT
A Leader always does the "right thing" but may not always do things right.

ACCOUNTABILITY
A Leader takes responsibility for his/her actions as well as the actions of those they lead.

HUMILITY
Self-importance is the enemy of Leadership.

COURAGE
Without Courage, there can be no Leadership.

HONESTY
Honesty, not political correctness, is the hallmark of a Leader.

GRATITUDE
A Leader frequently gives credit and thanks to many people.

Leadership – The 12 Commandments – Copyright 2012 – Anthony Wedo and Mainline Capital Advisors, LLC

Figure 16.1 Anthony Wedo's 12 Commandments of Leadership

17

Final Thoughts and Call to Action

PRESCRIPTION BEFORE DIAGNOSIS IS MALPRACTICE

In medicine, prescription before diagnosis is malpractice. In the world of leadership and corporate cultural transformation, it is likewise malpractice. There are too many organizations all over the world that are engaged in cultural malpractice. This must change. Start by measuring your culture. Engagement levels are determined by your culture. What must be measured? The health and vibrancy of your culture. You should survey all employees across all levels to get your finger on the pulse of how your organization is perceived by various employee and demographic groups, minimally by tenure and position level.

In our research, fewer than 15 percent of global organizations have assessed their cultures using an instrument that accurately measures those factors that determine culture. Many organizations confuse engagement or satisfaction surveys with culture surveys.

The two are not the same.

A culture survey is at best described as a leading indicator measure of engagement levels, customer satisfaction, and operating success. It is a good indicator of how people perceive the relative strength of the five predictor cultures in your organization: the "can do" culture; the "will do" culture; the "must do" culture; the "individual performance" culture; and the "team performance" culture—all of which combine to determine the health and vibrancy of your overall culture.

An engagement survey does not measure these factors, but it does measure an individual's reaction to his or her job and work environment. There are certain culture elements that do predict engagement levels, such as clarity of vision, and how motivating and compelling that vision is; however, a culture survey will yield a wealth of accurate information on why engagement is high or low, which a typical engagement survey will not. A culture survey will pinpoint clear action steps for addressing these challenges. Despite yielding better predictive information and a clearer call to action than engagement surveys, culture surveys are not nearly as prevalent in global organizations.

In our view, this state of affairs *must* change.

What else needs to be measured? First, your organization's readiness to transform. You must measure how ready your culture is to transform based on the results of your culture survey. There is a strong relationship between having a strong and vibrant culture and your organization's readiness to transform to something different and improved, such as being more innovative, customer-focused, and agile. Fewer than 10 percent of organizations use a readiness assessment to help pinpoint the cultural factors that will hinder or support their transformation initiatives.

In our view, this state of affairs *must* change.

Invest Heavily In Leadership Development for Senior Executives

It all starts at the C-level.

The CEO and C-level team must be the best-of-the-best leaders, possessing robust and vibrant inner cores and outer cores. Cultural transformation and operating originates at the crux of the C-level vibrancy. Fewer than 10 percent of global organizations invest in senior executive coaching that can help their leaders become even more effective. Senior executive coaching is aimed at helping incredibly successful senior executives become even more incredibly effective. Leadership weaknesses in the C-suite are translated into leadership weaknesses at all levels. There is no bigger impediment to your transformation efforts than weak leadership. This becomes especially dire if there is weak leadership at the top.

In our view, this state of affairs *must* change.

Invest Heavily in Leadership Development and Strengthen High-Potential Identification and Development Programs

Leadership at all levels must be strengthened. Leaders need to become more equipped, just like the C-level executives, to bring a stronger inner core and outer core to their work and lives. Organizations that succeed in building and sustaining a culture that is agile, nimble, and poised to handle the relentless disruption that defines business today and, most assuredly will characterize the future, will succeed to the extent they have equipped leaders and future leaders with the skills to also be agile in handling change, learning, and people. These three skills are in short supply globally; however, when these talents do exist in abundant supply in leaders and individual contributors, not only is the organization's culture stronger but their readiness to transform always is stronger. In our view, this state of affairs *must* also change.

Recognize It Is Not a Sprint, It Is a Marathon

To succeed with a transformation initiative, plan on a two- to three-year investment at a minimum. It requires incredible focus, persistence, passion, and patience. The C-level team must take the lead and be role models every step of the way. Unfortunately, most C-level teams neither possess the marathon view in their mind's eye nor do they possess the necessary focus, persistence, passion, and patience to run the required distance.

In our view, this state of affairs *must* change.

Positive transformation ignites when the ideology of comfort and the tyranny of custom are more painful than the ideology of different. Cultural transformation isn't easy. It takes courage, an unwavering adherence to your personal ethics, and a valuing of the other above the self. Are you ready to run your cultural transformation marathon? Have you prepared your organization, leaders, future leaders, and individual contributors to successfully compete in the marathon? Have you done all that you can do to ensure that you have prepared your employees and your organization to cross the finish line?

Remember, no longer is it about the organization you *want* to create; rather, it is only about the organization you *must* create.

Figure 17.1 offers an example of how John Mattone and his team work with clients to transform business cultures.

Here's How We Work with Organizations to Help Them with Their Culture and Culture Transformation Initiatives (Sample)

- Meet with the C-level team and sponsor team to learn more.
- Administer our *5 Cultures of Culture Assessment (5CCA)* to your employee population; debrief results and reports with C-level team and sponsor team.

Conduct C-Team Cultural Transformation 2-Day Bootcamp (Here's how it is structured):

Pre-Bootcamp

- Senior executive individual leadership assessments and coaching debrief with John Mattone.

- Administer our *Cultural Transformation Readiness Assessment 40 (CTRA-40)* to C-level team.

2-Day Bootcamp (with John Mattone)

- Discuss the latest research and ideas about culture and leadership.

- Debrief *5CCA* and *CTRA-40* results and reports.

- Discuss how to successfully transform your culture in support of operating goals and vision.

- Discuss how to lead as a C-level team to best support your transformation initiatives and ensure.

- Define your transformation/change imperative and set goals.

- Define your transformation, strategy-focused, leveraging culture strengths and address gaps.
- Implementation journey (2 to 3 years).
- Readminister the *5CCA* and *CTRA-40* at agreed upon intervals and course correct.

Figure 17.1

APPENDIX A

John Mattone's 20 Laws of Intelligent Leadership

Law #1 Align yourself with people of extraordinary character and competence.

Law #2 It is the disciplined pursuit of less that will give you more.

Law #3 Have the guts to look inside and admit that while you may be good, you are not the best you can be.

Law #4 Go forward every day committed to worthy achievement, being altruistic, and building rewarding relationships with the people in your life.

Law #5 The key to unlocking your massive potential is making the decision to be vulnerable.

Law #6 You have the choice to either accept or reject feedback; however, if you reject feedback you also reject the choice of acting in a way that may very well bring you abundant success and happiness.

Law #7 Great leaders commit to becoming more capable, committed, and connected today than they were yesterday.

Law #8 Success has nothing to do with money, titles, and possessions; success is only about committing—every day—to becoming the absolute best you can be.

Law #9   The most powerful leadership truth is that failure almost always precedes success, yet the most powerful leadership irony is that success is often the first step to failure.

Law #10   Great leaders engage in quiet, daily reflection: "Did I bring extraordinary value to my family, my team, and my organization?" And then they make the commitment to bring even more value tomorrow.

Law #11   If you want others to be happy be courteous, compassionate, and altruistic. If you want to be happy be courteous, compassionate, and altruistic.

Law #12   Your presence is determined by your reputation; your reputation can spiral up or down based on your "wow" factor—do you fall short or just meet people's expectations or, do you "wow" the people in your life?

Law #13   Nobody sees your inner core except you, if you choose to see it. If you do choose to see it, however, this becomes the key to unlocking your true greatness.

Law #14   The health and vibrancy of your inner core predicts the health and vibrancy of your outer core, which is what the world sees.

Law #15   Character won't determine your destiny; it will determine your ultimate destiny.

Law #16   The best predictor of your future is not past performance; it is the combination of your past, your willingness to accept your gifts and deficiencies, your willingness to commit to a plan in which you leverage your gifts and address your deficiencies, your willingness to execute your plan, your willingness to be vigilant to the results you achieve, and most importantly your willingness to course correct continuously.

Law #17   It's not about the organization you want to create; it's about the organization you must create.

Law #18   Positive transformation ignites when the ideology of comfort and the tyranny of custom is more painful than the ideology of different.

Law #19   Culture transforms when people transform. Results transform when behavior transforms. Behavior transforms when mind-sets transform.

Law #20   As in medicine, in the world of corporate reinvention and renewal, prescription before diagnosis is malpractice.

APPENDIX B

John Mattone's Cultural Transformation Readiness Assessment-40

JOHN MATTONE'S
CULTURAL TRANSFORMATION
READINESS ASSESSMENT-40 (CTRA-40)

General Instructions:

The following 40 factors listed predict your cultural change readiness. The factors listed on the left, to the extent they exist, will hinder your efforts. The factors on the right, to the extent they exist (or, you are planning for their existance), will support your efforts. To assess your organziation's overall cultural transformation readiness, please use a scale from 1 to 5 for each factor, with a 1 being representative of "inadequate readiness" in your opinion on that factor and a 5 being "strong readiness" on that factor. It is important to note that your cultural transformation readiness is highly correlated to the strength, health, and vibrancy of your current culture. The stronger your current culture is, the stronger the readiness is to change it.

Scoring Scale:

160–200: Strong Cultural Change Readiness

120–160: Adequate Cultural Change Readiness; however, some areas must be addressed

80–120: Low to Moderate Cultural Change Readiness and many areas must be addressed

40–80: Low Cultural Change Readiness and most areas must be addressed

0–40: Inadequate Cultural Change Readiness and all areas must be addressed

JOHN MATTONE

Factors That Predict Inadequate Readiness

1. People perceive no pain associated with not changing culture.

2. Success has led to complacency.

| 1 | 2 | 3 | 4 | 5 |

| 1 | 2 | 3 | 4 | 5 |

Factors That Predict Strong Readiness

1. The imperative to change is strong across all levels.

2. Everyone understands and feels the pain associated with the imperative to change.

Factors That Predict Inadequate Readiness

1. C-suite team and leaders are not aligned about the need for culture change.

   [1] [2] [3] [4] [5]

2. C-suite executives and leaders stuck in their thinking and actions and are ineffective.

   [1] [2] [3] [4] [5]

3. C-suite executives and leaders don't possess the capability and guts to look inside and accept their leadership gifts and gaps.

   [1] [2] [3] [4] [5]

4. Collectively, the C-suite team possess little willingness to accept the gifts and gaps of the organization.

   [1] [2] [3] [4] [5]

5. Individually and collectively, the leaders and C-suite team are unwilling and/or seem unable to accept the organization's gap pains.

   [1] [2] [3] [4] [5]

6. Individually and collectively, the leaders and C-suite team are unwilling and/or seem unable to leverage the organization's gifts and address the gaps.

   [1] [2] [3] [4] [5]

7. Individually and collectively, there is an unwillingness and/or lack of capability to communicate to the rest of the organization the gifts and gaps as well as the imperative to transform (the why?).

   [1] [2] [3] [4] [5]

8. Leaders are distracted, too busy, not personally committed to their role in change.

   [1] [2] [3] [4] [5]

9. No experience leading a culture transformation initiative.

   [1] [2] [3] [4] [5]

Factors That Predict Strong Readiness

1. C-suite team and leaders are aligned about the need for culture change.

2. C-suite executives and leaders are optimistic thinkers, with good emotions, and lead by example (Thinking Different; Thinking Big).

3. Willingness and capability to look inside and be vulnerable.

4. Willingness to accept gifts and gaps of the organization.

5. Willingness and capability to accept the organization's gap pains.

6. Willingness and capability to leverage gifts and address gaps.

7. Willingness and capability to communicate to the rest of the organization the gifts and gaps as well as the imperative to transform (the why?).

8. Visibly support culture change.

9. Experienced in culture transformation initiatives.

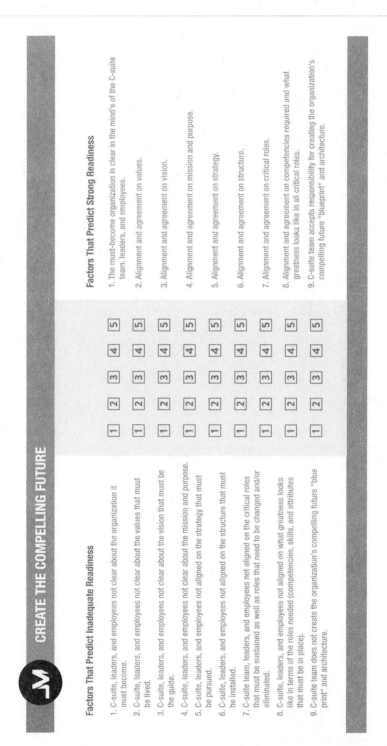

CREATE THE COMPELLING FUTURE

Factors That Predict Inadequate Readiness

1. C-suite, leaders, and employees not clear about the organization it must become.
2. C-suite, leaders, and employees not clear about the values that must be lived.
3. C-suite, leaders, and employees not clear about the vision that must be the guide.
4. C-suite, leaders, and employees not clear about the mission and purpose.
5. C-suite, leaders, and employees not aligned on the strategy that must be pursued.
6. C-suite, leaders, and employees not aligned on the structure that must be installed.
7. C-suite team, leaders, and employees not aligned on the critical roles that must be sustained as well as roles that need to be changed and/or eliminated.
8. C-suite, leaders, and employees not aligned on what greatness looks like in terms of the roles needed (competencies, skills, and attributes that must be in place).
9. C-suite team does not create the organization's compelling future "blueprint" and architecture.

1	2	3	4	5
1	2	3	4	5
1	2	3	4	5
1	2	3	4	5
1	2	3	4	5
1	2	3	4	5
1	2	3	4	5
1	2	3	4	5
1	2	3	4	5

Factors That Predict Strong Readiness

1. The must-become organization is clear in the mind's of the C-suite team, leaders, and employees.
2. Alignment and agreement on values.
3. Alignment and agreement on vision.
4. Alignment and agreement on mission and purpose.
5. Alignment and agreement on strategy.
6. Alignment and agreement on structure.
7. Alignment and agreement on critical roles.
8. Alignment and agreement on competencies required and what greatness looks like in all critical roles.
9. C-suite team accepts responsibility for creating the organization's compelling future "blueprint" and architecture.

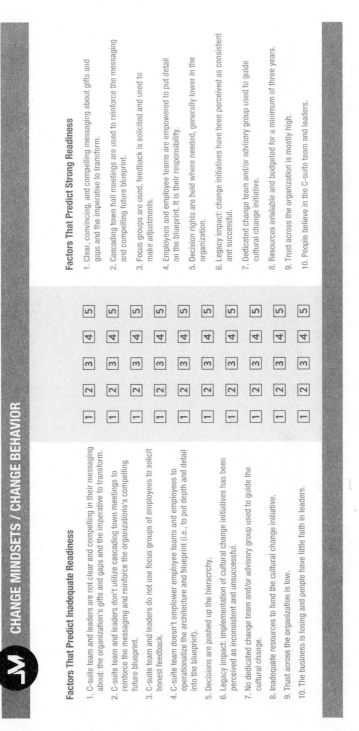

CHANGE MINDSETS / CHANGE BEHAVIOR

Factors That Predict Inadequate Readiness

1. C-suite team and leaders are not clear and compelling in their messaging about: the organization's gifts and gaps and the imperative to transform.

2. C-suite team and leaders don't utilize cascading town meetings to reinforce the messaging and reinforce the organization's compelling future blueprint.

3. C-suite team and leaders do not use focus groups of employees to solicit honest feedback.

4. C-suite team doesn't empower employee teams and employees to operationalize the architecture and blueprint (i.e., to put depth and detail into the blueprint).

5. Decisions are pushed up the hierarchy.

6. Legacy impact: implementation of cultural change initiatives has been perceived as inconsistent and unsuccessful.

7. No dedicated change team and/or advisory group used to guide the cultural change.

8. Inadequate resources to fund the cultural change initiative.

9. Trust across the organization is low.

10. The business is losing and people have little faith in leaders.

1	2	3	4	5
1	2	3	4	5
1	2	3	4	5
1	2	3	4	5
1	2	3	4	5
1	2	3	4	5
1	2	3	4	5
1	2	3	4	5
1	2	3	4	5
1	2	3	4	5

Factors That Predict Strong Readiness

1. Clear, convincing, and compelling messaging about gifts and gaps and the imperative to transform.

2. Cascading town hall meetings are used to reinforce the messaging and compelling future blueprint.

3. Focus groups are used, feedback is solicited and used to make adjustments.

4. Employees and employee teams are empowered to put detail on the blueprint. It is their responsibility.

5. Decision rights are held where needed, generally lower in the organization.

6. Legacy impact: change initiatives have been perceived as consistent and successful.

7. Dedicated change team and/or advisory group used to guide cultural change initiative.

8. Resources available and budgeted for a minimum of three years.

9. Trust across the organization is mostly high.

10. People believe in the C-suite team and leaders.

231

Factors That Predict Inadequate Readiness

1. There is little differentiation in rewarding employees and teams. A, B, and C players and teams essentially receive the same rewards.

2. Not measuring leader, future leaders, employee, and team competencies and skills and, therefore, this leading indicator information is not being leveraged.

3. Not creating a strong, vibrant learning environment in which leaders, future leaders, employees, and teams do have the resources and tools to develop and grow in support of the new vision of the organization.

4. Not selecting and promoting leaders, future leaders, and employees who do possess the required skills and competencies to help the organization achieve its new vision and mission (the must).

1	2	3	4	5
1	2	3	4	5
1	2	3	4	5
1	2	3	4	5

Factors That Predict Strong Readiness

1. A, B, and C players and teams are differentiated accurately and are rewarded appropriately.

2. Passionate and diligent about measuring the capabilities of leaders, future leaders, employees, and teams and leveraging this information.

3. Passionate and diligent about creating a strong, robust continuous learning environment where leaders, future leaders, employees, and teams can access and use resources that help them grow.

4. Selecting and promoting leaders, future leaders, and employees who do possess the required skills and competencies to help the organization achieve it's new vision and mission (the must).

MEASURE AND COURSE CORRECT

Factors That Predict Inadequate Readiness

1. Not measuring the effectiveness of our talent levers (i.e., recruiting, selection, promotion, succession planning, training and development for employees, leaders, and future leaders; and reward systems).

2. Not measuring employee and team engagement, commitment to new vision, mission, and purpose, and values alignment.

3. Not measuring the strength and vibrancy of the current culture.

4. Not measuring and capturing feedback from customers, suppliers, competitors, and so on.

5. Not making critical course corrections based on the world of feedback.

6. "Prescription Before Diagnosis" mentality does not exist.

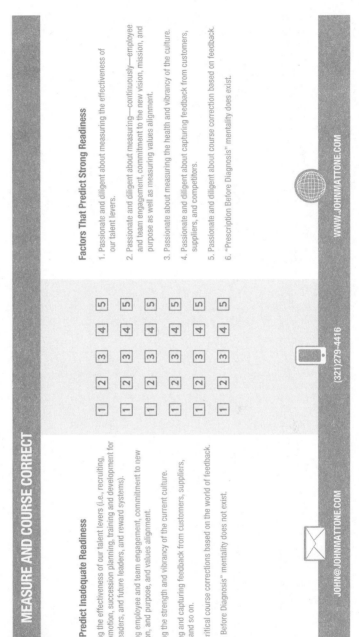

1	2	3	4	5
1	2	3	4	5
1	2	3	4	5
1	2	3	4	5
1	2	3	4	5
1	2	3	4	5

Factors That Predict Strong Readiness

1. Passionate and diligent about measuring the effectiveness of our talent levers.

2. Passionate and diligent about measuring—continuously—employee and team engagement, commitment to the new vision, mission, and purpose as well as measuring values alignment.

3. Passionate about measuring the health and vibrancy of the culture.

4. Passionate and diligent about capturing feedback from customers, suppliers, and competitors.

5. Passionate and diligent about course correction based on feedback.

6. "Prescription Before Diagnosis" mentality does exist.

JOHN@JOHNMATTONE.COM

(321)279-4416

WWW.JOHNMATTONE.COM

INDEX